How To Create
Powerful
Newsletters

Easy Ways to Avoid the Pitfalls
80 Percent of All Newsletters Face

Peggy Nelson

Bonus Books, Inc.

97 96 95 94 93   5 4 3 2 1

Library of Congress Catalog Card Number: 92–74455

International Standard Book Number: 0–929387–86–4

Bonus Books, Inc.
160 East Illinois Street
Chicago, Illinois 60611

Composition by Point West Inc., Carol Stream, IL

Printed in the United States of America

To a wonderful friend and mentor, Herschell Gordon Lewis,
who always gives his time, attention, patience and support
for which I'm forever grateful.

Contents

Acknowledgments

I want to particularly thank Dale Martin of First Marketing for his insight and focus and Don Sadler, my "private editor."

A warm thanks to Schlomitt Kreinberg. Without Schlomitt, nothing would seem possible. My mother, Margo Lewis, who always keeps me in line. Robert Nelson, my father, who was so patient and understanding when I was rushing to finish my book. And my very helpful, kind friends: Jodi VanCleve, Steve VanCleve and Gary Allred for lending their helping hands when everything was falling apart around me.

INTRODUCTION

Let me dispel a major newsletter myth:

Newsletters aren't simply products publishers sell by subscription any more. They're also powerful marketing tools which can help break through the clutter of everyday direct mail packages and conventional advertising methods.

This book is not — I repeat is not — about how to become an affluent newsletter publisher. If you're looking to crack your way into the business of newsletter publishing, look someplace else.

But if you're in the products or services industry, or a fundraiser, or church organization...if you're serious about boosting business profitability...or if you're looking for a guide to newsletters as a hot new advertising medium instead of as a product to be sold...you've come to the right place.

Why do I say newsletters can break through the clutter of every other type of advertising methods? Think about it . . .

Consumers, customers, clients, donors, prospects! You're

running in a never-ending rat race against your competition to win market-share. And today everyone has a fair chance to win that race.

New technology has opened floodgates to the world of business and has made it possible for fundraisers, private companies, and organizations of every type to target whomever they choose...to sway opinion, to bring in money, to espouse corporate philosophy, or just to show off.

As a result of our new computer-generated technology, new marketing techniques spew forth at an incredibly rapid rate, hell-bent on fortifying the growth of even the smallest businesses in even the smallest U.S. towns.

Have we, as business people and marketers, taken giant steps toward the benefit of greater market-share — or — have we stumbled into major technological overload?

Four nonexclusive techniques have evolved in advertising and marketing, spilling over into fund raising (which parallels commercial marketing more closely than some of its practitioners admit):

1. Mass-marketing or general advertising;
2. Target-marketing or direct response advertising;
3. Relationship marketing or personal service-oriented advertising;
4. Integrated marketing (a combination of direct and

general and relationship marketing within our existing client, customer or donor base).

In theory, we can research our markets through focus groups, surveys, and data bases. We can pinpoint our targets and we can use all our new technology to personalize our pitches. But let's take a hard look at what's really happening.

Has practice of this new technology made us better marketers? Or have we become lazy and dependent on our new-found "bag of tricks"? Have we become like the surgeon/technician who doesn't think of his patients as people but as body parts which have to be reassembled like Lego blocks?

Every day, on our jobs, we neatly confine and package the rest of the world. We can locate those people...but are we motivating them to buy? Are we giving the consumer what he or she wants?

As you're well aware, tidal waves of direct mail packages regurgitate from our mailboxes. Radio stations scream high- decibel sales-pitches. Television, magazines, newspapers, billboards, fax machines, computers, and even piloted skywriting messages assault the masses with the same shouts. Even those of us whose business it is to reach our audience only hear:

BUY! DONATE! BUY! SWITCH! BUY! OVER HERE! BUY!

How does that make me feel? How does that make you feel? And how does that make our targets feel?

In one word: Distrustful.

Is there any doubt why nobody listens to our messages any more? Is there any doubt why people head for the garbage can as soon as they pick up their mail? Everyone's vying for the same attention and as a result people are buried in unsolicited messages they're left to decipher. Believe me, they aren't taking the time any more.

Today, every person you want to reach wants proof of your promises *as well as your loyalty to him or her as a customer.* And today, you need to give that loyalty with a show of sincerity, if you're going to compete. This is the Age of Information. That means it's also the Age of Distrustful Minds.

You can do it. You've proved that. You want to help yourself and your company by looking at new alternatives...one of which is the newsletter as a vital marketing weapon. You can get past every padlocked skeptical mind — if it's done right. If it's pertinent. If it's relevant to your audience. Your newsletter will benefit your audience — while it benefits you.

I'm not professing a newsletter should by any means replace conventional advertising or sales programs. Rather, I want to show you how the newsletter can work as a catalyst for your other marketing methods by combining all four techniques of advertising/marketing/persuasion into one piece.

But while we're dreaming of a masterpiece, where do we go for help? When I began writing client/prospect newsletters for the purpose of business profitability, I found no help at all. Instead I found seminars, schools, and books about "How to break into the newsletter publishing business" which wasn't what I was trying to achieve.

Nothing existed then or exists now which can guide the entrepreneur, the marketing director, the head of fund-raising organizations, or the company CEO up the sure steps and along the path that's just being forged with no set guidelines. Until now.

The aim of this book is to give you who may have already begun a newsletter program, plus you who have yet to begin but are just starting the first stages of planning, a step-by-step guide to a hard-working, successful newsletter.

Let's forge ahead.

CHAPTER *1*

A Hard-Boiled Look at the Birth of a Marketing-Driven Newsletter Program

"But I only use my newsletter for public relations..."

I don't care what purpose you may be using (or thinking of using) a newsletter for—be it public relations, lead-generating, cross-selling, increasing revenue or profits from existing customers, or informing your clients, customers, donors, or prospective donors about what you're up to—the ultimate goal is your success. So from this point on I'll refer to these types of newsletters as sponsored "business-promoting-newsletters."

Parenthetically: Referring to fund raising as a "business" is *the* way to compete in the mid-1990s. Altruism has its place, but not when we're struggling in a murderously competitive fund raising ambience.

Successful Business-promoting Newsletters

You may think creating a successful business-promoting newsletter is easy. It *looks* easy, when you're criticizing somebody else's newsletter.

Nothing is ever as easy to create as it may seem to be.

But if it's worth creating, it's worth delivering the most you have to give. And if you have your wits about you, you have a lot more creativity than you think you do. The trick is to recognize areas in which you can add power to your project.

Creating a successful fund raising newsletter, or business-promoting newsletter program for your organization or company, is no different.

So, before we begin with the more enjoyable attributes of creating a newsletter—how to write better copy, how to grab attention with headlines, graphics, and format—the more mundane aspects have to be dealt with first.

Whether or not you're already sending out your newsletter...or if you're just beginning publication...or if your newsletter is still just a gleam in your eye...I'm sure you've been asking yourself the same three classic questions that have been asked by others before you:

> A. Does a promotional sponsor newsletter program really work?
> B. Is a sponsor-promoting newsletter logical for me?
> C. Is it even worth doing?

That third question invariably pops up after you've sweated through three or four issues and haven't collected mounds of inquiries and telephone calls from your clients or customers, bigger donations from your donors, or qualified leads from your prospects. Help! Is anybody out there?

Don't be discouraged or angry. It *is* worth doing, it *can* work, and you *can* track its progress. Hang in there and let's get to the nit and the grit of how this intricate business-boosting psychology can work to your benefit.

The Success or Failure Catalyst

Sponsor-promoting newsletter programs do fail. Self-serving fund raising newsletter programs do fail.

A lot of them fail. In fact, most of them. Why?

One surprisingly easy-to-do first failure is forgetting the purpose behind a newsletter program. The newsletter becomes a fluff piece **disguised** as a newsletter. It becomes a status symbol, an ego-extension. The company forgets what its purpose is: a business-booster in a news publication format.

Then it becomes a waste of your marketing dollars.

That's not the fault of the medium itself. It's the failure to understand how the medium is supposed to work to your benefit while it's performing as an apparent (and, we hope, true) benefit for your readership.

And it's the failure to remember the ultimate purpose of a promotional newsletter program is to work in *tandem* with your other promotional pieces and appeals to sell.

The Sponsor-promoting Newsletter Is an Advertising Medium, Not Your Product

The biggest reason a sponsor-promoting newsletter program can fail is because so many marketers, business people, and fund raising executives take their examples of newsletter format and content from newsletters which are commercial products sold by people in the publishing business.

For you, a newsletter is one medium you use to promote good will, stronger customer relationships, awareness of your organization, and ultimately, increase revenue. The newsletter is not your product as it is for newsletter publishers who subsist on subscriptions just like any subscription-driven newspaper or magazine.

The Difference Between Newsletters as Product and Newsletters as Marketing Tools

You're a subscriber to an investment newsletter published by ABC Publishing Company in New York. ABC gives you up-to-the-minute up-dates on investments. *You pay $100 a year for this information.*

You're also a Financial Advisor and your company sends out a newsletter to your customers and prospects on investment up-dates. The difference is: IF your newsletter is *hard-working and effective,* you're giving your customers and prospects a reason to use your services. You've shown them, through the content of your newsletter—you're the authority, you're the person they want to do business with because of the valuable **free** advice you give them four times a year.

ABC Publishing doesn't care who people hire as their financial advisors. You do.

Newsletters as Marketing Tools

Newsletters have been around for decades, but the newsletter as a marketing tool is a fairly new concept.

Even though the newsletter is the latest (and hottest) rage to add to marketing programs, practically every business and nonprofit organization labors over how to translate a newsletter into a successful, profitable marketing medium which convinces both existing customers/clients and desirable prospects to respond positively and favorably.

Client/prospect newsletter programs seldom are overnight successes. Newsletter programs are built to achieve *long-term* results. The un-paved road to their successes has very few road signs telling you which way to go.

We are the pioneers.

You may get some opinions from newsletter publishers or newspaper publishers as to how a newsletter format should look, or how to find your market for a newsletter and newsletter writing style. But remember, their goals are different from your own. They aren't trying to sell products, services or solicit funds. They're trying to sell subscriptions for the newsletter itself.

The best ideas you can take from newsletter publishers are how they sell newsletters. The direct mail packages that newsletter publishers use are wonderful examples of how you can sell your organization (not the newsletter) to your market.

You can also take a look at your own field of marketing for insight. But as you've probably already found out, an "overview" knowledge of marketing or even of integrated advertising techniques don't automatically qualify you to create a successful sponsor-promoting newsletter piece. Newsletters have a unique niche, and they demand a unique promotional approach.

Within the genre, the sponsor-promoting newsletter has a set of subtle and intricate techniques all its own.

This is where the marketing/persuasional road forks off into a different realm. New rules have to be formulated and met.

A bittersweet success story: The author's first attempts at promoting business via a newsletter

My first "attempts" at sponsor-promoting newsletters were, in one word: disastrous. I was hired by a company as a direct response copywriter. Among my responsibilities was to write a newsletter to promote the company.

Because the company I worked for was a marketing company, the overall theme of the newsletter was to give our clients and prospects new marketing techniques and tips on what was happening in their market.

The purpose of the newsletter was to convince our clients and prospects to think of our company as the marketing authority in its field and to use the services we offer.

Needless to say, I was thrilled to write the newsletter. I was so excited I completely lost track of the objectives behind the newsletter. (So did everyone else in the office, including the executives I worked for.) This was my chance . . . my chance to be the "voice" of marketing and my chance to sound my opinions.

That's exactly what our clients and prospects got—marketing news— nothing else.

After the first issue hit the presses and the mailboxes, I sat back and took a hard look at the newsletter. My eyes wobbled out of focus, I turned a few shades of crimson, and I thought: Uh Oh!

The readers of that issue received good value from its content —that is, the readers, not the company.

What's wrong with that, you ask? Aren't readers supposed to benefit?

Certainly they are. But so are *you* or you're either the most altruistic or most misguided promotional newsletter creator of the day. (You'll also be one of the briefest.)

Under what circumstances would the readers benefit and the issuer *not* benefit?

Think about it and you'll see why . . . as we did, *after* the fact. Nowhere did the newsletter tie our business in with the articles. In fact, I'm sure a lot of people didn't even know who sent the newsletter. Only in tiny 6-point type and very neatly tucked off in the corner on the third page did it read: "This newsletter was published by so and so. If you'd like more information please call: 555-1212." That was all, except for a b.r.c. (business reply card) asking the audience if they would like further information about any of the articles written in the newsletter.

BIG MISTAKE! It doesn't matter if it was a superb piece of writing and design. It didn't achieve its purpose.

Second Attempt:

Overcompensation. The newsletter became a piece of pure "fluff"—a bigger mistake than the first. Each article touted the company's marvels.

What were the reactions of the readers?

Confused. Some readers wrote: "I thought I was getting a newsletter about marketing techniques" . . . which they of course understood from the previous issue. Some more acerbic individuals wrote asking to have their names taken off our mailing list.

It's not easy admitting these mistakes. But they certainly are common ones when first starting a newsletter program.

These generalized examples should illustrate a basic point: Something which seems easily done, especially by experienced marketing or advertising professionals, isn't so easy when we add the dimension of *effectiveness*.

Without effectiveness, all we have is an exercise in either ego satisfaction or pedagogy. The business-promoting newsletter as an *effective* medium is an inexact science with its own set of rules. I've discovered some of these rules through brutal trials and errors...and the purpose of this book is to share them with you and prevent you from making them!

The Best of Both Worlds

By combining the two worlds of publishing and marketing we can create a newsletter which increases revenue or donations, increases profits or ratio of dollars-out to dollars-in, and positions you as a credible and trusted authority in your field.

But remember: We are the pioneers of a medium that hasn't quite evolved into a science—the psychologically effective, fine-tuned promotional newsletter.

Good intentions are plentiful when we first start a promotional newsletter program. As my own experience proves, it's much easier to lose track of newsletter program intentions compared with a typical advertising campaign.

The "why" of undertaking a promotional newsletter program often gets lost under a pile of technical or personality-serving mini-decisions. We get distracted, caught up in either producing the perfect journalistic effort or in fluffing and puffing up the company. The negative result: We lose track of *how* our readership is supposed to benefit.

It's *critically important* to recognize that the purpose of your newsletter program is to *increase the ratio of dollars-in against dollars-out.* Whether commercial or eleemosynary, that means: Increase business.

Repeat this over and over again. (In fact, it's a pretty good idea to glue it to the top of your keyboard.) Whether you're boosting better client relationships, building image, establishing community good will, or fundraising, your company's or organization's ultimate ambition is to increase business.

The procedures within the newsletter medium are different from your usual space ads, brochures or radio/television broadcast. (I'll help you translate, adapt, and replace some of those differences in Chapter Two.)

Begin at the Beginning

No matter what our business is, we all have to achieve the same group of objectives before a successful newsletter program can be realized. Let's take a look at some of them.

The New Concept in the Newsletter Advertising Medium

I'm going to suggest approaches that may be at variance with what academicians—who seldom get bloodied in competitive battles—may teach. The purpose of this book is, I admit cheerfully, to maximize effectiveness. That means sacrificing art directors' awards and inside-the-office "How clever you are" compliments for more practical objectives.

You may not agree with me as we begin, but your accountant should be thrilled when adding up the returns.

The following is a list of goals which need to be met to create a powerful newsletter.

Goal #1: Establish Market-driven Newsletter Objectives

Let's establish the marketing objectives for your newsletter program. Get a notebook or a sheet of paper and check off one or all the reasons, listed below, you may have for publishing a client/prospect newsletter. Any and all these objectives that apply should be tied into your newsletter. That, in fact, is the great wonder of newsletters: Newsletters are "the" medium today that can integrate all your marketing strategies.

> A. Do you want to improve or establish a certain image?
>
> B. How do you position your organization or business within your marketplace? How do you want to be perceived by your audience?
>
> C. Do you want to educate your clients or prospects about your services, products, or endeavors within the community?
>
> D. Do you want to gain confidence and credibility within your client/prospect base?
>
> E. Do you want to use the newsletter as a lead-generator?
>
> F. Do you want to cross-sell products and services?
>
> G. Do you want a public relations vehicle to create a broader awareness of your company or organization?
>
> H. If you're a non-profit organization, do you want to instill confidence and let people know how their dollars are being spent?
>
> I. Do you recognize the value of underscoring customer relations to the point at which customers know you recognize that value?

J. Have you recognized and implemented the implicit usefulness of a newsletter in establishing a "bonding" relationship with your customers, clients, or donors?

K. Are you working to reduce attrition among your existing customers and donors?

L. Are you recruiting new contributors?

This list is the guts of business-promoting newsletters. You can see how primitive psychology plays a large part in content. Another of the wonders of newsletters is their ability—assuming you have that grasp of primitive psychology—to generate a state of mind without the readers realizing *you're* the one who did the generating!

Once you have your objectives firmly down on paper, check them against your first (or next) issue. Check them again each time you begin a new issue of your newsletter, until you've settled into a comfortable internal and external set of relationships for each issue.

Question: Did you check most of these objectives?

If you answered yes, you're on the road to a hard-driving marketing newsletter.

Goal #2: Isolate and Attack Your Target-group

Okay, I'll apologize right now. I know this may seem overly basic and simple...but sometimes when you're writing a newsletter, it's easy to go off on an opinion-driven tangent.

An idea may inspire you and you'd like to shout it out in the newsletter. But be careful of projecting your personal inspirations! That idea may have nothing to do with the targets you're trying to reach.

A reminder—and I'd advise you to inscribe this point along with your list of objectives:

To whom are you writing? Write that down, as extensively and comprehensively as you can; and keep it in front of you. If you find yourself wandering away because you've abandoned your target-group and started to write for yourself, aha! It's time to refer back to your objectives and your market.

Goal #3: Match Your Client/Prospect/Donor Viewpoint

Austin Kiplinger, the original publisher of *The Kiplinger Letter*, once said, "Newsletters are in the business to help people adjust to the realities of life."

Kiplinger was speaking for all of us in the world of newsletters. Use his words to your advantage. "The realities of life" are ever changing. This is the Age of Information. . . and *informed skepticism*. Your clients and prospects won't take your company at face value. Relationships have to be built and your clients, donors or prospects need to be informed on *their* level. Once you've dragged them into your philosophical store, then you can start proselytizing to shift them to *your* level.

Competition is more ferocious than it's ever been. If you don't take the pains to keep your clients, someone else out there will.

After you've written your objectives, the next step is write down your clients' or prospects' expectations. What do they want to read?

> **Client/prospect/donor checklist**
> 1. Is your newsletter written within the experiential background of its readers?
> 2. Does your newsletter offer your client, donor or prospect a solution to problems you may have presented within the text?
> 3. Does your newsletter inform the reader about subjects he or she is interested in?
> 4. Is your newsletter seem to be loaded with ways to benefit your reader?
> 5. Will your readers perceive your newsletter as a benefit and not as a sales-pitch? If your newsletter doesn't benefit the reader it certainly won't benefit your organization.

Goal #4: Take Aim! Motivate Your Customers, Donors and Prospects

Once you've decided what you want to achieve from your newsletter program, who your market is, and how your audience should benefit from your newsletter, the next step is to make sure you're motivating your audience.

You're going to have to fight the urge to throw in too many blatant ads and puffery about your company or organization. Doing this emasculates the reader-value of any publication. You're eating up supposedly valuable space, space that's there for your audience to reap beneficial information.

The fine art of motivating your readers through the newsletter medium is much more subtle than would be the case were you distributing a piece of direct mail or a catalog or any other admittedly self-serving communication.

You'll reap the benefits of *credibility* if you have powerful, newsworthy articles which can be tied directly to your company.

Example: If you're selling radio spots to businesses, and you're using your newsletter to help you sell these radio spots, you won't get that business by letting loose with an obvious pitch for sponsor dollars inside your newsletter. Instead, your headline on an individual article within the newsletter might read something like this:

How to Get the Biggest Response from Your Advertising Dollars

The body copy would give hard facts and figures, plus the mandatory "How to . . ." suggestions. At the end of the article you might have this "kicker":

If you'd like more free advice about how to make your advertising dollars work harder for your company, call Harry at KBBB, 555-1212.

I'll get into the finer details of how to generate response copy later in this book. Using a newsletter to generate business does work, provided you aren't overly obvious within the newsletter articles themselves—leaving the more blatant pitches to response devices, separate appeals or direct mail packages which can be integrated into your mailing.

If you've truly taken aim, the information in your newsletter will motivate your readers to call you.

Response checklist:
1. Have you given your readers an abundance of motivating reasons to respond to you?
2. Have you included a b.r.c. (business reply card) or a b.r.e (business reply envelope) so you have a lead-generator?
3. Have you included phone numbers, addresses, and names of people to contact—by toll-free phone if possible?
4. Have you made your audience an offer they understand well enough to respond to?
5. Have you integrated your newsletter along with a specific appeal or direct mail promotion?

Goal #5: Decide How Often You Want to Publish Your Newsletter

Think about this one.

Will you publish weekly, monthly, bimonthly, quarterly, or semi-annually?

Consistency has to be maintained once you start scheduling issues. With brains, talent, determination, and a great deal of luck, your readers will be expecting their newsletter—if your readers perceive it as a benefit.

You don't want to take on the project if you can't meet your own deadlines. Don't make the commitment for a bimonthly newsletter if you can only manage to publish quarterly. The result would be ill-received and may have a horribly negative psychological effect on readers as a sign of unreliability or a reader-be-damned casual approach.

> The "Stay On Schedule 2-Step":
> 1. Develop a newsletter task force, each of whose members has specific authority and responsibility. Who will be in charge of development, research, writing, design, production, mailing, list maintenance?
> 2. Take into consideration other responsibilities each person has to accomplish besides the newsletter project. Does each person have enough time to meet his or her deadline?

IMPORTANT REALIZATION: Be sure you're realistic about the time-frame involved to reach your goals.

Goal #6: Match the Content of Each Issue to Your Marketing Plans

Most companies or organizations have their marketing plans laid out for a year ahead. What are your goals for the next twelve months? Are you ready to update them each month?

If you don't have designated plans, stop right here and make them. Your newsletter program as well as all your other advertising, public relations and appeal efforts will benefit from substantially increased results. (So will your budget and your peace of mind. You're less likely to lapse into a screaming fit.)

Conclusion

These first steps are admittedly very basic. But they do have a purpose that transcends the basic: They'll help you establish a hard-working and effective business-promoting newsletter program without encountering and stumbling into the pitfalls that have beset so many others.

Before beginning each issue of your newsletter and after you've completed your preliminary writing and layout of each issue, re-check your checklists you've put together as you read this first chapter.

By following these self-imposed guidelines, your newsletter will be clean and functionally able to perform. But you need more than that—your newsletter has to sizzle. Future chapters will show you how you can add the ingredients of *power sell*.

CHAPTER 2

The Success Psychology of a Fine-Tuned *Direct Response* Promotional Newsletter

Business-promoting Newsletter Psychology

Now that you've mastered the driving concepts behind a sponsor-promoting newsletter, the next step is understanding the subtlety of successful "sell-psychology" through the newsletter medium.

Don't worry. I'm not talking heavy stuff here. This isn't an academic exercise with a lot of technical terms to throw around. It's just seat-of-the-pants psychology based on logic. You already know how it's *supposed* to work or you wouldn't even be thinking of using a newsletter as a promotional or advertising medium.

Whether or not your company or organization is raising funds, selling toothbrushes or toilet paper, marketing canned green beans or books, generating sympathy or fun, or pitching health-help or financial services, the fundamental psychology of your newsletter is going to be the same.

Assumption

One basic assumption has always held true in newsletters of every type—people have grown dependent on newsletters as a source of information pertinent to their special interests. Newsletters are used to target a *specific* readership. They're read fast; the content is usually thought of as superior to other sources of information; and they're written in an comprehensible fashion. Plus: Good newsletters contain short, snappy and direct news briefs and articles so they can be used as an easy reference.

All these characteristics are what make the business-promoting newsletter work in your favor. Intensifying these characteristics: The reader should perceive your newsletter as *beneficial* and *impartial* to him or her—because the news content in each article is *proof* to the reader.

Whatever your product or service performs, the articles back up.

And here's where we touch on the very essence of how the psychology of a newsletter works when we use it as an advertising medium.

Myth Breaker

The decision to incorporate a newsletter into your marketing plan doesn't mean your program will work. Your newsletter program will only work when and if you incorporate the newsletter so that it melds seamlessly into the rest of your marketing efforts. What you're doing is adapting an accepted news medium and transforming that medium to work as a hard-driving *marketing medium*. Don't get stuck in the old medium. Yes, the word is *news*letter; no, "news" isn't the purpose; news is secondary to promotional value.

Reminder: Never think of your newsletter as your product. It's easy to do. But I can't stress this enough. The newsletter is your advertising medium.

Your "sell psychology" absolutely must follow your marketing efforts all the way or the rules outlined in this book will be futile. The reason why changing your own mind-set—to accept your newsletter as an advertising medium—can be difficult is that this type of communication has to follow two basic concepts:

> 1. The newsletter must be a standard newsletter in all respects.
> 2. The newsletter must boost your appeals, products or services.

Wow! Not easy! It entails combining the best advertising *and* force-communication approaches—image, awareness, education, positioning and direct response advertising.

Your data-base (hopefully) has been able to pinpoint the interests of your customers and prospects. You have their names because obviously they're interested in something you have. Let's expand on this:

Four absolutes exist regarding newsletters and the reasons why they get read...which are also the reasons why the newsletter is the perfect advertising medium for the mid-to-late 1990s.

1. In theory newsletters are *unbiased.*
2. Newsletters are the best source of information on a particular subject.
3. Good newsletters don't contain a lot of fluff (there's no room).
4. Good newsletters always give their readers something to keep. If the newsletter simply spouts its sponsor's glories without giving something to its readers, the newsletter doesn't contain any perceived value.

Don't assume I'm telling you to fool your reader or put one over on your reader. Newsletters that overcome reader-skepticism are the best advertising medium available to do that. But understanding the newsletter advertising concept is not enough. We have to work inside some hard, fast rules for using this successful sell-psychology peculiarly adapted to the newsletter advertising medium, in order for it to tie together as a whole working toward one common goal—promotion. That applies whether your promotion is achieving trust or promoting sales. Anyway, if you achieve trust, sales follow automatically.

The Ten Commandments Which Govern Successful Sell Psychology in Newsletters

I've read non-biblical lists of "Ten Commandments" so often I've come to feel this book would be derelict if we didn't include one. So here are the Ten Commandments for newsletter sales psychology—actually, Ten "Inclusions":

1. Include emotional motivational factors.
2. Include credible newsworthy information.
3. Include building blocks to strong client/prospect/ donor relations.
4. Include problem-solving answers and explanations.
5. Include success stories.
6. Include integrated advertising, without it seeming to be advertising. (I'd better explain this: This means selling without hard-core sales pitches. By "integrated advertising" I don't mean advertising recognizable as advertising. But in newsletters everyone gets stuck on one

objective. For the newsletter to be effective you have to combine all these: awareness, education, image advertising, sales, and customer relations. The newsletter is quite possibly the only advertising medium with which you can and should do this. Understand, please: A newsletter is *within itself* a total concept; it works as an integrated whole to drive your point across to your target. Don't bother writing and issuing a newsletter if you can't use it to its fullest capacity. You'll be wasting your marketing dollars, wasting time, and wasting staff.)

  7. Include strong demands for reader involvement.

  8. Include client/prospect/donor education.

  9. Include offers, response devices and special appeals with your newsletter.

  10. Include legitimacy (readers perceive a newsletter as a gift full of legitimate and beneficial information).

I'm going to assume you want the "complete" success of your newsletter. This means you'll get the most powerful results by using your newsletter to tie together *all* your marketing efforts. That's possible if your thinking isn't narrowed down to one objective. So promise yourself to follow each of these ten commandments in every issue of your newsletter.

Let's dissect the subtle ingredients that bind these ten commandments together to make a successful business-promoting newsletter.

Commandment #1 — Include emotional motivational factors

Emotional motivational factors

As you certainly know, hitting any reader on an emotional level that sparks a gut reaction drives your point across a hundred times more effectively than cold hard logic. You can base your appeal on one or a combination of emotional ideas. Emotion is the basis of your appeal.

The six greatest emotion-wrenching catalysts in advertising are:

  1. Fear
  2. Greed
  3. Guilt
  4. Exclusivity
  5. Egoism
  6. Envy

Ignite any one or all of these emotions and you'll get your audience to read what you have to say. You follow these three pointers:

1. Make it plausible.
2. Choose the emotion that pertains to what you're trying to achieve.
3. Find a common denominator your readers have for the emotional appeal you're using.

Remember the objectives which you wrote down in Chapter One? What are they? What's the purpose of your newsletter?

To get firm and unmistakable answers, take a look at who your target is. Then what is it your target audience wants? What will get their blood racing?

Example: Suppose you're a fund raising organization and the purpose of your newsletter is to create a broader awareness and peace of mind within your donor-nucleus about how you're using donated money and how the money is helping your cause.

Another objective would be to increase the total dollar amount of donations within your existing donor base.

What approach or approaches would you use to get your donors' attention and approval throughout the entire newsletter, culminating in the positive action you want the reader to take?

Try some motivators on for size.

Fear

Fear is probably the most hard-hitting emotion you can use to motivate your audience. It might seem I'm touting torture; I'm not by any means. If you're instilling an emotion of fear and you can touch someone else with that fear—it's pure emotion. And you then resolve the fear by giving your audience a solution.

It may seem appalling to say, "Scare the pants off of your donors." You don't have to go that far. I'm merely suggesting that you use this most powerful of all emotional appeals to get the attention of your readers.

NOTE: In order for this psychology to work, it must be centered on something your reader fears—not an abstraction centered on someone else, or the point you're trying to make won't be effective.

Let's try a fictional example. (WARNING: Keep remembering—this is a fictional example.)

Example: The National Organization of Women (N.O.W.) is trying to raise funds for pro-choice and they're also trying to get more women to join forces with them. What stance would you take? A headline might read:

17

What Would You Do If You Found Out The Baby You're
Carrying Has AIDS?

What would be the point of this headline, which may actually insult the
sensibilities of some readers? What, in fact, is the answer to the question
you've asked? Probably, *within this specific targeted readership*, the woman
may want an abortion. Probably she would get one. But that isn't the
point, because the headline itself is fantasy.

No, the point is: Did I get *your* attention? Did I raise an emotion of
shock or fear at the mere mention of the HIV virus? You bet I did. It's an
unmentionable in most circles. Did I get your attention with the abortion
issue? Unless you've spent the past ten years on the planet Mars, you bet
I did.

Now that my newsletter article has your attention let me say you probably have already formed some sort of opinion about me. I'm not saying
shock value is necessarily good. But the implicit image of newsletters is
that of a very conservative form of communication; and by using emotional
factors in this conservative, soft-sell form of advertising we get our point
across with unbelievable dynamic strength.

The reader comes to the arena accepting the newsletter as dispassionate. That means the reader isn't going to be skeptical. But in order to
achieve this—your target must first have something in common with the
premise you've stated.

**Can you see the benefit of knowing *who* your reader is? This
is the core of newsletter psychology!**

If you're writing for a readership such as N.O.W. you know your target
is primarily female. Your objectives (see chapter 1) don't change. They
are to: Build and maintain a quality image, inform your audience, raise
more money for your cause, and educate your readership in your favor.

Fear, like anger, works better and better as one approaches groups
with extremist positions. If I write a newsletter for machinists about the
danger auto exhausts pose for pantyhose, I'm not going to generate a lot
of fear.

The mixture of knowing emotional motivators and knowing the hopes,
dreams, and, yes, fears of your target-readers is an exquisite one. It's
what makes successful sponsored newsletters.

Guilt

This is an emotion someone feels when he or she knows something is
right...knows they can do something about changing whatever it is that's
being done wrong...and doesn't do it.

You can base your appeal on this emotion best when your target audience already has an instilled guilt. (It's difficult-to-impossible to present your argument, then try to form a guilt that wasn't already there.)

The best emotional appeal would be to combine Fear and Guilt together. This always seems to get the best response. Here's a good example of this (again, don't break the publisher's windows. This is just a fictional example):

Example: Your senior citizen newsletter has this headline:

> You Didn't Bother With Medicare "B" and Now You
> Have a $12,000 Hospital Bill You Can't Pay.

See the combination of fear and guilt? Can you imagine a person on Medicare passing this article without scanning it for meaty information?

Make no mistake: Combining fear and guilt is state-of-the-art. Unless you're already a polished motivational newsletter writer, start with a safer motivator, such as exclusivity.

Greed

Greed is human nature. If you're going to be a good newsletter sales psychologist don't ever disregard human nature. You may prefer to be altruistic and think others are—but sometimes you have to push altruism aside if you want to drive your point home. Speak to your target on his or her own level. We can all be greedy. The question is: What are we greedy about? If you're playing on the greed factor be sure you're playing it right. You can combine envy and egoism easily into your motivational factors.

The trick, in newsletter writing, is to project the concept of greed *without* guilt.

Example: You have this headline in a newsletter aimed at customers of a financial institution or financial planning service:

> What'll You Bet You Have an Extra $5,000 You Didn't
> Even Know About?

A more universal greed approach can be an article in a newsletter aimed at almost *any* readership:

> Sunday's Newspaper Costs You $1.00. Here's How to
> Make 15.75 Profit from that Same Newspaper.

(Don't be frustrated trying to figure this one out. The article might dissect some free-standing inserts, which always have discount coupons.)

Exclusivity

Exclusivity is a "natural" for memberships, because memberships themselves are (or, certainly, should be) exclusive. Too, exclusivity can be used as a tie-in with greed. If you use exclusivity, you're using it ultimately as a benefit too. You can't claim something is exclusive when it's not, *but* you always have a way to make *something* exclusive.

People like to feel they're a part of an exclusive in-group. They like to feel they're special and they're getting something not everyone can have because they'd like to be the envy of others.

Example of an exclusivity-based heading in a fund raising newsletter:

OPERA GUILD FORMS ADVISORY BOARD

The article either lists members of the Board; or, if the Board is too extensive for a name-by-name list (unlikely unless the list exceeds 200 names) the article is tied to a rubber stamp near the address area of the newsletter, which informs the recipient he or she has been appointed to the Advisory Board.

NOTE: The word "Private" has dynamic exclusivity-overtones and also applies to Envy as a motivator. See below.

Egoism

You're playing on somebody's ego when you're using exclusivity and greed. When you flatter or praise someone that person is going to want to keep doing whatever is bringing them praise or whatever will make people look up to them. (Like fear, you can be playing with fire using this one if it's not done right. Don't falsely praise or flatter someone. That will only inspire tremendous anger and alienate your readership.)

Example: Your newsletter circulates to employees of a chain of supermarkets. The headline on the lead article:

CLOSE COMPETITION FOR "EMPLOYEE OF THE
MONTH"

The article itself has photos and mini-biographies of the last three winners and a list of contenders for the current month's honors.

Envy

I believe the only way you can get away smoothly with this emotional motivator is to use it as if other people envy your readership.

Example: An "ear" at the top right corner of page one has this legend:

> The Financial Insider is Available Only to Individuals and
> Institutions Nominated by the Board of Governors to Re-
> ceive This Private Publication. Applications for Subscrip-
> tion Must Be Endorsed by Two Current Subscribers.

Commandment #2: Include Credible and Newsworthy Articles

Once you've decided on your objectives and the appeal of your newsletter, the next step is to plan your issue so it creates the perfect blend of
philosophy, sell, and appeal, tying your goals and objectives together. This
is where you really have to incorporate your "sell psychology" into
action. This is the crucial moment.

Example: Your newsletter circulates to investors. A main heading:

> NEW TAXES WILL DRIVE UNWARY INVESTORS TO
> THE WALL, EXPERT WARNS

Unless you have a genuine financial newsletter, not tied to a sponsor-
base, the expert is you or someone on your staff—a "Senior Analyst," for
example.

Careful, now. Don't let your customers or prospects catch you expounding your glories on their time.

Confused because you think I'm contradicting my own rule? I'm not.
Confused because your newsletter gives you tons of space to expound on
your glories, so why shouldn't you use it? Don't be.

What matters isn't what you think; it's what your readers perceive. If
they perceive expert advice, they act accordingly. If they perceive chest-
thumping, they react accordingly.

So it's as simple as this: Instead of using all this space to outright expound on your glories, tailor your newsletter articles in such a way that
your readers will be the ones spouting your glories. And this is easy to do.

The rule couldn't be simpler:

> Write as though you were writing for *Time* or *Newsweek*
> or *The Journal of the American Medical Association*. This
> will assure a "journalistic" appearance readers will ac-
> cept.

If you have the time and the talent, a sure-fire technique is to include in
each article a problem your clients/donors/prospects have, with tips (tips
are wonderful!) for eliminating that problem from their lives.

Commandment #3: Include Building Blocks to Stronger Client Relationships

Today's competitive market puts the consumer, client or donor in a position to choose whom he or she will do business with or give money to.

Your customers or donor nucleus are constantly getting wooed by other competitors. Your customers know they can pick and choose someone else who caters to their needs if they don't get satisfactory service from you.

You can't afford to treat your customers or donors as units, numbers that bring you income. Sooner or later they'll quit bringing you that income and go somewhere else. In my experience, creating newsletters for a number of clients who are just getting started in business, and even for those who have been in business for years, I've found most put the customers last. Once they've made a sale that's the end of the courtship phase of the seller-sellee relationship. That attitude doesn't fly today. And yesterday—a kinder, gentler time—people were never treated like a number.

That's another reason why a newsletter is an excellent medium for donor/customer relations. But don't stop there.

Commandment #4: Include Problem-Solving Answers and Explanations

Once you've posed a problem in your newsletter articles. Don't leave your readers hanging in midstream. Give them easy access to solve their problem.

A perfect example of this is Fig. 2-1, the *Tax $avings Report* newsletter published by the National Taxpayers Union. Look at the heading:

When to attach additional documentation to a return

The byline serves two purposes: It focuses responsibility for the opinions and suggests an authoritative or at least an investigative source.

Commandment #5: Include Success Stories

Success stories are the most reader-accepted means of convincing your donors/customers/prospects that you have a product or service they want to use. Special ways of reporting these success stories have to be used in order for them to be plausible.

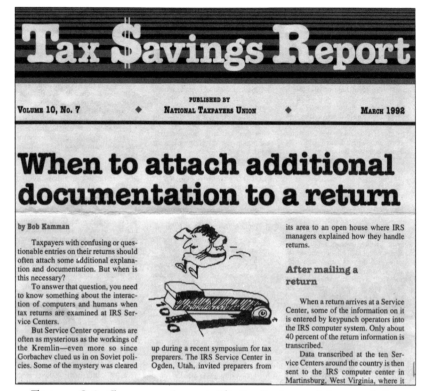

Figure 2-1. Commandment #4: Include problem-solving answers and explanations for your readers.

The easiest is "How I Did It." All you have to do is interview a cross-section of individuals who your readers might think are experts; then publish the opinions.

How does this serve *you*? Again, easy: The questions tie to your organization.

An example of this is the SRDS Report (Fig. 2-2). Heading:

> *Media Planning and Buying in the '90s:*
> *The Players are Leaner, Meaner*
> *and Looking for More*
> *'Bang for the Buck'*

The article itself is almost self-written—interviews with advertising agency people. Because SRDS is a media rate schedule publisher, any information of this sort enhances the corporate image.

the srds report

For the Professional Buyer and Planner of Media   March 1990 / Volume 4, Number 3

In this issue:

Dear Media Director:

In a Market Crowded with Titles, How do You Separate the Wheat from the Chaff?
page 2

Has the Consolidation of Advertising Agencies Impacted the Way You Do Business?
page 3

What Do You Really Want to Hear from Media Representatives?
page 3

Dear Media Rep:

Has the Consolidation of Agencies and Advertisers Impacted the Way You Do Business?
page 4

Has the Media Business Become More Numbers Oriented?
page 7

Media Planning and Buying in the '90s:

The Players are Leaner, Meaner and Looking for More 'Bang for the Buck'

All the world is a mega-merger or in some cases, a mini-merger.

Keeping track of the players as advertising agencies merge, re-merge and then spin off in new configurations is neigh onto impossible. Tracking the situation on the media side is no easier.

For example, in 1988 the Magazine Publishers Association monitored approximately 196 consumer publications. In 1989, the Association tracked a total of 286. The Association of Business Publishers monitored a total of 489 business publications in 1987, 560 publications in 1988, and a total of 588 in 1989. And that doesn't even account for publication mergers and acquisitions or what's been happening in trade, newspaper, broadcast or outdoor media.

How do agency media professionals keep up? How do they separate the "must sees" from the "please send a media kits?" What impact has the new leaner and meaner agency had on the way media representatives make sales calls? How do they now distinguish themselves from their competition?

We distilled the answers to those questions from interviews conducted with nearly a dozen agency media directors, planners and media representatives.

On the agency/client side, participants include: Jack Cohen, vice president, director of print and outdoor media buying for DDB/Needham Worldwide, Inc.; Michael Brink, manager of media services for Ben & Jerry's; Stephen Calder, vice president/director of media planning, for The Bloom Agency; Al Prior, media director at Hank Forssberg, Inc.; Bob Reuschle, senior vice president/director of administration at J. Walter Thompson, USA, Inc. and John Tully, vice president and account supervisor of The Parker Advertising Agency Co.

*Media representatives include: Linda Cohen, associate publisher of **Sassy**; Reed Foster, advertising director of **Redbook**; Sidney Ginsberg, **USA Network**'s vice president of sales administration; Constantine Kazanas, senior vice president/general manager of **Architectural Digest**; Richard Rabinowitz, vice president/advertising director at **Elle**; Jeffrey Schaffer, publisher of **Supermarket Business** and president of the Marketing/Service Publications Division of FM Business Publishing Inc. and Mark Tupper, general sales manager of **WCBS**.*

*Their responses appear in this issue of **The SRDS Report**.*

1

Figure 2-2. Commandment #5: Include success stories.

Commandment #6: Include Integrated Advertising Without It Seeming to be Advertising

Pack hidden punch into your sell without hardcore sales pitches. Punch can take one of four forms:

1. Image awareness;
2. Lead generation;

3. Customer/prospect/donor education;
4. Call to direct action.

The newsletter is an excellent means to achieve all four and pull them off without a hitch.

"Advice for the "Almost Empty-Nester"" (Fig. 2-3), from a credit union newsletter called Mountain America Life Styles, successfully straddles the gap between raw advertising and acceptable self-serving hidden punch. In an apparently statesmanlike way, the article steers the reader to the credit union's services.

Advice for the "Almost Empty-Nester"

Preparing for retirement is an eye-opener. Even with 15 to 20 years to go, you still wonder if there is enough time to prepare for what should be the golden years of life. More now than ever before, your ability to maintain the lifestyle you want during retirement will be a result of plans you make now. Perhaps this is the time to seriously prepare a financial plan and make the most out of what is financially available.

How can "almost empty-nesters" with college tuition for children still looming on the horizon manage to save, invest and make the most of time left before their incomes take a tremendous drop at retirement? Are the company retirement and investment plans going to yield a high enough return to support your daily needs and style of living? What laws in Utah do you need to understand to make the most of your retirement income? Will you have enough saved and invested?

Planning for Tuition

Many families, especially dual-income families, have postponed parenthood until well into their 30s. These families will find themselves nearing retirement age while still burdened with their children's tuition bills.

If you happen to belong to one of those families looking for ways

to finance your children's education, the following formula may be helpful in planning how much you may need to save:

Determine the current cost for one year at the college or university your child would like to attend (if unsure of their plans, you may want to use $5,300 for public institutions and $14,500 for private). Multiply this number by the inflation factor 1.3 if your child will begin college in five years or less. Multiply that number by the amount of years your child will attend school, and you should have a good indication of your child's tuition costs.

Traditional pensions have become less dependable, so funding a retirement for most people is up to them. Employers are cutting back on health benefits as well. A longer life span will stretch retirement funds out over a longer period of time. Inflation will erode the value of a fixed pension by a large percentage. Paying taxes, saving and keeping up with inflation takes planning.

Financial Services Available

Many financial services are available to member/owners at Mountain America Credit Union. Financial counselors are ready to assist with information on many safe investment options. Direct deposit programs have proved one of the easiest ways to accumulate

Retirement should be a time of leisure and relaxation. Many couples, balancing their children's college educations with their hopes for financial security during those golden years, find the investments and savings programs at Mountain America Credit Union an important part of their plans for today and tomorrow.

money for investments. Many member/owners of Mountain America who have made continuous payroll savings deposits now have large sums of investment capital.

Annuities appear to be one of the favorites for many member investors, because they provide a

tax shelter and a higher fixed or variable rate of return on funds. Mutual fund investments, municipal bonds, tax-free bonds, government trust bonds and worldwide government bonds are yielding impressive returns during this economic recession.

Another financial service are insurance offerings that include home owner, auto, health, supplemental cancer and disability insurance. These programs could

make a difference in the safety of your retirement investments.

In order to live well in retirement, you need to make plans and sacrifices today. Saving with a reputable financial institution, making smart and safe investments and working with a knowledgeable financial counselor could make the difference in financial comfort, leisure time and security during your retirement years.

Figure 2-3. This article straddles the gap between raw advertising and acceptable self-serving hidden punch.

Commandment #7: Include Reader Involvement

Since you're planning a newsletter program, you may as well use it to its fullest power. Make the newsletter interactive. Find out what your customers/donors/prospects think and what they want to know . . . what's important to them.

An insurance company's newsletter called "intouch" (Fig. 2-4) *almost* pulls this off under the heading "Services to Help You."

The insurance company has a booklet called "Owner's Manual." The text points out: The reader can get the manual "from your New York Life agent" or by sending $3.00 to the parent company.

Nothing really wrong with that, except . . . the $3.00 differential will generate as many negative responses as positive responses. If the newsletter circulates only to the insurance company's policyholders, a phone call to the agent is logical; but an outsider will assume, logically, the agent is going to deliver the manual in person and make a pitch. This venerable image of the insurance agent is one most companies are trying to erase.

What would I have done? I'd either have made it universally free, turning inquiries over to agents; or made it universally $3.00, using an over-stamp on *all* copies authorizing the recipient to get it free by calling the agent whose name and phone appear on the front page.

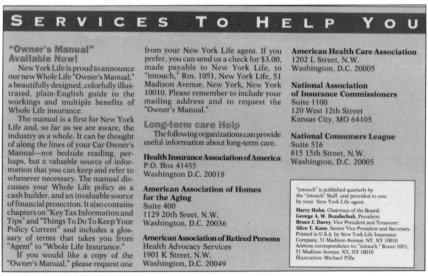

Figure 2-4. The insurance company offers a book called the "Owner's Manual." The $3.00 differential in the offer will generate as many negative responses as positive responses.

Commandment #8: Include Donor/Client/Prospect Education

No better way exists than a newsletter to educate your donors, clients, or prospects. If they don't know all the pros and cons of your services, products, or appeals—what's out there—what it can do and why they need it—why they should donate—they'll be in the dark. You don't want that, especially since with a newsletter you have the perfect and painless educational vehicle. Education (in the form of information) overcomes skepticism and overcomes fears of the unknown. . .especially if you're introducing a new technology people are afraid to try for one reason or another, or if you're justifying your own position in a competitive field.

Fig. 2-5 ("Caring") justifies the position of a health care group. The message is only partially successful because it violates a concept described in Chapter One—the disguise has slipped down and advertising-flavored, self-serving arguments seep through. Still, it isn't bad, because the point is made; and assuming the reader doesn't open the pages with a hostile attitude, the mild "selling" copy in the article headed "Cutting Health Care Costs" won't generate antagonism.

Commandment #9: Include Offers and Response Devices

It may sound trivial to include this commandment—but it's one of the most important, because it gives you a way to keep score.

Your newsletter could be a masterpiece with one small fault. Without telling your customers/donors/prospects what they can do and where they can turn to find out more or to enlist your services, it's a massive failure. All your creative and artistic efforts you may as well let sink to the bottom of the ocean.

Fig. 2-6 (The Levison Letter) is a primitive newsletter—two sides of a standard sheet of paper. Published by a free-lance writer, the newsletter includes some reasonable if obvious tips, then says:

> Want to avoid writing manufacturers' copy?
> Interested in putting me to work on your next letter, ad, flyer, etc.?
> Give me a call at. . .

Commandment #10: Include Legitimacy in Your Newsletter

What do I mean by legitimacy? Your newsletter should be perceived as beneficial to your readers. That perception depends on the belief—which you have to generate—that you sincerely want your newsletter to be factual, helpful, and correct.

With the other nine commandments in place, the tenth should be no problem at all!

INTERMOUNTAIN HEALTH CARE

CUTTING HEALTH CARE COSTS

IHC runs lean to keep patient charges low

Americans have been hearing about the high cost of health care for decades. Our nation's $700 billion annual health care bill accounts for over 12 percent of our Gross National Product. Demand for ever better health care is the major factor driving up costs. As a society, we want it all: state-of-the-art medicine and technology; instant access to the health care system; and low prices.

Although hospitals' share of health care costs has remained about the same in recent years, the share of costs attributed to other sectors of the industry has increased. Financial pressures on hospitals have forced record numbers to close—102 in 1988, 80 in 1989, and 63 in 1990—yet health care costs overall have continued to climb nationwide.

IHC's Contribution

Rising costs are a complex problem that needs to be addressed on a national level. But individual players can make an important difference. IHC hospitals work hard to save money, and these savings are passed along to consumers in the form of lower patient charges.

Here are some of the cost-cutting measures in place at IHC hospitals:

1. Strength of system. As part of a health care system, IHC hospitals take advantage of economies of scale which significantly lower their costs—and patient charges. For example:

■ **Volume buying**. Because IHC buys on a large scale for all its facilities, it negotiates greater discounts on goods and services.

■ **Consolidated services**. Many services (e.g., laundry) are performed at a central location for many hospitals, avoiding duplication of effort and lowering cost. Independent auditors found that IHC hospitals save over $36 million per year through centralized services.

■ **Self-insurance**. By self-insuring and managing risks, IHC hospitals save over $10 million in annual premiums.

2. Quality improvement. "Quality management" is the science of improving quality and efficiency. Some experts predict that quality management techniques, if widely implemented, could slash our national health care bill by as much as 20 percent. IHC hospitals have been leaders in quality improvement since the 1970s, and IHC recently received the nation's highest award for hospital quality *(see story on page 7)*.

3. Health Plans. IHC Health Plans offers three managed care plans which help businesses and employees reduce the cost of health insurance. Over 278,000 people are currently enrolled in IHC Health Plans.

Lower Patient Charges

IHC passes its cost savings on to consumers in the form of lower patient charges, improved facilities, and better health services. Analysis of Medicare data shows charges at IHC hospitals are an average 10.9 percent lower than charges at other hospitals in Utah. ▨

WHAT DOES "NONPROFIT HOSPITAL" MEAN?

"Nonprofit" (or "not-for-profit") means that the primary purpose of the hospital is to serve the community.

A type of charity. There are different kinds of charitable organizations. Some charities are primarily fund-raising groups; others provide various kinds of social services. While nonprofit hospitals engage in fund-raising, their primary activity is providing health care. (Note: All donations received by IHC hospitals are applied directly to patient care or to the purpose specified by the donor.)

Paying for charity care. No charity can mint money. Like all charitable organizations, nonprofit hospitals collect money from the public and redistribute it to the community according to their missions. When nonprofit hospitals give charitable benefits, the source of those benefits is money collected from the public in the form of donations or patient charges.

Patients who seek care in nonprofit hospitals are contributing to the charity care received by patients who are unable to pay. Yet patient charges are still lower at nonprofit hospitals because their margins are lower and their missions are to serve the community.

A margin is necessary. Any organization, whether for-profit or nonprofit, needs to take in more money than is spent, so that the organization can continue to satisfy future needs (improving facilities, expanding services, etc.) This difference between money collected and money spent is called an "operating margin."

Lower margins. Nonprofit hospitals exist to provide services to the community and set their margins as low as possible yet sufficient to continue serving. Nonprofit IHC hospitals set their rates to break even over the long run; for the past five years, this operating margin has been between two and three percent. All excess money collected by nonprofit hospitals is returned to the community in the form of improved facilities, better services, and lower patient charges.

For-profit hospital companies must provide a competitive return to stockholders from their margins in addition to providing reserves for the future.

Different behavior. Nonprofit organizations also act differently from for-profits. They undertake projects that are not economically rewarding but that are important for the community. For example, half of IHC hospitals are rural hospitals, operated at a collective loss of $4 million in 1990.

Nonprofit hospitals are historically tax-exempt. Utah's nonprofit hospitals must provide benefits to the community that are greater than their tax liability would be. IHC hospitals in Utah provide over $100 million in annual benefits, compared to a theoretical annual tax liability of about $7 million.

Figure 2-5. Commandment #8: Include donor/client/prospect education. This article justifies the position of a health care organization. The mild selling copy in the article won't generate antagonism.

reader faces, not the ones *they* face!

The bottom line is that if you're writing, or are responsible for copy of any kind, forget about *your* needs and problems.

Look at things from the *reader's* point of view and you can't go wrong.

Here's a twelve-point checklist of questions you can use to judge the effectiveness of advertising, direct mail, collateral, or package copy. I hope you find it of value!

✓ **Does the headline communicate a clear, compelling benefit?**

✓ **Does a subheadline elaborate on the benefit and increase reader interest?**

✓ **Does the first paragraph of the body copy expand on the headline and quickly get to the point?**

✓ **Am I using subheadlines to break up the copy and add visual interest?**

✓ **Am I keeping my paragraphs short for easy reading?**

✓ **Have I made the reader a compelling offer that's hard to refuse?**

✓ **Is ordering information complete and easy to understand?**

✓ **Is the vocabulary I'm using a good match for my readers?**

✓ **Can I use a guarantee to add credibility?**

✓ **Is the copy lively enough to keep the reader with me?**

✓ **Is my copy free of "cutesy", coy, or flowery language?**

✓ **Am I always answering the reader's crucial question, "What can your product or service do for me?"**

If you keep an eye on the basics I promise that your copy will get read and will produce the revenue-increasing results you're looking for.

* * *

Want to avoid writing manufacturers' copy?

Interested in putting me to work on your next letter, ad, flyer, etc.?

Give me a call at (415) 461-0672 and let's talk. I'd love to hear from you!

All best wishes!

Ivan Levison

IVAN LEVISON, an independent copywriter, works with clients like Bank of America, Levi Strauss & Co., Fireman's Fund, McKesson Corporation, Apple Computer, and Hewlett-Packard. He has won awards from the International Television Association, the New York Film Festival, the San Francisco Advertising Club, and many others. Mr. Levison has served as a judge at the American Advertising Federation's ADDY Awards competition and at the San Francisco Academy of Art Graphic Show. He is also a contributor to Inc. Magazine and other major publications.

Figure 2-6. Commandment #9: Include offers and response devices. (An off-the point suggestion: Don't use that word "etc." tell the reader what you mean.)

Conclusion

Let's put it all together. Use that checklist before you go any further in your newsletter program.

One key caution: These commandments won't work unless you know your target audience. Tailor your approach based on your own targeted readership. Don't load up a retirement newsletter with articles on child care. Don't load up a "See America" newsletter with articles on Madagascar and Borneo. Don't load up your hospital fund raising newsletter with articles on investment taxes.

But you already knew that.

CHAPTER *3*

Keep Your Newsletter on Target: Crucial Elements in Planning and Organizing Your Newsletter

"Seeing is believing."

You've set your sights. Your objectives are complete. Your goal (profitability) is engraved in your head. You now have a firm grip on where you're headed and how to go about achieving the perfect newsletter advertising piece. So what's the next step?

Beginning a newsletter program takes a little longer to plan than a conventional mailing piece or print advertising. After you've decided your format, however, subsequent issues should be easier to plan (if you don't stray from your original format).

Newsletter production should be allowed the same priorities and attention as your other advertising efforts. Many ambitious companies begin with good intentions but somehow the newsletter gradually takes a backseat because there's more work involved.

Don't let the ball drop. One of the main psychological ingredients behind your newsletter program's success is *consist-*

ency. Without consistency your newsletter—ergo, you—may be perceived even subconsciously as unreliable.

> Rule: The ground-breaking road to a cohesive hard-working newsletter is to first incorporate the elements that work into each newsletter.

Planning the content of your newsletter in each issue so you get the highest return is the same procedure you would use in creating a powerful written article. If it's going to be powerful, naturally it's going to influence your readers to your way of thinking. That's what the game is all about!

So what elements should always be incorporated into each article? Let's take a fast look.

Articles for Your Newsletter

Follow the "sell" psychology guidelines outlined in Chapter Two and originate some bylined or feature columns that will appear in every issue. Here are just a few suggestions:

1. **Gripe or Opinion Panel.** You can invite your readers to write to the editor about something they read in the previous issue. Then answer the questions in the next issue. If you have too many questions coming in (it should only happen!) — if you can't print and answer all the questions— be sure to answer them individually. This will give your readers a chance to participate and feel they're part of a decision-making process. They have a voice.

2. **Letter From The Editor:** Expounding his/her opinion about what's going on in the news at that particular time, relating to something which pertains to your business or organization.

3. **Marketing or Industry Trends.** Updates about what's happening in your industry or organization, events affecting your readers.

4. **New Research Reports and Analyses.**

5. **This Month's Spotlight Feature.**

6. **News Hotline.**

7. **This month's call to action.**

The Newsletter Timetable

Numerous factors play a part in the time needed to be set aside to get your issue out on the deadline date.

1. The amount of research you need to gather.

2. Are you going to have "outside" contributing articles?

3. Scheduling interviews.

I. Action Program: Newsletter Program

II. Objectives: Produce a **[number of pages the newsletter will be]** to:

1. Establish a communications between **[company]** and **[clients, donors, customers, prospects]**.

2. Build stronger customer relations.

3. To reduce attrition.

4. To educate and inform.

5. To cross-sell other products and services.

6. Increase revenue from existing clients.

7. Generate sales leads.

III. Goal: To increase profitability.

IV. What is your focus for this issue?

V. Strategy

1. To use **[internal or external]** resources to produce newsletter.

2. To use interviews of professionals in the field.

3. Solicit outside articles written by professionals in the field.

4. To use an editorial.

5. Success Stories.

VI. Tactics and Timetable:

1. Research Ideas for Issue:

2. Finalize Focus for Issue:

3. Gather materials, research and solicit outside articles from other sources:

4. Conduct Interviews:

5. Write case histories, filler material, response devices

6. First draft ready

7. Make corrections or changes to first draft

8. Send copies of articles to interviewees for verification of facts.

9. Choose art pieces for articles.

10. Final editing and layout

11. Layout submitted to newsletter committee

12. Submit newsletter to artist for camera ready material

13. Order labels

14. Letter from president

15. Proof back from artist and proofed.

16. Submit job for any corrections

17. Boards finalized

18. Check bluelines

19. Print job.

20. To mail house.

21. Send thank you notes to contributors.

4. How many department heads have to review the issue.

5. Are you using an attorney to make sure you haven't put anything in the newsletter which will be illegal?

6. Editing articles from outside contributors and getting their okays.

7. Design time.

8. Print time.

Most of these factors require time, and effort too, from others. The more time you allot yourself and others to meet deadlines, the better chance you have of making your deadlines.

You may find the mock-up schedule on page 33 helpful. Of course you may need to add extra items or delete a few of the steps.

(As previously discussed, your first step is to get a clear picture of the direction you've decided to go before you begin scheduling. Write it up—type it out—whatever. But keep it in front of you while you're producing the newsletter to keep focused on your plan of action and what you're trying to achieve.)

How to Track Your Timetable

Now you have the number of items you have to integrate into your production plan. How much time is each phase going to take exactly? That depends on how in-depth each issue can be *and how seriously this project is taken by everyone involved*. Keep in mind the time frame can vary from issue to issue.

I suggest working backwards. Work from the date you want your newsletter to be shipped and count the days backwards it should take to get the issue out on that date. You'll get the date you need to begin work on each newsletter issue.

Begin by planning what's going to go into one particular issue before you set a date. Some issues will take longer than others.

Big Factors Which Will Affect Your Timetable

1. Department figures.
2. Organization.
3. Chain-of-command confusion or arguments.
4. Executive ego.

Your First Step in Meeting Your Deadlines: Save Hair-ripping, Panic-stricken, Stress Attacks and Precious Time with the Fine-Art of Organization

Whether or not you're producing your newsletter in-house, or you're the advertising agency producing the newsletter for one of your clients, you must now encompass some of an editor's and writer's guidelines to getting the job done.

This doesn't mean you should turn around and get a new degree in journalism. It simply means you have to integrate some of a professional editor's organizational skills into your newsletter production. Don't worry, it's easy and painless—a lot easier than muddling through with no set guidelines. We'll just steal a few tips and tricks of their trade.

> "But this project is beginning to sound like a lot more trouble than it's worth!"

Nonsense! In fact this project will be a lot less trouble than you ever imagined if you know how to gun your psychological motorboat through the sea of over-whelming doubts of the "Where do I start?" and "This has to be done perfectly" syndromes.

Before committing the time, be sure you can honestly meet each set deadline. The best way to do this it to organize your time effectively. Begin by setting a pattern for organizing research, interviews, and articles. Once you can get your organization down pat you can breeze fairly easily through the newsletter. Your articles will not only read better, but by organizing what you're going to say and how you're going to say it will save you time in rewrites.

Being able to organize your issues will also negate any inkling to ramble or spew out too much uninteresting information.

A promotional newsletter can't be effective if it discourages your target-readers from scanning the newsletter. Newsletter pieces should be short, to the point, catching the interest of your audience, and selling them at the same time.

The Organization of a Newsletter

Your timetable has allotted only so much time to the researching, interviewing, writing, and designing of the newsletter issue itself. Let's break each component down so when you begin the issue you know exactly how much time you have to complete each task.

First of all, you have your objectives and your time frame in front of you. The next step is to gather all your materials, outlines, and research together and keep them in one notebook.

Step One—Organizing the Articles

Begin your issue by determining what you want to accomplish with each article. The most important key to remember when you begin organization of your articles is this:

> The purpose of your articles is to maintain your goal and objectives of your newsletter.

Don't stray. Your articles should slant towards your purpose—not roam in another direction. The best advice I can offer you is: Draft an outline.

Attention to just seven points *has to* result in an effective article:

1. What is the slant of your article? What do you want to communicate to your audience? Write it down in one sentence. (Choosing the most effective slants for your articles will be discussed in depth in Chapter 5.)

2. Think your story through.

3. Write down the important points which embellish or amplify your original explanatory sentence.

4. Organize each point so that when you start writing, these points will take the reader on a logical journey . . . and will let you know where *you're* going.

5. Write your lead.

6. Your lead should ease you right into your story. Use the points you've outlined to guide you through to the conclusion.

7. Don't get side-tracked. Keep your essential points in view and stay on a steady, comprehensible road map.

Step Two—Gathering and Organizing Your Research—How Much Is Too Much?

We can all get caught in the research trap. The research trap keeps you from ever finishing an article. I know if I gather too much information I'll get totally confused and lose track of the thoughts and ideas I had in the first place. Don't research more than you need. If you have an your outline of where you want your story to go—research only those parts.

Don't get side-tracked onto different roads that don't lead to where you've decided your article should go. If it's interesting save it for another article and just start writing.

The three-step formula for organized writing:

> 1. Organize your research before writing.
> 2. Combine all pertinent research you've gathered for each important point you want to hit in your article. Make a note of each point on your outline.
> 3. Begin writing.

Where can you find your research information? Number one, you should have some very good sources right where you work. But where else can you look for reference materials?

Consult your librarian. Consult an expert. If you can't find an expert, consult the *Encyclopedia of Associations*. Theoretically you shouldn't have a hard time finding an expert in almost any field, considering that your company or organization probably is associated with experts they deal with every day.

Consult trade magazines. Professional research services are also available. Professional researchers have their own resources and can often get the research you need right away, saving you time if not money.

Hundreds of "standard" resources are available and your librarian should know where to get them for you. Take my word: The information is out there and it's truly easy to find.

Step Three—The Elusive Art of Conducting the "Interview."

How to conduct an interview: Phone, in-person, or sending the questions to the interviewee? Rarely have I been so lucky as to have the benefit of being able to interview someone in-person for a newsletter interview. You aren't a publishing company, and this isn't the *New York Times*. It's economical and time-saving to conduct the interview by phone ...unless yours is a local newsletter and you'd more than likely be interviewing someone right in your own vicinity.

But most of the time your promotional newsletter may cater to a wider audience than your neighborhood. So let's assume you'll be doing most of your interviewing by phone. First, *before you lift that receiver*, you decide the slant the interview should take.

Seven key points to remember:

> 1. If you're going to use a tape recorder, be sure to tell the person you're interviewing that you'll be taping the interview. You could run into some legal problems if you don't.

2. Even though you're taping the interview, take notes. And I mean *take notes*. (A good yardstick for interview effectiveness: If you've conducted the interview in an interesting manner, you'll remember the most important points made. If not, believe me, something is wrong with your interview. Start over again. If you can't remember the interview, no one else will either.)

3. You may want to send the questions you'll be asking to the person you'll be interviewing beforehand. This way he or she will be prepared with information ahead of time and avoid any embarrassment or negative reactions to questions.

4. Give yourself plenty of time to get permission from the person you're interviewing and coordinate a set time and day. Don't wait until the last minute or you may not get the interview.

5. Do your homework. Research the topic of the interview so you have a clear direction of where you want to go.

6. After you've asked your questions, summarize what you understand from the interview. Be sure you're clear on all points.

7. After you have written the article, a good habit to get into is to fax or send the written article to the interviewee. This isn't for approval; it's just to be sure you have your facts straight.

Other tips to remember: Be sure you have the person's name spelled correctly. His title and where he works should be rechecked. If the interviewee refers to certain documents or dates, be sure they're correct too. If it's controversial get written documentation to back it up.

Receiving and Editing Articles from Solicited Outside Sources

Editing articles sent to you from outside sources often takes a lot of rewrites. Don't expect these people to be expert writers. Again you'll have to sort out the important key ingredients of the story and start over again to make it more interesting and comprehensible to your readers. *Be sure to allot time in your schedule for rewrites from outside sources.* Once you do edit the article, it would be good practice to let the contributor read it over before it gets printed.

The Department Figures Trap

Another problem stems from the company or organization itself—too many department heads having to approve the copy. Get this straight right away. Copy approval has to be done in a time-frame. If not the whole newsletter program could end up chucked out the window.

Step Four—Consistency: The Glue that Binds Your Newsletter to Reader-Confidence

Now that we've touched upon some of the major time traps and how to get past them, you should be able to approximate the time you need to get your newsletter out on schedule. You may have to start the newsletter three months ahead of time. Depending on who you are, three months, three weeks, or three days should be no problem.

Be realistic about your own capabilities. By the time you're finished with one issue it's usually time to schedule the next. No, there's never enough lead time between issues. Parkinson's Law applies, even if you're only producing twice a year.

Yes, but on the other hand...it's fun, challenging, and you'll reap its rewards for a long time. So don't hesitate, you're losing time!

CHAPTER *4*

Power-Propelling Design: How To Match Your Medium to Your Message

*"Design *!*-#!??"*

Why are some newsletters more appealing than others? Why do some newsletters grab their reader while others look forbidding, almost defying the target-individual to try to read them?

Howard Penn Hudson superbly describes the importance of newsletter design in his book *Publishing Newsletters*, as . . .

"Superior editorial content enhanced by appropriate design, typography, photographic quality, and printing quality."

Design isn't thrown in as an afterthought. Design takes a partner-position with the most important factor—your message.

Could you possibly be thinking that many newsletters you've seen have absolutely no design—yet you know they're successful?

First of all, a newsletter has to have an underlining design or it conveys no image at all. Use of photos or graphics is only a small part of the overall design of your newsletter. When I talk of design, I'm not thinking in terms of whether or not the newsletter integrates photos and graphics, but, rather, the grid or format; the typography; the color; the paper stock; callouts. If the newsletter isn't consistent in these important areas, it won't get read. In fact without these elements of design—guideposts to the reader—any communication would be impossible to read.

Second, you, as publisher of a sponsored newsletter, have a different set of reader-interest problems to contend with than do regular subscription newsletters. Subscription newsletters are solicited. People buy them for the information. They don't have to be lured into the publication, because they're anticipating the information. They've paid good money to get it.

Our problem is that sponsored newsletters are unsolicited. Your publication has to reach out and grab the reader the second he or she looks at it or your dollars are wasted.

You make the choice. Flimsy or strong, your design becomes the foundation on which you build your structure. It's just as easy to choose and implement a strong foundation. This enables the ten commandments underlying the basic ''sell'' psychology of a sponsor promotional newsletter to build themselves on solid ground. Design builds readership. Design is the only way a newsletter can reach your target audience and obtain your ultimate goal: *increasing your revenue.*

The Invisible Design Structure

Behind every project, behind every scheme or goal, if you look at the underlying pattern of how it was achieved, you'll notice the design. A design needs to exist to achieve your plan. And if the design matches your message your readers are comfortable and you've propelled your publication into success.

You don't have to drag out the heavy artillery. You don't have to spend exorbitant amounts of money for a commercial artist. You don't even have to use graphics or four color art work to create a hard-working design.

The only criterion you have to meet is to create your format so the design matches your message. . . and both medium and message match the group you're trying to reach.

Consider yourself ''master marketer'' because you've made the decision to create your own medium. Not only do you dictate what your message is, but you dictate *how* your readers perceive that message through your medium. This control over perception makes your message that much more targeted. And an effective, targeted newsletter doesn't cost any more than it would cost to run one ad for 12 months in one printed medium.

The important key is to exploit your newsletter to its highest capabilities.

Your Message Dictates the Design of Your Newsletter

Two easy rules here:

> 1. Design shouldn't contradict your message. Your message is your priority. The design works with your message to motivate your readers.
> 2. Don't use type, color, paper, photos, illustrations or construct a layout which hinders what you're trying to communicate.

Fig. 4-1 is an example of what not to do.

This is a newsletter printed every month by a Chamber of Commerce.
Target:
Members of the Chamber of Commerce. Business people.

What are the psychographic and demographic characteristics of this target? Professionals, for one. They're interested in marketing, in increasing business profitability. They don't have a lot of time to read their mail. (In this particular town the group is mostly male-dominated.)
Objectives:
1. Maintain membership;
2. Fund raising;
3. Establish credibility;
4. Increase participation;
5. Position the Chamber of Commerce as ''the'' organization which helps businesses profit;
6. Increase revenue.

I can think of quite a few marketing problems this newsletter *could* solve but doesn't even begin the job.
Message:
The Chamber of Commerce will help make your business profitable.

Does the Chamber of Commerce newsletter communicate this message? Are the points convincing? Are they credible? Will they increase participation? Will the newsletter help to increase revenue? Will the newsletter help to maintain membership? Does the newsletter help to establish and/or maintain a business-promoting image? And finally — will this newsletter combat member attrition, the deadly enemy of every organization?

St. George Chamber of Commerce
NEWS & VIEWS

With the Annual Installation Banquet behind us we look forward to 1992. We realize that during these competitive times the Chamber must constantly work to improve our performance if we are to meet the needs of our business community. While we tend to look at our successes, we are also concerned about spotlighting problems to determine where action is necessary.

> To better serve you, OUR MEMBERS, we need your support.

Would you please help us measure how well our organization is doing?

We look at our image, efficiency, financial stablity, services rendered, credibility, etc., to properly serve as we establish a base standard of measurement. We want to hear from you in defining problems or unique opportunities that we need to actively address as we plan for the future. Please take a moment and tell us what you feel are our greatest strengths and weaknesses; what you feel are the greatest opportunities and, YES, the problems facing St. George in 1992 that we should be focusing on. If there is one thing we could do better, OR DO that we're not presently doing, what would it be?

It is our intention to focus all our resources on priority objectives. We will be emphasizing results. We want to provide timely, thoughtful information to our members and keep you informed of progress, success in obtaining priority objectives.

We want to address issues and needs and yet realize the full potential of the combined strength of our membership working together.

We want to develop and utilize talents and resources and be responsive to specific member's needs.

We have great resources we feel we are not tapping, not only within our business community, but the retired community as well, and solicit input on how we can be more effective. Our objective is to develop a "WIN/WIN" situation where membership in the Chamber is a rewarding, positive experience, where you are insured a quality investment and feel a part of this organization.

Mission Statement "Create a Climate Where Businesses Can Operate Profitably"

It is truly an honor to work with the dedicated and talented Board members as well as others in the community who are willing to serve and give of themselves to help each other succeed.

Your response and input is valuable to us. Please respond by phone or in writing to help us accomplish the goals established for 1992!

Call 628-1658

Figure 4-1. This is an example of what not to do in newsletter design. First of all, the design isn't aimed at a business-to-business readership. Second, when typefaces are interspersed in the same sentence it makes for strained reading. Third, the choice of graphic borders are inappropriate for the target. Fourth, lack of headlines and subtitles make it difficult to tell where one idea begins and another ends.

44

If they achieve these objectives it won't be because of the newsletter.

You tell me: Why does the whole foundation of this newsletter get in the way of achieving these objectives? (Don't read on until you've reached your own conclusion.)

Okay, do we agree? It's inconsistent. The written message doesn't benefit its reader. The design isn't aimed at the business readership.

Budget isn't a factor here. Whether your budget constraints are high or low, no excuse is valid for turning out an inconsistent, imageless publication. Always maintain professionalism. This message and this design are communicating on a scrambled frequency.

Why? Take a look at the different typefaces. One or two different typefaces are all right to use, but when they're interspersed in the same sentence or paragraph it has an unprofessional effect which makes the reading strained.

The choice of graphics (hearts and flowers) is inappropriate for a business-to-business newsletter. The typesetting is inconsistent. The lack of headlines and subtitles makes it difficult to tell where one article begins and another ends. The copy lacks any beneficial information for the reader to use. No response devices exist. No motivating elements exist.

You're probably gathering: This isn't the way you'd put together this newsletter, after you've read this book...or maybe even before you've finished it.

More: The newsletter is aimed at businesses.

This newsletter is a business-to-business communications piece. But it's more suited to neighbor-to-neighbor. A touch of "mom and pop" in the newsletter isn't taboo because this is a small town community. But let's know when to draw the line. Maintaining professionalism is still top priority.

How to Match Your Medium to Your Target

What's your message? You're creating the medium and the design of that medium to match your message and your target readers. Let's get started.

Ask yourself this question: Let's say you're a fund-raising organization. You're raising funds for children in third world countries. And you want to put an ad in a magazine. Purpose: Prospecting. Psychographics tell you that your biggest target is the upscale woman over the age of 40. Where are you going to place this ad? In *Seventeen* magazine? In *Gentleman's Quarterly*? I don't think so. You'd get more response from *Lear's* magazine because the profile of your prospect is at least 100 times more likely to be reading that magazine.

Here's the parallel: When you're publishing a promotional newsletter, it should follow the same pattern. You've got an infinite gold mine in your hands. Don't blow it by designing a newsletter which would appeal to teenagers when you want it to appeal to seniors.

How to Choose the Right Design to Match Your Message With Your Target

Don't take the lead from "for profit" newsletters. You have totally different objectives that influence the way you'll format your newsletter. In earlier chapters we defined your market, your objectives, the "sell" psychology to use for your particular market and planning your topics of interest for your message.

The next step is to establish the look that will hook your targets and draw them into your newsletter. Any sponsored promotional newsletter will vary in its look depending on who its readership is.

For example, a fund raising newsletter should look different from a newsletter from financial advisors. How? Because the subject is more emotional, the layout should be warmer and more personal. That's what matching medium and message means.

But every newsletter usually contains these common characteristics:

1. Nameplate;
2. Subtitle (emphasizing the editorial content);
3. Logo of the association or organization;
4. Table of contents;
5. Masthead;
6. Headers;
7. Footers;
8. Headlines and subtitles;
9. Grid;
10. Title of newsletter.

Don't know what "headers" and "footers" and "grid" are? Not to worry.

Who are you?

Take a look at your logo or title of your newsletter. Does it express who you are and what you do? If not, scrap it and begin again.

How to match design to your message.

Who are you? Or, rather, who are you supposed to be as far as the recipient of your newsletter is concerned?

If you're assuming a statesmanlike posture—politicians, schools, civic groups, churches, libraries, hospitals, or other non-profit organizations—you need to pay specific attention to what you're conveying in your newsletter. The newsletter should maintain your *integrity* and establish *credibility*. That means the choice of paper stock, colors and graphics shouldn't imply extravagance. After all, you're ultimately asking for their donated money. You'll defeat the very purpose if it appears you're spending it on a newsletter when the money should be going to the benefit of your cause.

The newsletter in figure 4-2 may backfire for this particular health care system. It is a four-color, 16-page glossy. The design doesn't match the

Figure 4-2. This newsletter is four color and 16 pages of glossy paper. For that reason alone, the design doesn't match the message: "Non-profit hospitals lower health care costs."

47

SPRING, 1992

IN THIS ISSUE

- Tax time: getting ready to prepare your return.
- IRS hotlines: who to call for help.
- An IRA with us is anything but plain vanilla.
- Tax-free investments.
- Using equity to pare down your taxes.

SECURITY PACIFIC BANK

SIMPLY STATED

PUBLISHED FOR CUSTOMERS OF SECURITY PACIFIC BANK

A Few Words About Taxes

Helpful words, hopefully. And a few sympathetic ones as well.

That's the theme of this issue of "Simply Stated". We've culled some items from tax materials we've received throughout the year which may be useful as you prepare for your annual tussle with Form 1040. And we've included a few suggestions of our own which might take some of the sting out of tax bite.

A word of advice, too: despite promises for a more simplified form, it seems to get more complicated. We suggest that if you have any doubts whatsoever about your return, seek the advice and assistance of a qualified tax preparer.

It could save you a headache or two. And it just might save you a lot of money besides.

Ready!..Get set!...

Sharpen the pencils, get a new battery for the calculator and lay in a supply of aspirin. It's nearly that time. Tax preparation time. About as much fun to look forward to as a root canal. Unless, of course, you're getting a refund. If you are, congratulations. (You may want to check your withholding, too — see related article inside.) If not, well, there's always hope you'll break even.

To get you in the mood, we gathered the following bits of information from IRS materials.

The 5 Most Common Taxpayer Errors.

These errors accounted for a sizeable majority of the total number made by taxpayers on their 1990 federal returns. Watch for them; they could be costly.

1 Omitted an entry on return: 30.7%

2 Made an incorrect entry on return: 19.1%

3 Made at least one math error: 17.4%

4 Made an entry on the wrong line: 8.8%

5 Made an unnecessary entry: 7.7%

Another common error to watch out for: people go to all the trouble to prepare a return, then forget to sign it. Be sure to sign and date yours. It's probably the easiest way of all to avoid delays and possibly a penalty.

A Quarterly Newsletter On Hiring, Managing And Retaining Employees

Summer 1988

Hiring and Compensation—
The Key to Your Company's Growth

Are your company's compensation levels current with the rest of the industry? Do you ask the right questions during interviews with job candidates? Source Finance's *1988 Hiring and Compensation Guide* can help you find out.

The Compensation Guide is a valuable salary administration tool. Hiring managers can use it to review compensation levels and determine if their company's salaries are in line with industry norms.

Twenty-nine positions in public and private accounting are examined with salary levels given for varying levels of experience from staff to senior management. Positions examined are from the areas of cost accounting, financial planning/analysis, internal audit, and taxation.

Compensation information was gathered from a survey sent to tens of thousands of accounting and finance professionals at all levels and compiled by an independent research group.

The Hiring and Compensation Guide provides hiring managers with interviewing tips, techniques for getting offers accepted, as well as a checklist for reference checking.

Tips include:

Questions proven to provide the most critical information about a candi-

In This Issue

FREE Hiring and Compensation Guide See page 3.

date's skill level, professional maturity, compatibility, and creativity.

Areas of information most often misrepresented on resumes, and how to verify the details.

Who to call and what to ask when checking references.

The *1988 Hiring and Compensation Guide* is free to hiring managers. To receive your copy, simply fill out and return the coupon on page three.

Can Leadership Ability Be Learned?

Research indicates that most people believe leaders are born leaders. Most people go along content to accept leadership or to look to others for it, even though they hold management positions.

However, from observing hundreds of people considered leaders by others, studies now show important revelations.

Foremost, there are no clear-cut leadership traits applicable to all situations. Rather, these traits are recognized collectively by each group. It's a matter of how the group defines leadership qualities and then reacts to these in one of its own members.

Some of the key traits most frequently found in those perceived as leaders are:

- **self-confidence**
- **demonstrated competence**
- **good listening skills**
- **empathy**
- **willingness to compromise**
- **ability to influence others without manipulation**

And, yes—leadership qualities *can* be learned

Figure 4-3. Which newsletter design do you think matches its message?

message which is "nonprofit hospitals lower health care costs." The readers may perceive that the hospital could lower the costs even more by not spending so much money on this newsletter.

Ostentation is the number one mistake for non-profit organizations. So here's a blanket rule for non-profit organization newsletters: If you use graphics be sure they communicate sincerity, honesty, and an awareness of money expenditures. The use of color should be toned down. Black and one other color should be the limit. Paper stock should probably be low-weight bond. The size doesn't really matter—8½" × 11" is the logical standard size (although "standard" can decrease impact by looking like everybody else's publication); but the amount of pages should be a maximum of six to eight or you'll get into higher cost. The key is to look inexpensive but professional.

Financial institutions and business-to-business organizations can be bold. Use from two to four colors, glossy or textured paper, heavy weight. Even a simple black and white newsletter can achieve a look of excellence by the quality of paper it's printed on and by having the design of the nameplate, grid, headlines and subtitles, and the use of tint backgrounds giving off an air of top professionalism.

Figure 4-3 shows two examples of newsletters which fall into the same category but have two different readerships. The "Simply Stated" newsletter is a financial newsletter to the consumer. This newsletter uses four color process on standard 60# paper. The overall design provides an even flow for the eyes.

But do the design techniques match their message? I believe the graphics are stretching to match the headlines. For example take a look at the headline and the graphic that belongs to the article, *Your IRA: At Security Pacific, It's Anything But Plain Vanilla*. I don't know whether they were trying to match a headline with the only illustration they had, or didn't have any illustrations to match the headline.

It's the same story on the front cover: The illustration depicts a maze made up of tax returns. I don't see any article which matches the graphic on page one.

The newsletter "Hireline" is simple black and white on textured paper. It's a business-to-business newsletter for the person who hires accounting and finance professionals. The graphics, headlines, and use of tinted backdrops complement each other and make the newsletter readable and beneficial for the reader. "Hireline" proves production doesn't have to be elaborate to work.

Newsletters designed for promoting travel should communicate excitement, relaxation, and adventure. The example shown in figure 3-4 gives you an idea of what not to do when you're promoting travel.

This newsletter is promoting adventure travel—but the color of the paper is dull gray, the ink is black, headlines don't tell a story, the title doesn't say anything, and the graphics are passive instead of active and don't carry any cutlines—which leaves them dangling in the air.

Newsletters promoting public health, life insurance or health-promoting products and services should be "friendly and inviting." If you're going to use graphics, use people and/or photos which give an aura of care for the

---

92 Schedule of Trips:

JUNE:
Alaska Birding Expedition
3rd -14th $1,250 or $1600
Natural History Tour
6th - 17th, $2050.
ANWR Backpack.
19th-28th
28th July 7th, $1650
Kongakut River
16th-25th , $2250
Hula Hula River
25th-July 4th, $2250
Prince William Sound Kayak:
18th -24th,
27th-July 3rd, $1150

JULY:
High Arctic Exploration
7th -16th, $2250
Noatak River Canoeing
8th -17th, $2175
Photographers Expedition
15th -28th, $3400
20th -29th, $2950
Prince William Sound Seakayak
July 30th -August 5th, $1150
2 week Noatak Canoe
19th-Aug.1st, $2140

AUGUST:
3 National Parks of Alaska
19th -Sept.2nd, $3250
Natural History Tour
19th-30th, $2050
Sheenjek River
12th -22nd $2175
Ca. Academy Science Seakayak
Kenai Fjords
9th -17th ,$1510
Prince William Sound Seakayak
July 30th -August 5th, $1150

Alaska is Big!

Ultimate Wilderness!

The Brooks Range is located entirely above the Arctic Circle. An untamed land of wild beauty, rich in Eskimo, Indian and prospecting history, it was still little mapped or explored until a few decades ago. It's hard to describe the uniqueness of this vast wilderness. There are boreal forests of spruce and birch, but tundra dominates the landscape and gives a feeling of expansiveness. Magnificent glacier carved valleys dissect the rugged mountains and rivers flow for hundreds of miles with no sign of civilization.
An astounding abundance of wildlife populates the Brooks Range. You are always likely to see caribou, moose, grizzlies, wolves, dahl sheep, fox and even musk-ox...all existing in a natural state of undisturbed relationships. You can fish for salmon, grayling, pike, sheefish, lake trout, arctic char, whitefish and burbot depending on location and time of year. For the birdwatcher, the green tundra is peppered with over a 140 species of migrating birds. They migrate from as far away as South America and Asia.
The Arctic National Wildlife Refuge is remote and pristine even by Brooks Range standards. The ANWR is the summer home of the160,000 member Porcupine caribou herd. They migrate here every year from Canada to bear their young. Only a handful of people have run the rivers or explored the mountains of Alaska's ultimate wilderness.
Our trips explore the heart of these great areas, we invite you to join us!

Have you Driven A Fjord Lately?

Few experiences can match the magic of paddling a seakayak. From its' Eskimo roots thousands of years ago, it has developed into a modern, stable and comfortable craft.
We offer 3 to 7 day trips in Kenai Fjords National Park and Prince William Sound. These areas are famed for their spectacular scenery and marine life. If you don't believe us, just come and see...
The Kenai Fjords and Prince William Sound are mantled by extensive ice fields. The many glaciers have carved huge valleys that are now filled with ocean waters. Edging the beaches and coves are thick forests of spruce and alder. Hanging glaciers cling to the mountainsides creating hundreds of waterfalls. Below, thousands of sea birds and marine mammals raise their young. With our kayaks, we have the freedom to explore and gain access to the most beautiful areas.
No prior experience is necessary to seakayak and expert instruction will be given by trip leaders. We love to eat...kayaks carry about *three times* the food and gear that you could carry backpacking. We like to be safe...Rugged and remote as they are, these areas have calm waters and a mild summer climate. Come and see the Alaska that few have seen and learn why seakayaking is one of the fastest growing paddle sports.

2

Figure 4-4. Travel promoting newsletters should portray action graphics. The graphics in this newsletter are absolutely passive.

ABC'S of health

A publication of
Memorial Hospital Children's Center
Serving the children of South Florida

Home safe home —
Preventing accidents around the house

Parents always will worry about the health and safety of their children. One of the best ways to look out for your children is to be on guard against accidents. According to the American Academy of Pediatrics, more school-aged children die from injuries than from all diseases combined.

You can take steps to prevent some accidents from taking place. Start by teaching your children basic safety rules:

✔ Set a good example by always wearing your seat belt. Restrain children in car seats or with seat belts when driving.

✔ Bike helmets should be considered necessary equipment for all cyclists. Don't let your child ride a bicycle without one.

✔ When on a boat, see that children and adults wear life vests. Always supervise children near water.

Household chemicals should be stored in locked cabinets, out of the reach of children.

Child-proofing your home
A curious child can find many ways to get hurt when left alone for even a moment. Review your home for these potential dangers:

Cabinets/drawers — Use child-proof latches on cabinets and drawers where children might find harmful objects.

Electrical outlets —Purchase safety caps for all outlets. Unplug bathroom appliances, such as hairdryers and electric rollers, when not in use.

Household chemicals — Store detergents, cleaning products, cosmetics, medicines and pest killers out of reach of children and in child-resistant containers.

Household plants — Check in and around your home for poisonous plants. Harmful plants include dieffenbachia, oleander, azalea, spathe and aloe plants, English ivy, philodendron and others.

Plastic bags and wraps — Dispose or store out of reach all dry cleaning, produce, trash and other plastic bags. They can cling to a child's face and cause suffocation.

Furniture — Pad or cushion sharp corners and edges of furniture or fixtures. Be aware that reclining chairs can pinch fingers and trap small bodies.

Firearms — The best situation is not to have a gun in a home with children. When this is not possible, keep the gun

and the ammunition locked up separately — and be certain to keep track of the keys.

Electric garage door openers — Check to see that your garage door opener has a safety mechanism that reverses the door when it is stopped by an object. Children can become trapped if they try to sneak underneath the door.

Water heater — Adjust the setting on your water heater to 120° F to avoid serious burns, which can occur when children are left alone to play with the bathtub faucets. Also, purchase inflatable cushions to cover the spout, and non-slip mats for the tub.

Baby's crib — Remove pillows, extra blankets, loose bumper pads and stuffed animals from cribs, especially for infants under 4 months. Never hang objects over the crib, as this can lead to possible strangulation.

Everyday hazards
With all the media attention on subjects such as radon and lead, you might think that there's nothing you can do to protect your child. But you can. Start right within your own home and make it safer for your family.

Memorial Hospital Children's Center

Vol. 4 No. 2 Winter 1991

Figure 4-5. The overall appearance of this newsletter is inviting and caring.

individual reading your newsletter. Cold graphics such as charts and graphs are very impersonal. You're trying to get a humanized reaction, and you can't achieve that by aiming your graphics at the chairman of the board. Take a look at figure 4-5 and 4-6.

Figure 4-6. This newsletter would be more effective if the graphics matched the readership it was addressing. Personal photos or illustrations would have worked better. The graphics they have used make it difficult to read the copy (in fact impossible to read the copy).

These examples give you an idea of the overall tone of designs you should and shouldn't use.

Color

Let's decide which colors you would use to communicate your message even better. Colors can convey credibility, warmth, business tones, and the overall feel of your organization. If your budget allows you to use more than one color here are a few suggestions:

1. Blue communicates trust, quality, and stability.
2. Green usually signifies healthfulness, and relaxation.
3. Red is urgent, fast or forceful.
4. Yellow is usually a weak color.
5. Orange will tend to make people uneasy.
6. Pink is friendly.
7. Black is conservative and serious.

But don't get carried away on your second or third color. Use it to accent points you want to *stand* out in the newsletter, not *drown* out.

How to Choose a Paper Stock

The size, texture, weight and finish of the paper you choose all affect the cost of your newsletter. Too, deciding which typefaces and what type of graphics you want to use will have an influence on the quality of paper you choose.

If you anticipate using photographs and graphics, some papers are more absorbent than others and can impede visual clarity. Don't use small intricate type if you're using a soft, absorbent paper stock. Coated or glossy paper stock will give you a better quality of reproduction for photographs. If you're thinking of budget—especially if you're a fund-raising, non-profit organization—a 60# offset paper stock is low weight for mailing and is opaque enough for ink coverage on both sides.

What Type of Grid Should You Use?

The newsletter grid helps to maintain consistency issue to issue. It gives you defined horizontal and vertical margins for the page and reflects the image you want to achieve.

Classic Newsletter Format

The classic or one column grid is formatted to look like a typical letter style...the sheet is just a single column in which the line goes all the way from left to right. *The Kiplinger Letter* and many subscription newsletters

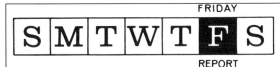

FRIDAY

S M T W T F S

REPORT

Published weekly by HOKE COMMUNICATIONS INC. • 224 Seventh Street • Garden City, N.Y. 11530 • 516-746-6700

October 18, 1991

THOUSANDS OF MAIL ORDER MARKETERS AND TELEMARKETERS have reportedly been identified by VISA for violation of their 1% chargeback rule and are in danger of being terminated if they don't reduce their chargebacks within 120 days, according to <u>Larry Schwartz</u> of the Credit Card Bureau and cofounder of the National Association of Credit Card Merchants.

VISA had announced that its new 1% limit on cardholder dispute chargebacks was created to terminate the merchant status of 175 sponsors of sex lines, but these new regulations are beginning to affect many other marketers. Schwartz says that a VISA insider told him that 4,000 "direct marketers" have been targeted. A VISA spokesperson denies this figure, claiming they have identified only 200 offending merchants. Either way, many marketers are on guard as the holiday season approaches, a time of the year when their chargeback volume typically increases.

Schwartz says one large bank has terminated 170 of its merchants since 8/1 "without allowing them sufficient time to apply elsewhere for merchant status and make an orderly transfer of their merchant account." Schwartz describes the effect as "panic," and says it has resulted in many marketers closing their doors. Other merchants are desperately seeking ways to reduce their chargeback rates below 1% and fearing the worst as their rates continue near 1%.

VISA recently issued another ruling, requiring catalog, mail order and telemarketers be divided by banks into six categories instead of one. VISA says this will allow them to add enhancements to their regulations in order to "reward low-risk and/or high-performance merchants." This ruling is optional until 4/1/92.

The six categories include <u>catalogers</u> (electronic or paper); <u>combination mail/phone and retail transactions</u> (which exceed 15% of sales) (e.g., most florists); <u>outbound and inbound telemarketing</u>; <u>continuity/subscription merchants</u>; <u>all other marketers</u>.

Rumors persist that heated discussions are ongoing between VISA and some of its member banks concerning raising the 1% limit on all 10 types of customer dispute chargebacks to 3%.

Schwartz says issuing banks are looking for ways to increase chargebacks because cardholders are purchasing less in this soft economy and rate of bankruptcies and failure to pay credit card bills has increased. Also, Schwartz pointed to a bill sponsored by Rep. <u>Charles E. Schumer</u> (D-NY), which, if passed, would force card issuers to disclose their interest rates, annual fees, grace periods and other information in every ad and on every envelope of every mailing.

Schwartz said merchants are taking precautions, including splitting sales into parts, stressing return policies, securing signed orders on purchases and deliveries, examining proprietary credit cards. ∎

Figure 4-7. This is a prime example of the classic newsletter format. This newsletter is a subscription newsletter—but it's deceiving—it also is a sponsored newsletter sold by subscription but selling its own services and products as well. It implies "late-breaking" news.

use this style quite often in order to cram all the information they can into a little bit of space. Their readers do read it and it projects a ''I have more to say than space permits'' image their readers expect.

But consider one point: These readers were solicited to buy the information inside the newsletter. They're expecting this information, they want the information, and they paid for the information.

But you have to grab the reader's interest right away. You may *only* want to consider this style if you're trying to imitate or be perceived as a well-established newsletter publisher such as the *Kiplinger Letter*. So a great many financial planners use the single-column ''letter-effect'' style.

But I wouldn't recommend this style for a sponsored newsletter. Your purpose is to motivate and get your readers to respond. It would take exceptional know-how from an experienced newsletter promotional writer to pull it off without generating a negative comparison with the well-known newsletters. Figure 4-7 is a prime example of the classic newsletter format.

If you insist on this type of format, the classic newsletter style can be used best to imply the immediacy of late-breaking news. The message appears to be urgent. Careful with graphics in this format: The use of graphics will often look disproportionate to the newsletter's contents. If you have multiple articles or sections, you have to make careful use of typefaces so your messages don't get lost or mistakenly tied together in the pages.

My personal opinion: A single column format makes for dull and hard reading when you're trying to push your product or service.

Two Column Formats

This type of format is almost too symmetrical. It would, however, be a good format to use for senior citizens who need to read a larger typeface. Your use of graphics can be limited. And two columns can break the natural flow of the eye. Take a look at figures 4-8 and 4-9.

Three Column Grids

Personally, I like three column grids. Most newsletter publishers will tell you this isn't a true newsletter because it's impossible to use typewritten text. But three columns help us create articles the way they should be—short, snappy and to the point. It's easy to do this with a three column grid. It has a clean effect and can increase readership by giving the reader a variety of places to look. If you feel there's too much monotony in the design of a three column grid, take a look at figure 4-10.

The Levison Letter

ACTION IDEAS FOR BETTER MARKETING COMMUNICATIONS

THE SUBJECT:

A TWELVE POINT CHECKLIST FOR AVOIDING "MANUFACTURERS' COPY"

Professional advertising copywriters refer to a certain kind of writing as "manufacturers' copy" -- the kind that manufacturers themselves write (or would write) for their own products.

IVAN LEVISON is an award-winning independent copywriter.

Instead of viewing the world from the customer's point of view, the owner of the company sees things through his or her narrow perspective.

The result?

Selling copy is heavy on personal horn-blowing and short on benefits.

One of the ways to find out if you're writing or paying for manufacturers' copy is to look for vocabulary danger signs.

Do you constantly talk about "commitment" and "dedication" and use inflated phrases of all kinds?

Watch it. You may be heading down a slippery slope.

Let me give you some specific examples of the kind of manufacturers' copy you see all over the place. (All the examples come from a recent issue of Forbes magazine.)

Manufacturers' copy from Consolidated Freightways:

"We pride ourselves on being an integral part of your business, in industries ranging from automobiles to aerospace, computers to retailing. That means playing a vital role in Just-In-Time manufacturing, inventory management and distribution. It means dedicating ourselves to increasingly sophisticated levels of communication, and providing the flexibilty to make your business more competitive. But above all, it means truly understanding and responding to your needs."

The reader doesn't care what you pride yourself on. They want to know "What are you going to do for me?"

Manufacturers' copy from the New Federal States of Germany:

"For decades, the words 'Made in W. Germany' have set the standard for product excellence. And for decades, West Germany has been equal to the challenge this standard implies. Now we face a new challenge. By dropping the "W," we extend this mark of excellence to include the New Federal States of Germany. And in realizing this aim, we create investment opportunities of unparalleled proportion for companies large and small around the globe."

The New Federal States of Germany should focus on the challenges the

Figure 4-8. This is a perfect example of confusing the reader's eye.

Equity Liner

What will the next decade bring?

In the '70s, Americans binged. In the '80s, they purged. And in the '90s, look forward to paying it all back! So says John Rutledge of California's Claremont Economics Institute in a recent *Changing Times* article. Rutledge, a superoptimist, also predicts more growth and less inflation for the coming decade. "The long term looks a lot better than most people think," he forecasts.

"Whatever the economy will do . . . any forecaster who accurately predicts the future will do so out of luck."

Forbes magazine

The '90s are coming!

The beginning of a new year marks a busy time for economists. 'Tis the season to review past trends in an attempt to predict what lies in the months ahead. And this year has a special twist — it's not just a new year — it's a whole new decade!

Educated guesses point at a recession sometime in the new decade — more likely later than sooner. Data Resources, Inc. estimates a 50 percent chance for 2 percent to 3 percent growth through 1991 — *without a recession.* This prediction also estimates a 9 percent fall of the dollar and a slight increase in interest rates.

Fortunately, job growth looks good in many metropolitan areas. In fact, Ohio, along with other Midwestern states, is secured to weather the potential recession.

According to a *Business Week* feature, a recession would cause only minimal disruption to Industrial America. Businesses are better prepared for — and therefore less vulnerable to — an economic downturn. We wouldn't experience the widespread layoffs that characterized the recession of the early '80s. This would keep consumer confidence levels surprisingly high in the Midwest.

Expect shifts in the population and government, too

The '90s will be marked with an older population as America's baby boomers enter middle age. These folks who were known for their spending and borrowing will turn over a new leaf and focus on saving. Good news for U.S. companies, this trend will reverse the capital shortages that force them to be dependent upon foreign investments.

As economists keep an eye on the government, they see a glimmer of promise for less defense spending in the '90s. This opens up billions to be spent on education, industrial modernization and debt retirement, according to Jeff Kosnett, *Changing Times.*

Compare and contrast those forecasts you read . . .

. . . for predicting the future is a tricky trade. And, as you gather information from various media during the next few months, you'll probably encounter conflicting theories. That's because economic forecasting isn't an art or a science. It's a matter of opinion . . . with a hefty dose of luck!

N HB NATIONAL CITY BANK

Figure 4-9. If you use the two-column grid, you can counteract this effect by designing the two columns off-center leaving a band of white space to the left or right of these columns. This way your headlines and graphics won't get in the way of the flow of your newsletter.

IRS reveals average deductions

by Julian Block

Whether the Internal Revenue Service computers pick your return for an audit can depend on how your itemized deductions compare with the average amounts claimed by other people in your income category. Take a look at the table to the right, which is taken from IRS statistics, to see how your deductions stack up against the averages. These figures are based on AGI, short for adjusted gross income.

The figures in the table are based on returns filed in 1990 for the 1989 tax year—the latest year for which information is available.

Keep in mind that changes introduced by tax reform eliminate or curtail deductions:

* Previously, medical expenses were allowable only for amounts

in excess of 5 percent of AGI. Now, however, the nondeductible floor is 7.5 percent.

AGI	Medical	Taxes	Contributions	Interest
$25,000-30,000	$3,128	$1,975	$1,109	$4,314
30,000-40,000	2,849	2,342	1,184	4,887
40,000-50,000	3,546	2,947	1,318	5,400
50,000-75,000	4,713	3,943	1,607	6,271
75,000-100,000	6,448	5,713	2,108	8,531
100,000-200,000	10,090	9,020	3,532	12,150
200,000-500,000	24,134	19,645	7,213	19,853
500,000-$1 million	40,556	43,499	18,374	29,788
Over $1 million	66,478	148,529	83,929	68,303

* Sales taxes ceased to be deductible after 1986.

* For 1986, interest payments on consumer loans, such as car payments and school loans, were 100 percent deductible. For 1987, only 65 percent of such interest was allowable, 40 percent in 1988, 20 percent in 1989, and 10 percent in 1990. After that, the deduction vanished.

The IRS releases its statistics with a standard warning to forget the averages. You are entitled to claim only your actual payments. The tax collectors can insist on proof in the form of

canceled checks, receipts and similar documentation.

Despite that warning, these averages may provide an important clue for your chances of examination. Your risk is greater if your deductions stand out as unusually high compared to amounts being claimed by other taxpayers in your income class. It is immaterial that you have actually spent and are able to substantiate every dollar claimed. Even worse, above-average deductions might prompt the IRS to challenge *other* items on your return, and also to scrutinize your returns for earlier years.

What if you discover that your itemized write-offs fall significantly below the averages? Perhaps you neglected to claim some perfectly legal, but often missed, deductions like out-of-pocket expenses incurred to do volunteer work on behalf of charitable organizations. These averages should prompt you to take a closer look at filing time.

A final reminder: Just because you claim average deductions does not mean you can forget about an audit. There can be trouble ahead unless you hang on to receipts, checks, etc., that support deductions and other items until the statute of limitations runs out for an audit— usually, April 15, 1995, in the case of a return due in April, 1991. ♦

Julian Block is a former IRS agent and attorney in Larchmont, NY. He is the author of The Homeowner's Tax Guide *(Runzheimer International).*

The Bush tax plan: stay tuned

Congress is currently debating the President's tax proposals designed to spur the economy. *Tax Savings Report* will have extensive coverage of the following proposed tax breaks, if and when Congress acts to pass or modify them:

* A cut in the capital gains tax from the current 28 percent to as low as 15.4 percent for assets held over a certain period.

* A $5,000 tax credit for first-time homebuyers over a two-year period.

* Homebuyers would be able to withdraw money from their Individual Retirement Accounts (IRAs) without a penalty to use for downpayments.

* Homeowners who sell their properties at a loss would get a deduction.

* Interest payments on student loans for college would become tax deductible. Families would also be able to withdraw money from their IRAs penalty-free to pay for college costs.

* A $500 increase in the tax exemption of $2,150 for each child under age 18.

* Deductions for health insurance premiums and "refundable tax credits" for low income Americans to use to obtain insurance from private companies. ♦

> **Coming next issue . . .**
>
> ■ **Boosting deductions for auto use.**

Figure 4-10

A number of techniques can be used to break monotony. Opinion: These techniques should be used in all sponsored promotional newsletters. Sidebars, screened backgrounds, and headlines can span the entire page, or span two columns if you're using the three column format.

Four and Five Column Grids

These are the most versatile grids because you can double the columns, vary the widths, and make use of white space with headlines and subtitles. (see figure 4-11.)

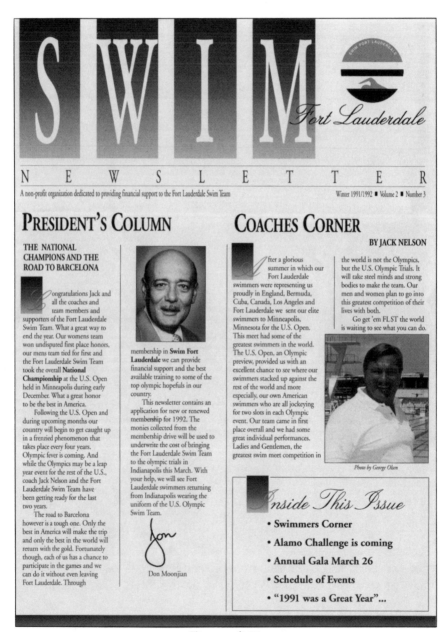

Figure 4-11

Dear Media Director:

Has the Consolidation of Advertising Agencies Impacted the Way You Do Business...

...Or the way you find the media now trying to do business with you?

Al Prior: Yes it has. Our media department is smaller. So it has made it tougher, because I handle account supervision in addition to media, where traditionally they had been two separate functions. So certainly there has been a change in terms of time management.

And as a general statement, I think there's a lot more individual negotiation going on to meet the individual needs of the given advertiser. Things are being brought to people that are more customized to what they're trying to do.

These are things that fall under that lovely heading of *added value*. But from straight pricing to positioning, merchandising—all those different things—they're being presented to us in a more customized approach.

[And that makes sense.] If you're competing in a larger pool of alternatives, you have to figure out what you're going to do to make yourself more valuable to buy than somebody else. And there are more alternatives out there.

Jack Cohen: No. I think we're doing business in the usual manner. With the merger of agencies, I think in some cases you ran into certain conflict situations. But business is still being done in the same way.

Are you finding that now it's a case of less people doing more?

Jack Cohen: Well, that's been holding true for awhile. But that's not just because of the merger situation. I think both on our side and on the side of the media, you're seeing more work being done with less and less people.

That's the agency business in general, and for that matter, the media business in general. I think the reps don't have as many people working for them as they did at one time. There've been cutbacks in that area.

Stephen Calder: We're talking about agencies running leaner and meaner. I would agree that the lean and mean agency is the agency of today. The most major impact I see on our side of the media desk is that senior [agency] media management is regularly involved in every aspect of a client's media planning—much more so than in years past.

The other advantage we now have in dealing with [the lean and mean] situation is a constantly increasing use of new computers and software to be able to manage the quantitative aspects of the business. We have a personal computer on every planner's desk and that enables us to respond a lot more quickly to client requests and to examine a wider variety of options for every marketing situation than would otherwise be impossible and it really

allows us to run a more efficient shop.

On the other side of the coin—in terms of the sales reps who call on us—there is a trend towards the media assigning one rep to visit a given agency rather than a category of client.

People magazine recently restructured their sales force to do that and from my side of the table, it's an incredibly good idea, because I really don't have the time to see them all. Previously I may have had four or five reps assigned to me from one magazine, and from a time management standpoint, that's totally impractical.

Bob Reuschle: Overall, people are handling more business in terms of dollars. I haven't seen an attempt to put an inflation factor on that—like have we really reduced the number of people per unit of work if you will. But generally, I think we are handling more business with fewer people.

However, on the whole, we've got more [tools] to help us do that. We've got more equipment, more computers, more data bases and more machines to do the number crunching and a lot of the laborious jobs that people used to do by hand and used to take hours. So people can spend a lot more time conceptualizing and the computers can process the numbers for our explorations and document and sort out what makes sense and why. ◆

Dear Media Director:

What Do Y...
Hear from

Stephen Calder: The most i... thing to emphasize is that me... need to present their stories i... my client's business needs.

We have too many reps ... and they tell us all about *thei*... or *their* network and then the... "What kinds of clients do yo... might be applicable to this he...

They really need to do th... work ahead of time before th... here and not just give me the... *schtick*. They should really tr... there is a fit for a client on m...

The other things I would ... they emphasize are special ed... portunities, which may have ... with our products, and value-... opportunities. These are incre... important and we need to kn...

Figure 4-12. If you received both those newsletters, which one would you be more likely to read?

The DeLay Letter

A twice-monthly report to top management on news, perspectives and trends in Direct Marketing

Vol. 4 No. 9   May 8, 1989

OVERVIEW OF THE 6TH ANNUAL CATALOG CONFERENCE Despite the recent overdose of meetings, the 6th Annual Catalog Conference (jointly sponsored by DMA and CATALOG AGE) at the Chicago Hyatt Regency, May 1-4 was a first class affair. Lots of people (more than 2,200) and good level of programming. Chicago is the right place for this meeting. A few less exhibit booths, but still a strong trade show. Some exhibitors are choking from the demands of too many local and national events.

Although relatively good business continues to be reported by many catalogers, there was an obvious note of caution in the air concerning the next 18 months. Veteran Eddie Smith (National Wholesale) shared the results of his ongoing survey of catalogs received -- down dramatically the first three months of this year. Admittedly, the postal rate increase, segmentation efforts and less use of outside lists, all contribute.

Consultant Jim Alexander warns that late sales during the holidays last year saved some marketers but points to two less selling days between Thanksgiving and Christmas this year! Obviously, last fall's election prompted a late buying start. But well-run operations, watching the numbers closely, are still doing a profitable volume.

The Lost Arrow Corporation's Patagonia catalog was named the Catalog of the Year by guru Dick Hodgson. And, to no one's surprise, L.L. Bean got the accolade for the Catalog of the Decade. Twenty-nine Gold Awards were also presented by the American Catalog Awards sponsored by CATALOG AGE.

INSIDER'S REPORT The announced acquisition of Carson, Pirie Scott means CPS Direct Marketing (Phoenix, AZ) should be moved even faster than projected. Asking price was $50 million when Carson's put it on the block recently. Doubtful there will be any buyers at that price although large inventory, receivables and building property could be translated into healthy dollars.

• According to the most recent study from Mediamark Research, about 80 million American adults a year will pick up the telephone or write to order a product from a catalog or mail order service!

• A recent study from Decision Research found that catalog shoppers regularly read magazines and newspapers and are moderate users of all kinds of TV. What that means is that rather than seeing other media as competition, you can view them as support systems for your efforts in catalog.

• Junk Fax was highlighted in a feature by THE WALL STREET JOURNAL last week prompting reports of privacy invasion. Sixteen states have bills in the hopper. I don't believe it is a long-term threat. Results of such advertising can't be good. Failure to get returns will happen before legislatures get around to restrictions! Fax unto others as you would have them fax unto you.

OBSERVATIONS OF THE QUINTESSENTIAL MERCHANT When legendary Stanley Marcus (chairman emeritus, Neiman-Marcus) was introduced as the luncheon speaker at the Catalog Conference, he was aptly described as "the quintessential merchant of his time." It was, indeed, a most deserved salute to a most admired man.

Typeset or Typewritten Newsletters

A typewritten newsletter goes hand-in-hand with a classic style grid. Typewriting implies "late-breaking" news and fresh copy. But in practice the decision depends—as so many newsletter decisions do—on your reader and the message.

A financial advisor may want to use this style along with the classic format if he or she wants readers to believe they're getting fast financial tips. Remember, though: You're giving your readers an unsolicited newsletter. The classic style could backfire because its look isn't "professional."

If you want to achieve a skilled or professional look which commands a perceived value, typeset the newsletter.

Capture Your Readers

Grab your readers with callouts, tint blocks, graphic inlays, subheads, and photo captions.

Most people skim a newsletter to see if it's of any interest to them. A skillful use of these techniques will pull your readers into your publication . . . and hold them there.

Text Alignment

Should your text be flush-left, flush-right, centered?

Readership studies favor flush-left and ragged right. Go with these conclusions. The formal effect of flush-right isn't reader-inviting.

Conclusion

Remember: Your message shouldn't be lost in the design of your newsletter; rather the design should emphasize the message.

Don't add confusion to your newsletter by using too many typefaces, too many graphics, or running photos too small to decipher. Don't use graphics if they mix the message. The key is to communicate to your readers. If you haven't done that, you really haven't issued a newsletter at all.

CHAPTER 5

The Winning Combination: Effective Editorial and Promotional Copy Mix

How "flair" conscious are you?

True or false?

1. Sponsor-promoting newsletter editorial and copy should be planned and written with a journalistic flair.

2. Sponsor-promoting newsletter editorial and copy should be planned and written with an advertising/promotional flair.

If you answered "true" to either of these statements, chances are you don't fully understand the total notion of *sponsor-promoting* newsletter editorial and promotional copy blending. Assuming that either of these two "flair" directed statements is correct is more than conjecture; it misreads the purpose of a sponsored newsletter, because the aim is inward, toward the writer. . .not outward, toward the reader.

Remember, please: We're paving a brand new road. You not only hold the key to *effective* sponsor-promoting newsletter copy, you're the one who turns that key in the reader's intellectual lock. But first, the formula needs to be broken down.

What's the difference between conventional journalistic editorial matter and sponsor-promoting newsletter editorial matter? What differences exist between promotional/advertising copy and sponsor-promoting newsletter copy?

Recognizing the difference is a far more significant key: the key to a newsletter whose effectiveness is directed rather than accidental...a newsletter reflecting image-projection rather than individual ego.

Journalism and Sponsor-promoting Newsletters

The premise behind sponsor-promoting newsletters is that the newsletter doesn't have the appearance of, or echo the "hype" of, a typical sales brochure; nor does it parallel the unrelenting drabness of a coldly analytical annual report.

That, in fact, is the magic of sponsor newsletters. The content of a sponsor-promoting newsletter must be *newsworthy and informational,* for two reasons: 1) If it's to be worth the reader's attention; 2) if the reader regards the newsletter as beneficial.

Of course we don't throw journalistic talents out the window. The difference is that a newspaper journalist is usually trained to be unbiased and to report the facts. Good—although in the post Woodward/Bernstein era, a dangerously huge number of journalists regard their mission as muckrakers rather than fact-diggers.

If you hire someone with a journalism background to write and plan your editorial, I'm afraid the writing could aim itself at one of two extremities: barren or sensationalized. I'm not saying journalists are poor writers—on the contrary—but newsletter writers have to be marketers as well.

Oh, sure...a pure *journalistic approach* to the editorial and copy style might make the newsletter interesting. But from the sponsor's viewpoint, the newsletter couldn't be as effective. What I mean by "as effective" is this: In sponsored newsletters, effectiveness is the reaction an article or editorial generates *toward you,* not just toward the informational core.

Any interesting article you put into your newsletter that gets the attention of your reader won't necessarily hinder you; but that same article will be much more effective if it causes your readers to understand that you are the company or organization to turn to if they want to donate money, buy a specific product, or use specific services. The reaction—or even a change or reversal of state of mind—occurs because of the effect of your newsletter.

A word of caution: Because your editorial and copy are newsworthy and thought-provoking doesn't mean you're the organization your customers, donors, or prospects use. *Be sure you aren't opening the doors for your competition too.* A journalistic style approach in this case would counteract the effect you're trying to achieve.

Other problems you may face with a journalistic approach is the tendency to crusade and write about controversial issues that can offend any number of your readers. Please, please! Don't crusade, unless your newsletter is aimed foursquare at an "in-group" whose religious, political, economic, environmental, or civic philosophy absolutely parallels your newsletter.

Why run the risk of alienating any client, customer, donor or prospect? You are, after all, *promoting*...not *reporting*.

Another problem with straight reporting is that the reader doesn't know what to do, who you are, or why you're bothering to send them your newsletter. To describe this circumstance in two words: *a waste.*

Let's take a look at figure 5-1 for an example of how strict reporting can be detrimental to what you're trying to achieve.

Figure 5-1 shows a newsletter from a mortgage company, its target is real estate agents. Its purpose: nudging the agents to direct their clients to the bank for a mortgage.

Or is it? Read a few paragraphs.

The "boiler-plate" interpretation of sales certainly has to generate resentment among professional real estate people who take exception to being lumped into generalizations about "sales" as a not-quite respectable profession.

And what information or viewpoint is transmitted? What image does the newsletter create for its issuer?

Undoubtedly the mortgage company has other advertising efforts aimed at real estate agents, but why not use the newsletter to bring the agents and their customers "into the loop"?

As you can see, this newsletter isn't particularly beneficial to real estate agents. It offers generalized advice about selling, unrelated to real estate. It stops short of effectiveness, because it's inspirational without specificity. (This suggests a syndicated newsletter, more loosely targeted than in-house editing makes possible.)

I spoke to the real estate agent who receives this newsletter without that person knowing my reasons. She had very good things to say about it—she saves them—yes, because it offers her excellent references and "gung-ho" advice. It's beneficial to her, she said, in that it helps keep attitudes high. She accepts it, then, on generalized terms unrelated to knowledge of real estate sales problems.

Is it beneficial for the mortgage company? In one way, yes, because the newsletter is retained and kept for reference, but not because of the mortgage company. The customer or prospect thinks of the *newsletter* as beneficial, but there's no reason for the customer or prospect to think of the *company* as particularly beneficial.

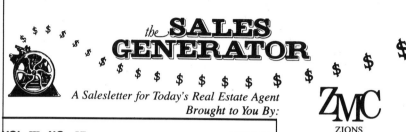

the SALES GENERATOR

A Salesletter for Today's Real Estate Agent
Brought to You By:

ZMC
ZIONS
MORTGAGE COMPANY

VOL. III NO. VI   **JUNE 1991**

THERE IS BUT ONE

CHOICE

When you ask people to rank professions that they view as being riddled with deception and an overall lack of integrity, you will find sales to be ranked right up there at the top of the list along with politicians, attorneys and television evangelists.

Although we've come a long way in terms of making our industry more professional, we've still got a long way to go. The general perception held by the public is that a salesperson is not to be trusted. Whether you agree with that point of view or not doesn't really matter. What does matter is that it's a perception held by the general public and it's something that you have to combat as you're striving to build your successful real estate business. So, how do you go about stemming the tides, turning back the wave of popular opinion and proving to others that you're different?

It begins by being sure that your own house is in order.

All of us arrive, thrive and survive based on our repeat and referral business. There is only one way for that referral business to grow and that is for us to have an outstanding reputation. Our reputation is the most valuable asset of our business. Is yours above reproach?

There are those in this business who will tell you that the key to success is working hard and going for the numbers. They suggest that you put the deal together any way that you can. Just get those numbers up on the board. Close them hard. Get the name on the dotted line and work out the details later. The philosophy is that success breeds success. Sales produce more sales. Get momentum going in your favor and you'll become unstoppable and

on and on the story and the "hype" goes.

That's all fine and good. However, you will find that the people who take that "rammin' jammin'" approach to the business are often "flashes in the pan", unable to sustain success for the long term. What causes these people to crash and burn? What makes the difference between those that succeed just for a little while and those that succeed for the long term?

The answer is quite simple. Cause and effect.

For those people who experience the temporary success, they are often left wondering what happened. It doesn't occur to them that they built their entire business on the shallow foundation of being out for a fast buck, regardless of who they had to step on to get it. They really thought that success was going to continue to come to them regardless of how they behaved within their business. In their minds, bending the rules to put a deal together was just the way things were done. Taking advantage of someone who was lesser informed was just smart business. Pulling a "fast one" on a competi-

(continued on next page)

Zions Mortgage Company • 4460 South Highland Drive, Suite 100 • Salt Lake City, UT 84124 • (801) 524-4720

Figure 5-1. This is a good example of a newsletter which doesn't benefit the reader or the organization. This particular mortgage company doesn't tell its readers what they want them to do.

This company inserted one so-so house-ad at the bottom of page two. Only one article comprises the entire newsletter. The newsletter says it's for "Today's Real Estate Agent" but nothing in the text mentions mortgages or services for real estate clients.

Result: When the real estate agent is asked about mortgages by a client, the agent isn't going to think of this mortgage company as the result of this newsletter.

So why bother?

Point: Editorial content should be planned to hit the specific marketing needs of the mortgage company as well the interests of the real estate agents. *That's* a proper editorial position...and unless the mortgage company is buying a syndicated newsletter whose editorial content is necessarily broad, it's just as easy to mount—provided the mortgage company actually has on its staff someone who understands real estate sales psychology.

An example of "off the wall" reporting of fun-and-facts-only is "Overnight News" in figure 5-2. This newsletter is mailed to clients and prospects of an advertising copywriting company. The purpose is obvious: a light-hearted reminder of the two principals as a creative source. Outsiders wouldn't have an inkling of why it was sent. They may enjoy reading it but it wouldn't help those who sent the newsletter.

This newsletter is *fun* and *humor*. But is fun and humor driving home any beneficial point? Or is it just fun and humor for no reason at all? This company is an advertising copywriting firm. With giants of industry, I think the two principals would be digging their own professional graves; but are giants of industry their targets?

To smaller advertisers—those who may fear the "three-piece suit" syndrome often associated with advertising executives—this is disarming. The reader feels he/she can call these fellows without running up a huge consultation bill.

Without this analysis, the point of the newsletter may be blurred. It's nice to keep in touch with your clients, customers, donors, or prospective customers. It's good public relations. Hard-nosed purists may argue: If that's what you're going to do, especially on a monthly basis, give them and yourself something from which to benefit.

This newsletter does contain a device for reader involvement and it tries to give the readers something to look for in the next issue. Quite deliberately, the subject matter in which it gives the reader something to look forward to isn't of any value. ("Q. What do Sir Laurence Olivier, Don Knotts and Dick Van Dyke have in common? Answer next month.") What a challenge! Will a marketing executive be looking forward to next month's issue to find out the answer?

Maybe. That isn't the point. The point is that this is about as low-key as a newsletter can get, and it has a certain comparative value for that reason alone.

THE MONTHLY NEWSLETTER THAT DOESN'T TAKE UP MUCH OF YOUR TIME (OR OURS)

OVERNIGHT News

VOL 1 • ISSUE 10 • NOVEMBER 1991

MARTY PEKAR / GREENWICH, NY

DAVID BURD / EAST STROUDSBURG, PA

STAMPS TAKE A LICKING

Here at Overnight Inspirations we pride ourselves on personal, one-on-one relationships with all our clients and associates (this means you). That's why it saddens us so to say goodbye to those cheery and colorful stamps that used to adorn our monthly mailings. Say hello to cold, impersonal postage metering. Actually, our printer insisted on the change. The metering, done by a machine, is quicker and costs less. And the stamping, done by hand, is time consuming, and tastes terrible.

THEM, HERM, AND HESHE

What is wrong with the English language that we can't have a singular third-person pronoun that isn't sexist? When referring to someone whose gender you don't know, you have to resort to the awkward sounding he/she or him/her. Often we'll try using "they" which is unisex but ends up either being sloppy or requiring a rewrite of the sentence to make it plural. Why not coin a word that will cover both a male or a female person? Combining words to form something like *heshe* (pronounced "heesh") is one idea. (It becomes *herm* in the objective case.) Or else make up a fresh word like *tren* or *sliv*. If a reader has a suggestion and if he/she/ they sends us his/her/their idea we'll print it and give credit to him/her/them.

IMAGE PROBLEM

How do you know a lawyer is lying? (He's moving his lips).

What do you call 1000 lawyer on the bottom of the ocean? (Not enough).

The list of lawyer jokes goes on, seemingly without end.

Now, in order to put an end to the jokes, and to the unsavory image of lawyers in general, a 3,800 member trial lawyers association has decided to take action by funding an advertising and PR campaign. Citing successful image building campaigns for cholesterol-rich beef (Real Food For Real People) and fat-laden cheese (Don't Forget The Cheese), these ambulance chasers hope to put a positive light on what they do.

We'll be watching to see what they come up with. Meanwhile, here are some slogans to get them started:

Lawyers. Lien On Us!

We've Got The Rights Stuff!

If You've Got The Money Honey We've Got The Time!

Don't Forget To SUE!

"Image is everything."
Andre Agassi

MISSING THE POINT

The following is quoted from a letter to the editor, printed in the record collectors' publication, Goldmine.

"Excuse me, but who the hell does Bob Dylan think he is? Enough is enough. You practically dedicate the whole July 26 issue to this so-called singer. Can anyone understand his lyrics?

"If you need an article on a real singer's singer, try Tom Jones. This Welsh-man can cover all vocal ground. Show me another singer who can cover songs from Sinatra to Jagger and everyone in between."

Thomas Terry, Raleigh, NC

HOLIDAY HOURS

With Thanksgiving just around the corner, we'd would like to take this opportunity to announce our holiday work schedule. This year, as every year, we will be available to work on all holidays and their respective Eves. We say this not so much to tell you how devoted and dependable we are but to remind you how lucky *you* are to have a day off. Happy holidays!

"To be effective, a billboard should not have more than seven words and two things to look at."
Glen Lane
NEVER TRUST A CALM DOG AND OTHER RULES OF THUMB

A̲D OF THE MONTH

Tie Rack For Real People.
Our battery-operated motorized tie rack is the ultimate in down-to-earth practicality. It works like a dry cleaner's carousel, storing ties and rotating them toward you for easy selection. Uses minimal space, fits most closet bars, and even has a light.
VP320 $29.95

Finally! A down-to-earth motorized tie rack that we *regular* guys can enjoy. If you find a fine product like this, fax the ad or catalog page to (717) 424-5248.

BRING BACK BELLS!

Ever since the electronic revolution hit the telephone, the familiar sound of ringing bells has been replaced by that annoying, synthetic "chirping" noise. Getting used to the sound of it was bad enough, but living out here in the country adds another wrinkle. There's a wild bird that lives in the woods that makes a chirping sound EXACTLY LIKE A PHONE. Every time one of these feathered friends finds a worm or hatches an egg, we go running to answer the telephone. Since there are no birds that ring like a bell, it seems a good argument for switching back.

"Q: What do Sir Laurence Olivier, Don Knotts and Dick Van Dyke have in common?"

Answer next month

Overnight News is published by Overnight Inspirations, an advertising copywriting company serving the world from two remote locations. Call Marty Pekar in Upstate New York at (518) 692-9902. Call David Burd in the Poconos of Pennsylvania at (717) 424-5245. Or, in New York City, save the long distance charges and call (212) 869-4430.

Illustration, design and production of *Overnight News* by Das Illustration & Design Studio (518) 346-2713.

START 'EM EARLY

We recently discovered an interesting vending machine at the local K-Mart. For 25¢ it dispenses 2 (count 'em—two) baseball cards. With packs of 15 baseball cards selling for 50¢ at the registers, the economics didn't add up. Why would anyone pay 12.5¢ per card from the vending machine when they could pay 3.3¢ at the counter? Are kids that bad at math? Are kids that anti-social?

We asked an expert (a kid who was buying cards out of the vending machine) and discovered the insidious truth...

What appeared to us to be a vending machine was actually a *gambling device!* The cards in the machine were not current 1991 cards...all were three or more years old. As you may know, the market for old baseball cards is so vast today, they can be easily converted into cash at well-established values. To entice young gamblers to try their luck, the machine displayed valuable rookie cards on the outside. *Come on Bo Jackson...baby needs a new pair of Nikes!*

We invested a quarter in this slot machine for kids and suspect that we struck out...anyone know what a 1988 Jeff Blauser or Benny Santiago is worth?

SORRY, WRONG FAX

"Sorry, wrong number," is a fast and efficient way to handle those annoying calls that want Bruno's Bakery and get you by mistake. But what do you do when someone's fax machine incorrectly dials your phone number? You pick up the receiver and get that familiar computer tone, but you can't very well tell it to call back on your fax line. Most fax machines also have an automatic redial feature so they will keep trying, and keep beeping at you *all day long.* Once we were out of the office for a few hours and came back to find the answering machine had taken 16 messages all the same: BEEEEEEEEEEEEEEP, followed by number 17, "Call me, your fax machine isn't working." Ah, modern technology!

GARN BUT NOT FORGOTTEN, 9

Our capsulizations of the wisdom and philosophy of Roy Garn and his fabulous fifties book, *The Magic Power of Emotional Appeal*, is undoubtedly the most looked-forward-to feature in Overnight News. But, in all fairness, we can't keep ripping the guy off this way! We did look into actually reprinting the out-of-print tome, but for now this will be our last Garn But Not Forgotten column. Hopefully we've given you enough insight to set you on your way to doing some Magic Power thinking of your own.

Let's examine emotional appeal at work in politics. Garn tells of a Rhode Island election in the days shortly after the Civil War. Two candidates for the House of Representatives, both former soldiers, were campaigning. One made a speech, "During the war I was a general, a man of great responsibility. My opponent was merely a private. Vote for me, *the general*!" The other candidate responded, "It's true that he was a general and I was a private. So on Election Day, generals vote for him, privates vote for me!" Guess who won.

A school teacher who was having trouble motivating her students used the Recognition appeal to encourage study. Instead of passing out marked test papers discretely, she wrote each student's name on the blackboard with the individual's grade next to it. On the next test the ego-conscious class improved their scores by an average of 26%.

Here's an example of a modern-day use of Garn-ism in our own experience. One of our readers tells us that she had a summer home for rent. She was prepared to draft a typical real estate ad listing specs like "two bedrooms, eat-in kitchen, close to town." Then, remembering our article about appealing to the emotions (issue 6, still in stock) she wrote instead about the "enchanted cottage" with its "magical charm." Our friend got 65 phone calls asking about the property!

Our reader took advantage of Emotional Appeal and made it work. We can all do the same. Every time you create or evaluate an ad, brochure, direct mailer, or TV commercial, ask yourself, "Does this appeal to the emotions? Does it break through the reader's preoccupation and touch their inner desire for Money, Recognition, Health or Romance?" Good luck!

Figure 5-2. Does fun and humor drive home any benefit? Can you find any beneficial information value for the readers of this newsletter? Can you see where this newsletter could be beneficial for the company itself? The point of this newsletter may be blurred in the eyes of the target readers.

Promotional/Advertising Copy and Sponsor-Promoting Newsletters

An advertising copywriter is concerned with (or should be concerned with) benefit-oriented copy. You do want reader benefit-oriented copy in your advertising or direct mail. This is the number one "safety net" for the newsletter medium too, because concentrating on reader benefit prevents straying off the point of why you're issuing a newsletter in the first place.

You want copy that will tell your readers what to do, where to go, and whom to ask for when they get there. But be careful if you're thinking that's all you need. Pure promotional copy and advertising placed in a newsletter format will make your readers angry. Include newsworthy, beneficial storylines along with your promotional copy...interesting, newsworthy articles which pertain to your target audience. You're *courting* your readers as well as *convincing* them you're a credible, reliable, and thoughtful organization who caters and fulfills the needs and wants of your clients, customers, or donors...and will too, for your prospects.

Pure promotionalism will turn your piece into a brochure, one big giant space ad, or one big giant mail order piece. You don't want this...or if you do, then create one. Don't use the newsletter as your medium or you'll lose your credibility and your objectives won't be met. Newsletters are *long term* relationship builders with these two ultimate goals: 1) to build and maintain long term confidence-based relationships with your existing donors and customers; 2) to draw in new prospects.

If you want short term sales or revenue don't use a newsletter. Get an advertising copywriter and have that person write your direct mail pieces, space ads and brochures. That's a different, shorter-term, more straightforward marketing program.

Take a look at figure 5-3. This example shows a direct mail piece in disguise. One point of using the newsletter medium is to overcome skepticism. Does this guise overcome skepticism? At first, yes. On analysis, no. The cover looks like a newsletter because it has an issue date, a nameplate, and a subscription rate of $10.00 in the above right hand corner.

As we open this 24-page "newsletter" we find it contains 14 pages of hard-core sales pitches, 11 pages of which are a letter from the president selling his services. The cover is an excellent means to pull the reader inside...but under false pretenses. The package contains good information, but the promotional portion is overkill.

If this newsletter is mailed a second time, readership has to drop off. It's obviously designed as a single shot, coattail-riding on the newsletter format and using newsletter techniques to create an attitude that bleeds over to the hard sell.

One admirable aspect to a questionable technique: The "tips" do exist and are universally helpful...if already known to most professionals. So

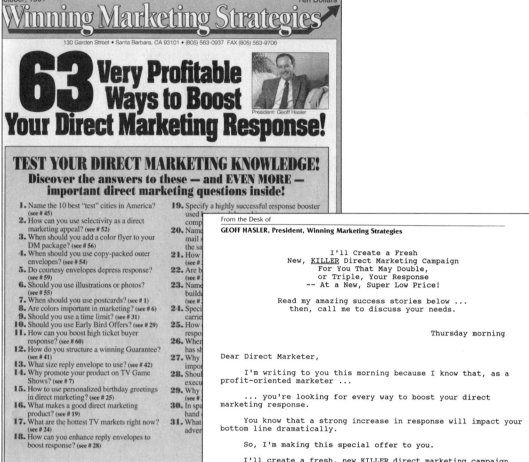

Figure 5-3. The aim of a newsletter is to overcome skepticism not instill more. This newsletter begins with beneficial headlines and information which promises the readers something of value. But after the newsletter is opened the readers find nothing but a hard-hitting sales pitch. This type of format wouldn't work as well the second time around because the readers are already wise to the pitch.

to the novice, the issuer of this newsletter becomes a knowledgeable source, which adds to the credibility of the not-so-hidden sales pitch at the close of the sales letter which comprises exactly half the book: "If you want to *DOUBLE, OR TRIPLE,* your direct marketing response rate...*BOLD, INNOVATIVE, AND IMAGINATIVE* direct marketing is the answer. So, *CALL ME TO DISCUSS YOUR NEEDS TODAY.*" (Note: That word "needs" as a noun isn't a professional-appeal word.)

Figure 5-4 is an example of how you can provide your readers with a wonderful blend of promotional and informational editorial. The useful informational content keeps readers inside the newsletter and reading.

The newsletter provides beneficial information *aimed precisely at this specific readership* and lets the readers know who's behind giving them this information. The newsletter gives the reader plenty of benefit-oriented reasons to join the Senior Alliance Group, plus it integrates its public relations program, markets its various senior programs, keeps its customers and prospects informed, works on customer retention, builds stronger relationships and gives the readers plenty of means to respond—and it sells. See how easy it is?

Easy to Follow Newsletter Editorial and Copy Formula

Before you start writing your newsletter, take your plans (outlined in earlier chapters) and outline where you want the articles in the newsletter to take your readers. Once you've done this, write down what you're trying to accomplish with these articles.

Keep asking as you go: Do you want to cross-sell any products or services? Do you want to raise money for a particular appeal? Do you want to get your audience to join a cause? Do you want to generate qualified sales leads and build a prospect list? The newsletter articles need to work together as a whole effort. Don't try to cram too many offers, ideas, or news articles about totally different services, products or appeals. Weave them together so you have an underlying theme.

Step One: An Easy and Foolproof Startup Exercise

Whatever your business or fund-raising venture may be, ask yourself this question:

"Why am I really creating this newsletter?"

I know you may argue that you aren't trying to sell—you simply want the audience to know where their money is going, or what activities they should be attending, or you're trying to build qualified leads, develop a

SENIOR Alliance, Inc. NEWS

For Californians age 50 and BETTER! Winter 1992 Edition

SENIOR ALLIANCE PROGRAM NEWS

SENIOR ALLIANCE Adds Pharmacy Savings!

IN THIS ISSUE

Features

SENIOR ALLIANCE PROGRAM NEWS

SENIOR ALLIANCE Adds Pharmacy Savings . . . . Page 1

To start the New Year, SENIOR ALLIANCE is offering a new savings program for members. As of January 1, 1992, participating pharmacies will offer SENIOR ALLIANCE members without a prescription drug benefit in their health insurance plan, a discount of 10% on prescription drugs!

Most participating pharmacies will also offer discounts to SENIOR ALLIANCE members on selected over-the-counter items. The over-the-counter discount program will vary depending on the individual pharmacy.

Look for the SENIOR ALLIANCE logo at your local pharmacy to determine whether your pharmacy is participating in this program or ask your pharmacist. The pharmacy may not have received our logo yet or may be unaware of the program. If your pharmacy doesn't know about the program, give them our toll free number: (800) 289-3949. We'll be happy to

explain the program and s them all the materials they to partipate.

Currently, our network participating pharmacies i strongest in Los Angeles, Orange, San Diego, Ventu San Francisco and Alame counties. Other counties t have participating pharma may not yet have coverag your particular area. A few counties have no coverag However, we are adding pharmacies to our discour network on a daily basis. your pharmacist or call us (800) 289-3949 to find out pharmacy in your area is a SENIOR ALLIANCE partic By the time the SENIOR ALLIANCE NEWS arrives mail, your area may be co

Your SENIOR ALLIANC membership card is your t to discounts and services. card is the only way the pharmacist can identify yo eligible for the SENIOR ALLIANCE discount.

PAYING FOR HEALTH CARE

Health Care—Who Pays for It!

We are introducing a new section of the SENIOR ALLIANCE NEWS this year that will keep you up-to-date on one of the major issues of the 1990's—in light of ever-increasing health care costs, how can we pay for adequate and appropriate health care?

Medicare—What's Old, What's New, What's Wrong

SENIOR ALLIANCE members, age 65 and over probably know the basic facts about Medicare. However, for our members age 50-65, and especially those who will become 65 this year, following is an overview of the Medicare program. This information can also be helpful to readers closer to 50 than 65, who wish to better understand their parents' health insurance needs.

With changes occurring almost annually, Medicare has grown so complex that many long-time beneficiaries are uncertain about some rules of coverage.

What is Medicare?

Medicare was enacted (as Title XVIII of the Social Security Act) in 1965 as an acute care health insurance program for individuals age 65 or older who had enough work credits to be eligible for Social Security or Railroad Retirement benefits. In 1973 the program was extended to people under age 65 who were receiving disability benefits under Social Security or Railroad Retirement for at least two years and to certain individuals with end-stage renal disease.

Medicare is actually two programs: Part A, Hospital Insurance and Part B, Medical Insurance.

Part A of Medicare is automatic for people who are eligible for Social Security or Railroad Retirement benefits at age 65.

Part B of Medicare is voluntary, requiring a monthly premium which is usually deducted from the beneficiary's Social Security check.

In 1991, of the approximately 32 million people age 65 and over about 30.3 million had Part A of Medicare, and some 29.8 million had Part B coverage. Some of the 1-1.6 million without full Medicare coverage probably have other sources of health insurance, but at least 300,000 people had neither Medicare nor private insurance coverage in 1988 (the latest year for which there is compiled data).

What Does Medicare Cover?

Part A of Medicare pays for all reasonable inpatient hospital care for the first 60 days minus a deductible for each benefit period (the period associated with one acute illness). For 1992, the Part A deductible is $652. From day 61-90 in the hospital, the beneficiary must pay a copayment ($163 in 1992). Beyond 90 days, beneficiaries may choose to draw upon a 60 day lifetime reserve, each day of which requires a copayment of $326 this year.

If certain requirements are met, Part A will pay for up to 100 days of skilled nursing care or skilled rehabilitation services (i.e. if the patient has been an inpatient in a hospital for three days prior to admission to the skilled nursing facility, if the care is prescribed by a physician and if it is related to the condition for which the patient was treated in the hospital.) The first 20 days may be paid by Medicare at 100%, but from day 21 through 100 a copayment of $81.50 is required. From day 101 to 365, a copayment of $163 must be paid.

In addition to care in a skilled nursing facility, Medicare also will pay 100% for medically

necessary home health care benefits as well as hospice care to terminally ill beneficiaries. No copayments or deductibles are required for Medicare-certified home health care or hospice care (hospice care under Medicare has a separate set of benefits and requirements).

Part B of Medicare pays 80% of reasonable charges for most covered services after an annual deductible of $100 is met. Beneficiaries who enroll in Part B also pay a monthly premium, which is deducted from their Social Security payments. This year, the Part B premium is $31.80. Covered services include medically necessary physician services, laboratory and other diagnostic tests, X-ray and other radiation therapy, screening mammography, Pap smears, outpatient services at a hospital or comprehensive outpatient rehabilitation facility, rural health clinic services, home dialysis supplies and equipment, certain artificial devices, physical and speech therapy and ambulance services. Medically necessary home health care visits may also be covered under Part B.

Annual Increases

Except for the Part B deductible of $100 which can only be changed by federal law, the co-insurance and deductible amounts for Medicare Part A and Part B increase every year, as does the Part B premium amount.

Gaps in Medicare Coverage

Services not covered by Medicare include outpatient prescription drugs, routine physical exams, non-surgical dental services, hearing aides *Continued on page 5*

Continued on page 5

Figure 5-4. The newsletter works well because it provides a perfect blend of promotional and informational editorial aimed precisely for the company's specific target readership.

73

prospect list, keep people dedicated to a cause, create goodwill, maximize their customer potential, and/or use the newsletter tool as a public relations vehicle.

Fine. All these reasons are what the newsletter medium is all about. But why do you want to achieve these objectives? It's because you're trying to convince your audience to react, to formulate an attitude, to buy or donate something. You're selling something you want someone else to buy, whether a product, a service, or an idea. And you want them to buy from you. So ask yourself: What are you *really* selling?

After you've answered the question, write down the answer. Then write *about* your answer so that you describe its benefits, why your audience wants it, what type of enjoyment or fulfillment will come from it. Do this in as many ways as you think are possible. Answer the question so that you describe its benefits...why your readers want it...what type of enjoyment, fulfillment, or problem solving will come of your product, service, or appeal.

Once you've done this, keep it in front of you as you plan your articles. Your articles should slant towards these fulfillments, solutions, and benefits and instill the intended desire in your audience.

Step Two: Tie Your Objectives into Your Editorial Content

Next ask yourself how you can get your targets to buy or donate money over a long term period.

Turn back to the main objectives of the newsletter. We know your ultimate goal is to increase revenue. But your objectives to accomplish this may be obliquely different from the goal. Your objectives are to: build strong customer relations, keep people involved in your cause, maintain or establish credibility—you've got your list. Now, the only reason you have these objectives is to increase revenue; and you will if you meet your objectives over each short period of time (i.e., each issue of your newsletter).

Now describe to yourself—taking the firm position of reader, not writer—how you're going to get your audience to perceive the qualities you want to project in your objectives. And there you have it—your editorial foundation. All your articles, in every issue, should slant toward these particular points.

You can write till your fingers fall off...and that's okay as long as you've matched the slant of your piece to the right target. Here's an example of an editorial outline that you can use for your newsletter editorial formula.

Newsletter Editorial Outline

Target: _____

Overall Theme of This Newsletter Issue: _____

1. Objectives: (What do you want to happen?) _____

_____

2. Product, Service or Appeal: _____

_____

3. How will your product, service or appeal benefit your readers? ___

_____

4. Copy Tone: What type of voice will appeal to your readers?
   ☐ conservative ☐ mom and pop ☐ open ☐ friendly ☐ funny
   ☐ opinionated ☐ olympian ☐ professorial [*not recommended*]

5. Style Approach:
   ☐ hard-sell ☐ soft-sell ☐ fact ☐ fiction ☐ interpretive
   ☐ theoretical

6. What type of slant should your articles take? _____

_____

7. What type of feature articles will help solve specific marketing problems? _____

_____

8. Motivational factors: _____

_____

9. What offers tie into your newsletter articles? _____

_____

10. Response devices: _____

_____

11. How will you generate qualified sales leads? _____

_____

12. What devices will you use to build a prospect list? _____

_____

13. What content stimulates existing clients or customers to intensify their relationship with you? _____

_____

Successful Editorial and Promotional Blends for Sponsor-Promoting Newsletters

In one summation: Success *usually* lies in a 50/50 blend of promotional coverage and editorial matter, or less promotional percentage to a higher editorial percentage.

Careful, now! By a 50/50 blend I don't mean you should create 50% flagrant promotional copy. I'm talking about promotional material which also has beneficial, newsworthy content in addition to editorial content which doesn't speak of your company or organization and which pertains to the interests of the readers.

Develop Your Own Editorial Style

For totality—completeness in pre-production preparation for the great battle with potential readers—you have yet another set of questions:

> 1. What types of features and information will you carry in each issue?
> 2. What other points of interest will blend with these features?
> 3. How much content will be straight editorial and what will be promotional copy?
> 4. How will your editorial content "interface" with your promotional articles?

Determine the Interests of Your Market

Don't create editorial content which talks only about your products, services, or cause. Instead, determine the reasons why your readers would buy, use your services, or contribute to your cause.

For instance, if your company sells health insurance, don't simply state the benefits of this type of health insurance, but also include articles which will help your readers stay healthy. This benefits your readers and your organization as well.

Figure 5-5 is an example of how this company blends targeted interest articles throughout their newsletter. This newsletter targets AAA members. The purpose is customer loyalty, retention, and cross-selling products and services. The newsletter writes about more than just proprietary products and services: In these pages the editorial staff has integrated articles such as car care, and why gas wasting is detrimental. These subjects *have to be* of interest to the readers of a newsletter aimed at motorists and are not out of context with the products and services the sponsor sells.

Effective Promotional/Editorial Slants

For sponsor-promoting newsletters, the slant (how you present your topic to your readers) has a great influence on whether or not you generate the attention and response you want. Some different types of successful sponsor-promoting newsletter slants include:

1. **Testimonials or success stories.** The slant is your sales pitch, and the style of writing should be newsworthy, creative, and delivering answers to your readers about how to do something better. "How I did it" or "How they did it" are obvious approaches.

Success stories are good slants for a sponsor-promoting article if targeted right, because people identify with others who share their same experiential background.

Take a look at figure 5-6. Here's a success story placed in a newsletter from a newsletter company. The target? The health care industry.

This company's business is to sell sponsor-promoting newsletters to the health care industry. The purpose of this newsletter is to prove to people in the industry that newsletters are excellent promotional vehicles. By featuring a success story written by someone who has achieved promotional success through newsletters, the publisher uses a potent key: A peer within the targeted group's own field of work is more reliable and convincing than direct editorializing. Too, the success story is believable and reliable because the article *doesn't* ramble forever about the person's newsletter; rather the mention of the newsletter is only a minute part of the feature—but a strong selling point for others in the industry who might be interested in promoting through newsletters.

When you plan your success stories, however, beware of the implicit danger of these stories appearing too much like a sales-pitch.

Figure 5-7 is an example of a pseudo-success article. The format is standard; the style of copy is testimonial-based, but it fails to maximize techniques conducive to overcoming skepticism.

For example: Instead of lining up photographs and putting each person's testimonial underneath the photo, the writer would have achieved greater reader-acceptance by setting up the article as if it were a question/answer interview, with the answers not obvious from the first word.

Let's move on to. . .

2. **"How to" articles.** This type of article is beneficial for the reader *if* you target it right. You don't want to put a "how to" article about planting a vegetable garden in a newsletter about condominium living.

Figure 5-8, "How to use your telephone in emergencies" is a good example of a "how to" article in sponsor-promoting newsletters. Why is it a good example? What does it do for the organization?

From the first paragraph, every subhead tells you that you're getting useful information. Content implies thoughtfulness on the part of the company, which in turn breeds customer loyalty. It also positions this company as an authority in telephone emergencies, and that position instills confidence in the company. The subject matter pertains to the industry and is of interest to their target.

AAA Rates Two Domestic Cars Best New Models Under $15,000

ORLANDO, Fla., December 30 — The American Automobile Association has rated the 1992 Ford Escort the best new car model available for under $10,000 and the 1992 Saturn Sports Coupe the top scoring auto in the $10,000 to $15,000 price class.

Seven other models round

out AAA's new car picks for 1992. The selections are based on 16-point evaluations of more than 100 new models reviewed in the motoring federation's 1992 book, AAA AutoTest.

Other cars ranked highest in their price class by AAA were the Honda Accord, $15,000 - $20,000; Oldsmobile 88, $20,000 - $25,000; Mercedes-Benz 190E 2.3, $25,000 - $30,000; Volvo 960, $30,000 - $35,000; Lexus SC 400 and Acura Legend (tie), $35,000 - $50,000; and Mercedes-Benz 400E, over $40,000.

These cars exceeded all others tested by offering the most outstanding combination of design, quality and performance in their price category.

In naming the best new models for 1992, experts under the supervision of AAA automotive engineers rated vehicles on the basis of a point system that assigns from one to five points in 16 categories including acceleration, braking, handling, economy, comfort, convenience and workmanship.

The total number of points represents a car's overall score with a maximum possible score of 80. The cars on AAA's list scored highest in their price class, with the Mercedes-Benz 400E scoring highest of all with 71 points.

Car buyers' needs and preferences vary and motorists should

consider AAA's list as only a starting point in their search for a new car. The best way to avoid wasting time and money in the crowded new car marketplace is to know which cars will meet your needs and expectations before entering a dealership.

Cars evaluated for AAA Auto-Test include all price ranges and most popular models. Each review highlights the car's best and worst features, its specifications, price,

safety features and performance. There are easy-to-read tables, a point-rating system and two pages of text and photographs on each car.

The book also contains information on selecting a new car, test driving, negotiating the best deal, auto maintenance, warranties and resolving disputes.

AAA AutoTest is available in bookstores and many AAA club locations. 🅰

AAA Marks 90 Years Service To Members Traveling Public

The American Automobile Association — which has grown from fewer than 1,000 members in 1902 to more than 33 million today — marked its 90th anniversary March 4.

AAA was founded by pioneer automobilists to safeguard the interests of motorists and aid in the development of better roads and services to car owners. Today it is one of the world's largest travel organizations.

"While we have become more sophisticated in our ability to provide quality auto and travel-related services, the fundamental AAA principle of promoting safe and enjoyable travel for members and the traveling public continues to guide this organization," said AAA president Paul R. Verkuil.

AAA, which reached one million members in 1940, grew at the rate of almost one million members annually in the 1980s. During that period, AAA membership increased 48 percent.

AAA members currently represent approximately 18 percent of licensed drivers in the United States and own 21 percent of the nation's registered passenger cars.

Throughout its history, the association has been instrumental in the fight for better roads.

AAA supported the 1903 "Good Road Bill," federal legislation establishing the U.S. Bureau of Public Roads. It worked for adoption of the first federal aid highway act in 1916 and was instrumental in passage of the 1956 Federal Aid Highway Act, which created the Interstate Highway System.

In addition to responding to more than 21 million emergency road service calls each year from members, AAA has been a pioneer in developing public service programs, such as school safety patrols, driver education, drunk driver rehabilitation, pedestrian safety, energy conservation, and gasoline price and availability surveys.

AAA has consistently led the fight against increased fuel taxes for non-transportation purposes and unreasonable levies on air travelers and vacationers.

Presently, AAA is working with the federal government, General Motors Corporation, the state of Florida and the city of Orlando in developing this country's most comprehensive intelligent vehicle/highway systems program. The one-year TravTek test program was kicked off in late March in Orlando, Florida.

"During this decade and beyond, AAA plans to be at the forefront of the nation's efforts to help find solutions for traffic congestion, vehicle safety and environmental concerns," Verkuil said.

4

Memo's From Motor City

The term "tune-up" has been in the automotive vocabulary for quite some time. But if you plan on hauling your vehicle into the shop because you think it may need a "tune-up," you'd better be sure you and the mechanic have the same definition of the term.

A recent survey of 150 repair garages completed by the Autolite division of Allied-Signal found that mechanics listed twice as many items that should be checked as part of the catch-all tune-up than consumers.

"Mechanics view a tune-up as analyzing the vehicle's operating condition — not just replacing parts," explained Mark McIvor, Autolite marketing vice president.

A survey of 2,000 consumers was also completed to gauge current perceptions of car care. Then an industry roundtable group was assembled to discuss the results. When asked why they have their

vehicles tuned-up, 51 percent of consumers surveyed said they wait for engine trouble, poor gas mileage or starting problems.

Of the survey respondents, 35 percent said they do their own vehicle maintenance; 31 percent bring their vehicles to a repair garage; and 31 percent go to a dealersip for service.

The prime motivation of do-it-yourselfers: Sixty-six percent claim cost savings.

"While we can only hypothesize about why people wait for trouble before bringing their cars in for a check," said Tony Molla, managing editor of Motor Age magazine and member of the industry panel, "our feeling is that today's car owners have a false sense of security about their car's ability to maintain itself."

Motorists will see real financial savings by keeping their vehicle in top operating condition, the panelists concluded. That means a program of regular preventive maintenance and periodic "health checks" on their vehicle's overall condition.

"Most consumers see their car as an appliance, not something they need to care for," concluded Tony Molla.

• • •

EVEN BACK IN FDR'S TIME WASTING GAS WAS A "NO-NO"

Some things never change. Not even in a half century. In fact, today with energy conservation often a topic in the news media, the message burns stronger than ever: waste not, want not.

February 2, 1942, NEWSWEEK MAGAZINE. A letter from two observant Newsweek readers at the Southeast Missouri State College, Cape Girardeau, gives Franklin Delano Roosevelt's economic wizard, Leon Henderson, a tap on the wrist for wasting gasoline. He left his car idling at the curb.

With the letter, Newsweek obligingly reprints the picture that

triggered it. Sure enough, as the letter's author, J.M. Muscovalley and H.W. Huber point out, "The picture of Leon Henderson's automobile definitely shows the motor to be running and Leon is off to distant whereabouts."

"Perhaps Secretary of the Interior (Harold) Ickes should speak to Henderson concerning the conservation of gasoline."

More significant than their discovery, however, is their observation: "If 30 million cars and trucks in the U.S.A. left their motors idling for one minute, a total of approximately 291,666 gallons would be consumed."

Commenting on this nostalgia, Car Care Council President Donald B. Midgley observes that energy conservation was vital to the war effort. "Today it is essential to our energy independence and our balance of trade," he says. "What's more, vehicle population pushes the gas consumption figure into the millions of gallons.

"Air quality is more of a matter of concern, too, as an engine sitting at idle is a heavy polluter."

It is tempting to let the engine run to keep the car cozy and warm, says Car Care Council, but it is a bad habit. Another no-no, long periods of idling with the air conditioner running. Not only is this habit particularly wasteful, it also can cause the engine to overheat.

Shut off the engine if you expect to sit for more than a minute, concludes the Council, and keep the engine properly tuned for optimum fuel efficiency and minimum exhaust emissions.

Figure 5-5. *This organization integrates special interest articles into their newsletter rather than straight promotion of their products and services. Articles which appear to be indirectly related to your organization or business have a positive psychological effect on your readers. If targeted properly, special interest articles keep your readers interested and keeps them reading your newsletter, which in turn benefits your bottom line.*

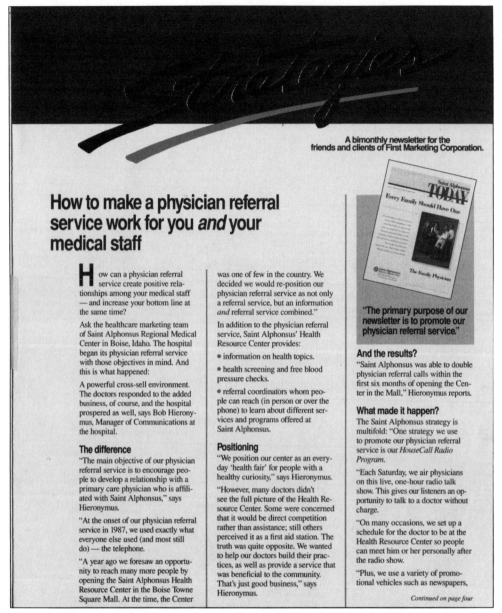

A bimonthly newsletter for the friends and clients of First Marketing Corporation.

How to make a physician referral service work for you *and* your medical staff

How can a physician referral service create positive relationships among your medical staff — and increase your bottom line at the same time?

Ask the healthcare marketing team of Saint Alphonsus Regional Medical Center in Boise, Idaho. The hospital began its physician referral service with those objectives in mind. And this is what happened:

A powerful cross-sell environment. The doctors responded to the added business, of course, and the hospital prospered as well, says Bob Hieronymus, Manager of Communications at the hospital.

The difference

"The main objective of our physician referral service is to encourage people to develop a relationship with a primary care physician who is affiliated with Saint Alphonsus," says Hieronymus.

"At the onset of our physician referral service in 1987, we used exactly what everyone else used (and most still do) — the telephone.

"A year ago we foresaw an opportunity to reach many more people by opening the Saint Alphonsus Health Resource Center in the Boise Towne Square Mall. At the time, the Center

was one of few in the country. We decided we would re-position our physician referral service as not only a referral service, but an information *and* referral service combined."

In addition to the physician referral service, Saint Alphonsus' Health Resource Center provides:

● information on health topics.

● health screening and free blood pressure checks.

● referral coordinators whom people can reach (in person or over the phone) to learn about different services and programs offered at Saint Alphonsus.

Positioning

"We position our center as an everyday 'health fair' for people with a healthy curiosity," says Hieronymus.

"However, many doctors didn't see the full picture of the Health Resource Center. Some were concerned that it would be direct competition rather than assistance; still others perceived it as a first aid station. The truth was quite opposite. We wanted to help our doctors build their practices, as well as provide a service that was beneficial to the community. That's just good business," says Hieronymus.

> "The primary purpose of our newsletter is to promote our physician referral service."

And the results?

"Saint Alphonsus was able to double physician referral calls within the first six months of opening the Center in the Mall," Hieronymus reports.

What made it happen?

The Saint Alphonsus strategy is multifold: "One strategy we use to promote our physician referral service is our *HouseCall Radio Program*.

"Each Saturday, we air physicians on this live, one-hour radio talk show. This gives our listeners an opportunity to talk to a doctor without charge.

"On many occasions, we set up a schedule for the doctor to be at the Health Resource Center so people can meet him or her personally after the radio show.

"Plus, we use a variety of promotional vehicles such as newspapers,

Continued on page four

Figure 5-6. Low-key success stories which soft-sell your product or service have a positive effect on your readers.

"How to..." articles don't have to be labeled in your newsletter as "How to...", but those two magical words have a power few substitutes can muster.

Take a look at figure 5-9. In business-to-business publications, showing someone how to improve specific marketing problems is your foot in the door. This particular article—"New insight for targeting your healthcare newsletter"—is pointed and targeted, assuring that it will be beneficial for

Figure 5-7. Testimonials such as these can only increase reader skepticism. You can make this work better by simpy changing the style of the format. For example: Why not set up this obvious piece of advertising as a newsworthy interview?

the reader (*and*, then, automatically beneficial for the company issuing the publication).

Take a look at Figure 5-10. The company sells marketing services. Without directly telling their clients or prospects to buy their services, they illustrate in their newsletter that they know what to do and how to help solve a company's specific marketing problems. The benefit of this example is recognition of a common business circumstance: A high-profile supplier of goods or services may not want to appear overtly promotional. The newsletter not only fills the semi-promotional gap; it adds a patina of service to the company's position within the business community.

What other medium can match newsletters for the magical combination of image-building *and* business building?

And on to...

3. **Question-and-answer** articles are excellent pieces for promoting customer relations. This type of article can get customers or donors in-

How to use your telephone in emergencies

When a disaster hits, especially an earthquake, people pick up their telephone to call family and friends. Too many people calling at the same time causes a major problem with the telephone system. Please remember, it is important to limit your calls to emergencies only. This prevents overloading the system and helps critical calls get through.

Don't call 9-1-1 or the police to ask if there's a major disaster like an earthquake. Only use 9-1-1 to report a specific emergency. Listen to your radio or television for information about major emergencies.

Protecting the telephone system
To avoid system overload, Pacific Bell and long-distance companies may block some calls. This means that when you pick up your phone, you could get a busy signal or no dial tone at all for a brief period.

Blocking is an important safety measure that limits the number of calls in the system. It directs some calls to an "all circuits are busy" recording or to a "fast busy" signal (twice as fast as a normal busy signal).

Establish an out-of-area contact
Before an emergency occurs, select someone outside your geographic area to be your emergency contact. The Red Cross recommends an out-of-state contact. When a disaster hits, call this person after the immediate danger has passed. Ask the person to pass on information to relatives and friends. By having an out-of-area contact notify your family and friends, you will help reduce the volume of calls into the affected area so that critical calls can get through.

Emergency calls after a disaster
If you need to place an emergency call:
• Lift the receiver and wait for the dial tone. You may have to wait a minute or longer due to the number of people trying to place calls. **You will delay your call further if you hang up and start over before you get the dial tone.**

• If you reach a recording that says "all circuits are busy" or hear a "fast busy" signal, try your call again.

• If our equipment or your telephone wiring is physically damaged, it may be impossible to complete your call until the damage is repaired and service restored.

9-1-1 emergency telephone service
Use the 9-1-1 telephone number only for reporting specific emergencies. An emergency is a situation that threatens human life or property and demands immediate attention. Every 9-1-1 system includes police, fire fighting and emergency medical and ambulance services. The inside front cover of your Pacific Bell telephone directory lists any other agencies in your area that may be available by dialing 9-1-1.

Non-emergency calls
Seven-digit telephone numbers for non-emergency calls can be found in the White Pages of your directory. Most directories have these numbers listed in the Government Pages beginning on page one. In other directories, these numbers are listed alphabetically under the city or county name.

For further instructions on what to do in an emergency, see the **First Aid and Survival Guide** section of your Pacific Bell White Pages directory.

Figure 5-8. The magic of this "how to" articles is in the way the company has positioned itself as an authority in telephone emergencies.

volved and make them feel they're a part of the company. This has a positive psychological effect useful to everyone in the world of newsletters, in one way or another. It also helps the company or organization know what their readers want from the organization and what type of information they want to know more about.

Questions/answers are particularly helpful for certain hard to understand services, appeals, and products which first require information and education in order for the readers to be comfortable in using the specific product or service.

Figure 5-11 shows a question-and-answer article which walks the customer through a usually difficult, hard-to-understand technological update. It's written for the lay person—rather than putting information into technical terms which transcends their readers' comprehension and automatically locks the non-technical reader out of the mix.

Although the article itself isn't particularly appealing to the reader's eye because of the typeface, the basic idea is there for you to see.

Take a look at figure 5-12. This is an excellent Q&A article which gets

New insight for targeting your healthcare newsletter

Do you ever ask yourself whether you're absolutely *on target* with your newsletter? In other words, are you accomplishing your main objectives?

There's one way to find out: a readership survey.

A recent readership survey conducted by Decision Support Systems, Inc. (DSS) of Arlington, Texas, helped determine how members of PARTNERS National Health Plans felt about their First Marketing Corporation newsletter, *Partners Today*. The survey revealed some major factors which help determine the direction a healthcare newsletter should take.

Methodology

Some 6,000 members were randomly selected from the newsletter mailing list. Components of the mail survey consisted of a cover letter, current newsletter, questionnaire and return envelope.

The readership survey was designed to gauge:

- Are members aware of the newsletter?
- What percentage of the members read it?
- Is the newsletter readable?
- Is the information useful?
- Which articles have led people to take action?
- What topics are members interested in reading?
- From what other sources do members receive healthcare information?
- Do members want to continue receiving the newsletter?
- How long have readers had their healthcare plan?
- Are they satisfied with the plan?

A total of 712 people completed the questionnaire. DSS estimated that 20 percent of the questionnaires were not delivered because of various address problems.

By pinpointing who your readers are, you can determine the direction your newsletter should take.

Results provide valuable insight

PARTNERS achieved interesting results from their readership survey … results which could also benefit you. For instance:

- The readership survey supports the common belief that a woman is the major healthcare decision maker in most households. (Studies indicate that women are responsible for about 70 percent of the family's health-care decisions.) And indeed, 70 percent of the people who responded to this study were women.
- A higher ratio of married couples responded to the survey than single people.
- The 35-and-older group read the newsletter more thoroughly than the younger members.
- The longer an individual has been a member of PARTNERS, the more he or she reads at least some of the newsletter on a regular basis.
- People who are satisfied with their healthcare plan usually read the newsletter on a regular basis.
- Over 20 percent passed their newsletter on to friends or associates.
- Members 45 years and older shared their *Partners Today* with friends and associates more than did younger members.
- More important, those who read 50 percent or more of the newsletter, married couples and those who have been members for more than three years, were most likely to take positive

action regarding their health because of articles they had read in their publication.

Members pinpoint value

Members gave four dominant reasons why they want to continue to receive regular newsletter communication:

1. Information;
2. Interest in subject matter;
3. Staying abreast on healthcare issues;
4. Usefulness.

What do these results tell you? They tell you *your members or your community want information*. And as a result of the information you give, plus inclusion of a proper response vehicle, they *can* and *will* take action.

Newsletters that work!

You can have a newsletter researched, written, designed and produced to reach your specific market. More important, you don't have to spend a lot of time or money to get a newsletter that works.

First Marketing Corporation is the nation's leading publisher of *customized* newsletters for the healthcare industry.

If you're interested in more information, put the enclosed reply card in the mail today.

Figure 5-9. "How to" articles must be targeted. Here's a classic good example of how to draw readers into a newsletter with pertinent information for its readership.

the readers involved—it asks the reader to get involved—and it gives the reader a specific contact-person to write. the effect is to give the customer or prospect a forum.

When it comes to fund-raising the Q&A column in figure 5-13 bridges the gap between the donor and the organization. Too many donors today

INDUSTRY LEADERS SURVEYED ON STATISTICAL MODELING IN LIST SELECTION

By Denice M. Swain
Director, Market Management

The results are in and they reveal increasing use of sophisticated methods of list selection.

Based on Dun's Direct recent survey, one third of you, the leaders in direct marketing, use statistical modeling to identify your business-to-business mail targets. Among those who have tried statistical modeling techniques, 55% said that they have found them to be quite successful and have begun to use them on a regular basis.

Respondents who have found statistical modeling successful stated that, in addition to improving the profitability of mailings, its advantages are that it is easy to use and is easily understood by "non-technicians". Twenty-seven percent of those who have used statistical models describe their experience as questionable. Among their concerns are that some compiled files lack sufficient information to produce a reliable model, and that modeling can be time-consuming.

Our survey found that the main reasons for not having tried statistical modeling are that it is perceived to be too expensive, the procedures are too complex, or that mailers are satisfied with the results they get from compiled file mailings. However, even among those Industry Leaders who have not used statistical modeling yet, there appear to be plans to test it in the near future. Several respondents to Dun's survey indicated that they are currently conducting major file-cleaning efforts, are converting to new systems and/or having custom programming done in order to capture the information necessary to perform statistical analysis.

Not surprisingly, two out of three companies that use statistical modeling employ it to segment their customer database. But nearly as many said that they use modeling to segment compiled databases as well. A smaller, but substantial number of respondents use modeling on response lists.

MARKET BRIEFS

POSTAL ALERT!

Here is the latest update on bulk mail rate increases that became effective in April.

Regular rate
Bulk third class

Minimum per piece:	Old Rate	New Rate	% Increase
Basic	12.5	16.7	33.6
5-digit	10.1	13.2	30.7
Carrier Route	8.3	10.1	21.7

For more detailed information, write us and ask for the POSTAL UPDATE.

UPDATE ON THE 8-DIGIT SIC CODE

Dun & Bradstreet has recently completed the hierarchy structure and definition of the 2 + 2 SIC code enhancement. The codes have been sent to the DMA's Business-to-Business Users Group for review and comment. In addition, Dun's account executives are currently channeling clients' suggestions on specific SIC code extensions to Dun's Direct headquarters. If *YOU* have any specific suggestions, please call your local Dun's account executive or Jerry Reisberg at our headquarters, 201-299-0181.

LATE BREAKING NEWS...

Dun's Business Executives at Home file is now available from Dun's Direct. The file of over 5.5 million business owners, professionals, top and middle managers allows direct marketers to target top executives in Corporate America. Key lifestyle data combines with broad based compiled information to provide a highly selectable source of decision maker names. To find out more, contact your local Dun's Marketing Account Executive.

In summary, we should expect to see more and more mailers increasing their marketing precision by making use of statistical modeling techniques such as Regression Analysis in list selection. Good targeting!

PITFALLS OF STARTING UP A BUSINESS CATALOG— AND HOW TO AVOID THEM

1: **Company fails to have a plan.**
Solution: Define goals and objectives; examine the market; make sure product and catalog creative are unique; project detailed financial growth.

2: **Company fails to develop a unique niche.**
Solution: Products or services and catalog presentation should be unique. Offers and customer service should set you apart from competition.

3: **Company doesn't know who its customers are or where they come from.**
Solution: Capture information on customers and maintain purchase history on a database. Involve marketing and data processing people in information gathering discussions.

4: **Company does not understand the creative subtleties of cataloging.**
Solution: Covers must attract attention; inside front and back covers should feature high-margin, high-volume products; pages should be tied together to establish a flow for customer; photography must present products to customer; order form should be easy to use; and telephone number should be emphasized throughout the catalog.

5: **Development of the customer list is disorganized, ill planned, and often delegated to the lowest level of the organization.**
Solution: Someone within the marketing group should track growth and performance of customer list. Front-end and back-end analyses are essential.

6: **Company fails to have adequate financial skills to make the catalog profitable.**
Solution: Your business catalog should be financially driven. Know your business plan; control costs, operations, systems, inventory; analyze financials, know break-even marks and have resources to grow business.

From Direct Marketing, Garden City, N.Y.

Figure 5-10. This newsletter not only fills the semi-promotional gap; it adds a patina of service to the company's position within the business community.

feel as though they're left in the cold after they donate their money. Where does it really go? What is the organization really doing with the money? And what part of total activity does the organization actually cover in the appeals?

This column might be improved by giving the reader a name to write to with the reader's own questions (unlikely to happen but a good promo-

Getting the Most From WP5.1 Win

WordPerfect for Windows has been shipping for almost four months. We asked Customer Support to look at the questions callers were asking over that period to see what were the most common areas of concern.

In the following three articles you will see many of the answers to the questions you asked most often. We hope these will help you with your major concerns. And don't forget: if you still need help, call Customer Support.

But first, the most often-asked questions:

Questions and Answers

How do I convert my WordPerfect 5.1 for DOS files for use in WordPerfect 5.1 for Windows?

No conversion is necessary; WordPerfect 5.1 for DOS files are completely compatible with WordPerfect 5.1 for Windows.

Can I use the same printer drivers I use in WordPerfect 5.1 for DOS?

Yes! WordPerfect 5.1 for Windows uses the same printer drivers (.PRS files) as WordPerfect 5.1 for DOS. However, WordPerfect printer drivers which require a TSR (Terminate Stay Resident) program to function in WordPerfect 5.1 for DOS will not work in WordPerfect 5.1 for Windows. These include: DP-Tek LaserPort, Eicon Script, Fujitsu dexNET 200 Faxmodem Driver, GammaLink GammaScript, Hayes JT FAX, Intel Visual Edge, and all LaserMaster and Raster Device drivers. You can print to the LaserMaster and Raster Device's Trendsetter printers using Windows printer drivers.

How can I speed up WordPerfect 5.1 for Windows?

We strongly recommend using a 386 machine or better with at least 4M of RAM, although WordPerfect 5.1 for Windows will run on a 286 machine with 2M of RAM. If you are running multiple Windows applications, you may consider purchasing additional memory. You may also reduce the number of applications running in the background to conserve Windows system resources. You can also reduce the number of icons (minimize several groups) in the Program Manager because they use system resources.

WordPerfect 5.1 for Windows, and most other Windows applications, generally run faster in Standard mode; type **win/s** when launching Windows. You can also enhance performance by using a disk-caching utility such as SMARTDrive which ships with Windows. (Be careful not to allocate too much memory or you can decrease speed.)

You can increase the file handles in your CONFIG.SYS file. When you see *FILES=x*, increase the number. Microsoft recommends at least 30. WordPerfect 5.1 for Windows will also launch more quickly without the Ruler, Button Bar, or the Horizontal/Vertical scroll bars selected as defaults.

Why does my screen not always display correct fonts?

In the Windows environment, screen fonts (the ones displayed on screen) sometimes differ from printer fonts (the fonts built-in or downloaded to your printer). WordPerfect printer drivers use only printer fonts, not any of the Windows screen fonts. When using WordPerfect printer drivers, WordPerfect 5.1 for Windows will select the best screen font to represent the printer font you have selected. While the screen font may display differently, your document will always print with the selected font, as long as it is available to your printer. Installing a third-party Windows font package will give you more screen fonts to match your printer fonts.

Should I use WordPerfect or Windows printer drivers?

Each has advantages: Using WordPerfect printer drivers, you can use the same

Figure 5-11. When you know your customer, donor, or prospect will have trouble understanding certain elements of your organization's activities, services or products, a question and answer article written for the lay person is a simple approach to educating your readers and building your sales.

Meet Judy Clough

Your Customer Relations
Manager

DOLLARS & SENSE

Energy Dollars That Work For You

You can count on it — your electric bill arrives on time every month. And, thanks to summer heat, your next one may be higher than usual. It's a necessary cost, but one you can help control. Here are a few tips to make your energy dollars work smartest for you:

Choose Equipment Wisely

If you live where you must have a central air conditioner, it should be the right size for the area it needs to cool. Put the unit on the north or east side of your house in a shady spot. Make sure the vents are clear of grass or shrubs and the air can flow freely through the unit.

If you use a smaller unit, still keep the vents clear. Also, you can use a pedestal or ceiling fan to circulate the cool air.

Don't Forget The Appliances

Your washing machine uses very little energy. Most of the energy is for hot water. You can save dollars by using the coolest setting that will still get your laundry clean.

Make sure your dryer's lint filter is clean. Don't dry heavy and light fabrics together. Set the timer carefully; don't overdry.

You can keep the cost of running you refrigerator in line by simply keeping the door shut. Make sure the seal is intact and the door closes tightly. Then, limit the times you must open the door.

Finally, get in the habit of turning the lights out when you are leaving a room.

Making these few changes can save you a few energy dollars. ❏

Your ideas, comments and opinions are important to us at JCPenney Life Insurance Company. The more we hear from you, the better service we can provide.

While our Customer Service, Telephone Sales and Claim Representatives are available to answer your questions when you contact us on our toll-free numbers, Judy Clough, our Customer Relations Manager, is working behind the scenes representing your voice within the Company. She works with all departments to ensure that we are listening to what you have to say and that we are responding to you in a manner that meets your needs.

Judy along with our Service Representatives plans to use this Q and A column to share with all our JCPenClub members answers to many of your frequently asked questions. Judy feels this is one way we can communicate useful information to you... the most important part of our business.

Q If I am unable to get your claim form completed by my doctor, would you accept the doctor's statement?

A Yes, we will be happy to accept the doctor's statement as long as it contains a diagnosis and date(s) of treatment. We need a medical diagnosis from your doctor, so we can pay you the correct benefits in accordance with the provisions of your policy.

Q Why is my signature required on your claim form?

A We need your signature for the release of information when we request you or your dependant's medical history or information about your claim. When we don't have your signature, we must take time to obtain it from you and this could delay your benefits.

Q I have high blood pressure (hypertension). Can I still get insurance?

A Very likely. Most people are surprised to learn that they are insurable even though they have controlled hypertension or other condition.

That is why you should give us complete information when applying for one of our coverages. If we have complete information on your application, we can process your application more quickly. ❏

Figure 5-12. This is an excellent Q&A article which gets the reader involved.

tional ploy), thereby making it more personal, even if no specific person actually answers the letters.

The Q/A column could also include more specifics in its introduction.

For example, instead of saying "If you have a question..." be more specific—about what? You may have a huge number of people writing to your organization. Be sure this effort doesn't backfire. If you're unable to answer all the questions you receive, add a sentence:

86

DONORS ASK

Our Donor Services Department answers some of the most commonly asked questions from CARE contributors. If you have a question, please contact us at:

CARE
Donor Services
660 First Avenue
New York, NY 10016

Question: *How much of the food and supplies that CARE sends overseas actually makes it to the people in need?*

Answer: Virtually all of it; less than one percent of all goods that CARE transports overseas annually is lost due to transportation damage or pilfering. A representative from CARE is always on site when goods are unloaded from ships and transferred to warehouses. CARE then works with reliable local organizations to ensure that supplies reach the needy.

Question: *What is CARE doing to help the environment?*

Answer: First of all, CARE helps plant more than 20 million trees each year to stop soil erosion and help farmers improve productivity. Trees also provide shade, fruit, firewood and fodder. In addition, CARE encourages the use of organic pesticides and fertilizers. And CARE works in concert with other environmental organizations. Together, we help farmers manage their land more effectively, so that they won't abandon it and press into fragile regions like the Amazon rain forest.

Question: *Because I prefer to give once a year, I'd like to receive fewer letters. Is this possible?*

Answer: Absolutely. If you wish, you can choose to receive letters from CARE once, twice, or four times a year. To make such an arrangement, write to us at the address above.

Question: *I see a lot of ads on television and in magazines for child sponsorship programs. Does CARE offer this type of program?*

Answer: CARE does not have a program in which a person can sponsor an individual child. However, we do have a program called "CARE for the Child," in which members make a monthly pledge of $12 or more to support CARE projects that help children. In return, members receive photographs and letters about the children they are helping. Through these pictures and letters, members learn what it's like to be a child living in the developing world. They receive detailed feedback about how their gifts are helping specific children.

If you want to learn more about our CARE for the Child program, fill in the coupon on the last page of this report and send it to the address above.

Starbucks: A Cup of Coffee to Warm the Heart

Thanks to Starbucks Coffee Company, steaming cups of premium coffee will be awakening minds to the plight of the developing world's poor.

Starbucks is the largest West Coast sponsor of CARE programs, and has pledged to raise awareness among its customers about CARE's work in the developing world.

"Since CARE works in so many of the countries in which we buy coffee, this is a logical way for us to give something back," says George Reynolds, vice president of marketing for Starbucks. "And you can be sure that anybody who comes into our stores will know we're involved with CARE."

To accomplish this, Starbucks has publicized its partnership with CARE in its Fall and Holiday catalogues and through a special promotion in its retail stores during the month of January.

Starbucks' financial contribution will support mother-child health projects in Indonesia and Guatemala, and a children's educational magazine published by CARE in Kenya.

From its inception in 1971 as a single store in Seattle's Pike Place Market, the privately-held company has grown to employ more than 1,300 people, with more than 120 retail stores located throughout Washington State, Chicago, Portland, Ore., Los Angeles, and Vancouver, B.C. Starbucks also operates a mail-order business and a restaurant/wholesale division from its Seattle headquarters. ∎

At a CARE-supported nursery in Ethiopia, a CARE worker (right) shows a farmer how to tend tree seedlings. CARE photo/Santha Faia

Figure 5-13. This Q&A column helps bridge the gap between donor and the organization.

We would like to publish all the questions we receive from our donors, but due to the number of questions sent, your questions may not all be printed. We will write to you personally with a response to your question. Thank you for being involved.

And on to . . .

4. **Reader involvement columns (i.e., puzzles, quizzes).** Do you think coaxing the reader to become involved in your company or organiza-

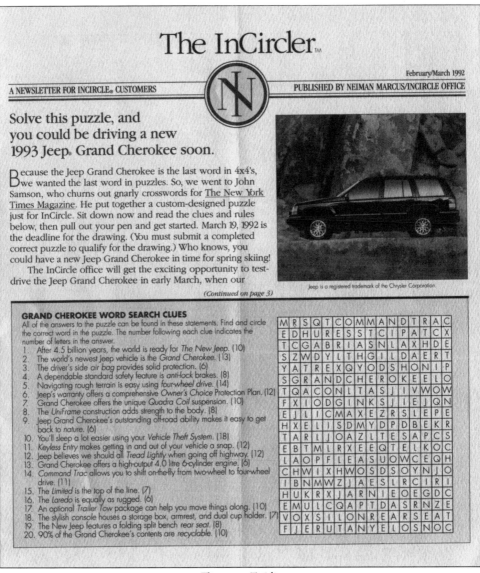

Figure 5-14

tion's message is difficult? Not at all. It becomes easy if you use blatant involvement devices such as a crossword puzzle or test.

If you're going to use devices such as these, be sure it ties into your organization in some way. Merely adding something for the reader to do without tying it directly to yourself is a waste of time and newsletter space.

Figure 5-14 shows an example of a puzzle which gets this company's readers involved even to the point of taking it to the mail box. It's a word search puzzle, with clues leading to a substantial prize—a Grand Cherokee Jeep. The puzzle, on page one of the newsletter, not only gets the

COMMUNICATOR

Upward communication

Take this quiz to evaulate your communication with your supervisor

How well you communicate with your boss can make a big difference when the time comes for performance reviews, pay increases, and promotions. Effective communication requires effort on everyone's part, and you can start by evaluating how well you and your superior are communicating. Place a check mark next to every statement that's true about your situation.

- **I can ask** the boss for help without being embarrassed.
- **My supervisor recognizes** good work when he or she sees it.
- **I understand** what my boss expects of me.
- **The boss coaches me,** helping me to improve my job performance.
- **I am aware** of the reasons for the major decisions my superior makes.

- **The boss understands** my personal goals.
- **I know** at least two specific things I can do to improve my rating at my next performance review.
- **The boss lets me know** when I've failed a task, but without humiliating me.
- **I feel free** to disagree when we talk.
- **The boss knows** about the basic difficulties I must deal with in my job.

Scoring

10: Your communication should be problem-free.
8-9: Good.
6-7: Average.
5 or less: Your communication with the boss needs some work.
(*Innput*, La Quinta Inns, Inc., P.O. Box 790064, San Antonio, TX 78279)

Public relations

Stretch your PR budget with some creative thinking

You say you want to boost your organization's image but don't have a lot of money to spend on a major public relations effort? Here are some strategies that should help you stretch your budget enough to increase the visibility and public opinion of your company or association:

- **Beg.** Go to other groups you do business with and ask for their help. For example, one swimwear manufacturer got some advertising assistance from the company that produced the cloth it used in its suits. How did it get the money? Someone went to the manufacturer and asked.
- **Borrow.** Look for resources you can use at least temporarily in your industry or community. Equipment, office space, or sometimes even personnel may be available when

they're not needed elsewhere. Repay people with a letter of appreciation and public credit for their work.

- **Improvise.** Look for unexpected solutions to your PR problems. One manufacturer who wanted to conduct a survey convinced several newspapers to print the survey and forward the results.
- **Sponsor.** Contribute to an event or a cause that will reflect your organization's strengths and values. Be sure to mention your sponsorship in your advertising.
- **Be creative.** Offer something different, like a special inaugural lunch for all the people who weren't invited to the real event.
(*IABC 'toban*, International Associoation of Business Communicators, Manitoba Chapter)

Improve quality by inventing problems

Shake up the creative process by occasionally using a backwards approach to problem solving. Think of all the ways you could *lower* the quality of work you're doing. Then figure out ways to counter these fictional bad practices. You should come up with some fresh ideas on raising quality standards. □
(*Together*, NWNL Group, 20 Washington Ave. South, Minneapolis, MN 55401)

Avoid computer fatigue with regular breaks

Working at a keyboard all day leaves you vulnerable to muscle soreness as well as eyestrain. Get into the habit of relaxing your hands and eyes at frequent intervals. Clench your fists for a couple of seconds, then stretch your fingers, and finally shake out the kinks while holding your arms loosely at your sides. Also, every few minutes take your eyes off the screen and focus on a distant point. □
(*Bank Notes*, Toronto Dominion Bank, P.O. Box 1, TD Centre, Toronto, Ontario M5K 1A2)

Watch for symptoms and cures of burnout

Burnout caused by job boredom or stress can strike anybody. Symptoms include increased eating, smoking, and drinking; excessive fatigue; feelings of anger, apathy, and/or depression; dread of going to work and difficulty showing up for work on time. To deal with burnout, learn to pace yourself. Don't just run from one crisis to the next. Eat lunch away from the office, and if necessary, take a mental health day. Also, be aware of what you do well on the job, and what you enjoy doing. Don't push yourself to do something you hate if you don't have to. □
(*DNA Focus*, Dermatology Nurses' Association, Box 56, Pitman, NJ 08071)

Phones emphasize careless speaking

The telephone can exaggerate careless enunciation. Clients and colleagues will get irritated trying to decipher what you've said, so when the phone rings, concentrate on speaking each word clearly. Don't make callers have to constantly ask, "What did you say?" □
(United Telephone Systems, 112 Sixth, St., Bristol, TN 37620)

Figure 5-15. This is a good example of how to get your readers involved.

reader involved but gets the reader to appreciate both the newsletter and the department store issuing the newsletter.

Another example of how to get your readers involved is to give them a test or quiz they can answer. Figure 5-15 is an example of a test one newsletter used for the readers to self-evaluate how well they communicate with their supervisors.

Notice that any reader of this newsletter can take and score the quiz easily. That's mandatory. A quiz whose answers lie deep in hidden lore will infuriate readers. If they want that kind of challenge they'll try to work the *New York Times* Sunday crossword puzzle. Your quiz should be helpful, ingratiating, and non-threatening.

For instance, if you're a fund-raising organization seeking contributions to save the whales, give your readers a relevant quiz—what they know about whales and the destruction of whales, and how these matters affect them. Be sure to give the answers elsewhere in the newsletter. Then, in a box adjacent to the answers, ask the readers if they'd like more information, and give them a way to respond. This can help qualify your prospective donors for that specific appeal.

The checklist in figure 5-16 gets the reader involved and also gives the reader a reason to keep the newsletter.

Note, too, the word scramble on the same page. The reader's conclusion: This newsletter is fun.

5. **Marketplace news, or a product news column.** A simple column for new products or services which can benefit your readers is not only useful; if you take the of proving your position within your business or fund raising community, it's a necessity.

The trick is for the column to contain products or services just "hot" off the market, being careful to choose items catering to your readers' interests. Report these products briefly and clearly. Preferably the byline should be by someone well known in your industry. Don't use the entire newsletter to "sell" the product or service; do be sure these products or services pertain to the newsletter's overall purpose.

Granted the newsletter in figure 5-17, states on the front page that it's "devoted specifically to new and proven popular mailing lists . . ."; but this particular issue is not a "newsletter," but a self-serving catalog.

If the recipient accepts it as a catalog, fine; if the recipient thinks, at first glance, it's a newsletter, not so fine. Fight the tendency to use too much "what we have for sale" product or service information.

The back page contains only one "news" article, "Make your database asset work in tough times." This is the only article included in this "newsletter," and even it evolves into a sales pitch. If this were a true newsletter it should contain information along the following themes:

       a. Data base information
       b. How to know your list is working
       c. How to clean your list
       d. Product news column
       e. Direct marketing tips

90

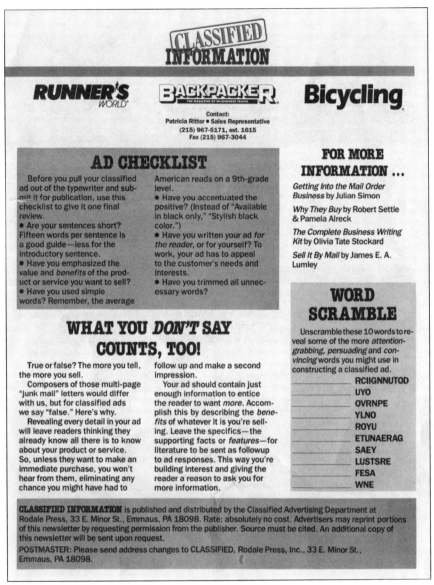

Figure 5-16

Within this framework the newsletter can include plenty of self-serving information without having the reader conclude the entire piece is puffery.

The newsletter in figure 5-18 devotes an entire page to new products, plus a feature review. These products are beneficial to the target-readers (financial services marketers). This six-page newsletter promotes membership in the Bank Marketing Association. The ''new products'' column blends well with the marketing mix and has the proper tone of newsletter conciseness: It doesn't give the impression of page after page of sales pitches for the sponsor's products.

Published by Action Direct Marketing Pty. Ltd. (inc. Action Mailing Lists), Level 12, 10 Queens Rd., Melbourne, Vic. 3004 Tel: (03) 820 4644, Fax: (03) 820 4951
A NEWSLETTER OF INFORMATION ABOUT THE LATEST IN LISTS FROM ACTION MAILING LISTS.
Print Post Approved PP 381667/00005

Vol 4. No. 1 1992

New and popular lists for 1992

This issue of the List Report is devoted specifically to new and proven popular mailing lists that should work well for you in 1992. Of course it does not represent all local and international lists that AML can provide but should give you a good feel of the wide range of lists available from AML across all consumer and industry sectors.

Many niche and speciality lists have been avoided for this issue but profiles are available on request from AML.

Education

This sector continues to boom despite the uncertain economic climate and problems on how best to administer education for our Australian children.

AML's basket of education lists has been used for 100's of successful campaigns many of which ADM undertook the distribution or fulfilment.

An example includes the complex fulfilment component of a campaign which involved matching pupils to schools and matching computerised information of each school to AML's schools list address labels.

The list comprises 11600 schools and has a deliverability guarantee of 99%.

What's more any format can be delivered within 48 hours.

It has become the main educational tool for publishers, school suppliers, computer companies and others who have a need to market educational products and services.

A fully detailed, easy-to-understand statistical breakdown is available.

Selections • Telephone numbers available • any enrolment size • by religion • by any school type or category • personalised to any generic title • by boarding/non-boarding • by State, city, metro or country area.
Ask for list no 74.

Kindergartens

AML's launch of this list which included half price rentals to the first three renters was snapped up within the first two weeks. (See The List Report, Vol 3 No 3).

It is the most extensive list of kindergartens and child minding centres in Australia.

There are 3600 kindergartens and 2500 childcare centres on the file.

Telephone numbers are available for telemarketing follow up.

A generic title of your choice can be inserted.

Deliverability is 95%.

An ideal educational list that works well with AML's highly accredited schools list.
Ask for list no 42.

Libraries

A new comprehensive list of every library in Australia.

You can select by type of library, i.e. public, government, corporate and so on.

An additional bonus with this list is that all public libraries are fully personalised to the head librarian.

Any generic title can be inserted for non-personalised categories of libraries.
Ask for list no 43

> **AML has more than 240 of the best mailing lists in Australia**
> **Tel: (03) 820 4644**
> **Fax: (03) 820 4951**

AUTOMOBILE

4-wheel owners

A recently compiled listing of 49500 4-Wheel drive vehicle owners sourced by a market research company.

The majority of records are personalised to the home address.

Telephone numbers are available for telemarketing purposes.

A high profile list of owners who enjoy the outdoor and who have leisure time to develop other interests.

Ideal for travel, car, or credit card prospecting.
Ask for list no 83.

Car Owners

The list owner is a car servicing company operating in NSW, ACT, VIC and QLD.

The company uses direct mail to generate on-going business from its database and is continually adding new records as cars are serviced.

All 8100 records are active (except NSW), 90% of business is repeat.

Information is captured from actual work dockets and guarantee forms.

AML also manage another car owners list which has 350000 identifiable vehicles nationally.

The list is mailed twice yearly by the list owner and cleansed 12 times per year.

The file increases by about 10000 records per month.

Deliverability guaranteed at 95% with 96% of records to the home address.

All records are fully personalised.

A highlight of both these lists is the wide selection criteria.

It includes make, model of car, speedo reading, no of kms travelled each year, age of car, male/female driver.

Detailed yields on 55 makes of vehicles can be provided.

Ask for lists 15 and 55.

Other lists to consider:

• *List no 59 — 11200 NZ motorists*
• *List no 130 — 33000 SA motorists*
• *List no 131 — 11500 4WD subscribers*

COMPUTING
Macworld

This list is comprised of 4800 subscribers to the only Australian magazine devoted exclusively to MacIntosh computer users.

Macworld subscribers are a diverse group of business and professional Mac product users and buyers.

The MacIntosh computer owner and user represent a captive market for computer software, products and services.

Ask for list no 44.

PC World

Subscribers to Australian PC World are PC users who buy or recommend PC products and services.

Subscribers are kept informed about changing trends, new technology, product comparisons and comprehensive hardware and software reviews.

The list of 13500 represents an ideal vehicle for targeting PC users who have a desire to be well informed and kept abreast of the latest in technology.

Renting this list will provide access to PC users who buy, recommend, approve and evaluate personal computers, software and peripherals across all brands.

Ask for list no 64.

Pacific Computer Weekly

Australia's oldest computer publication, first published in 1971.

It is targeted at the computer and communication managers, decision makers and technical staff in the industry.

It is an ideal file for those wishing to strike 15400 decision makers who are in need of information, services, training courses, software and hardware updates.

Ask for list no 62.

Computerworld

20800 of Australia's top spending MIS/DP individuals and organisations.

This active, highly targeted subscribers list reaches industry professionals.

Job title criteria covers 22 different positions.

Type of industry can also be selected.

Ask for list no 18.

Other lists to consider:

• *List no 303 — 64700 Computing Aust. subscribers*
• *List no 120 — 5000 Your Computer subscribers*

MEDICAL
Doctors

This doctors list of 42000 is highly recommended and credentialled.

It's so finely tuned that selections include male/female doctors, age, qualification, discipline, fields of practice, secondary medical interests, employment type, non-medical interests and more.

The list is continually being updated with new doctors or as doctors change their specialist area.

This is an excellent doctors' list that offers the flexibility to target by specialised profession.

Guaranteed at 95%.

Ask for list no 25.

Hospitals, nursing homes

 A specialist file of 620 who are prime prospects in NSW and QLD for detailed information on wheel chairs, medical aids, etc.

The list is activated every six weeks by the owner who mails the entire file a newsletter to their business address.

Records are constantly updated via returned mail and the use of directories.

Ask for list no 155.

Pharmacies

 A list of 900 retail pharmacies in NSW and QLD which are sent a newsletter every quarter.

To compliment this list AML has another popular pharmacist file with national coverage of 12200.

Ask for lists 156 and 66.

Veterinary Surgeons

A national list of 1700 private practicing veterinary surgeons who are mailed detailed information on veterinary products and equipment each month.

70% of records are fully personalised.

Ask for list no 157.

Other lists to consider:

• *List no 9 — 6900 subscribers to Australian Hospital*
• *List no 11 — 85000 NSW nurses*
• *List no 139 — 3250 hospital and health services*

**For mailing lists
Tel: (03) 820 4644**

WINE AND FOOD
Wineries and vineyards

 A customers in-house database of 745 records covering Australia (617) and New Zealand (128) wineries.

This comprehensive listing which includes specific job titles for targeting, has been compiled and researched by the owner for a very popular annual publication.

The list is updated quarterly by the owner from a circulated update questionnaire.

A generic title of your choice can also be inserted for each record.

Ask for list no 152.

Wine and food lovers

A list of 21250 qualified wine and food connoisseurs, mostly in Victoria and NSW.

This prized targeted list can be accessed by three segments - wine newsletter subscribers, wine drinkers who receive "monthly specials" and those who attend special wine and food dinners, seminars and exhibitions.

The list is fully personalised to the home address. Deliverability is 95%.

This list provides a one-stop source to tap into Australia's serious and committed wine and food lovers.

An ideal market for liquor, or strong image products and services.

Ask for list no 91.

Other lists to consider:

• *List no 39 — 15300 Hospitality, convention industry.*
• *List no 311 — 26270 Liquor license holders.*

BUSINESS
Corporate executives

This list is comprised of 8000 decision makers in NSW and VIC.

It contains managing directors, chief executive officers and personnel managers across all industry sectors.

98% of all records are fully personalised.

This file is activated every six weeks by the owner and all updates are processed prior to each mailing.

Deliverability is guaranteed at 97%.

An excellent list to access the highest levels of management.

Ask for list no 20.

BRW

Business Review Weekly is Australia's most respected and largest selling business magazine.

Over 88% of all readers earn in excess of $30000 p.a.

The average age group is between 25-49 and represents 63% of the total file.

This list of 56250 provides a unique opportunity to target decision makers and entrepreneurs who are motivated to succeed and who desire to keep abreast of current affairs and developments.

Figure 5-17. The issue of this newsletter is a self-serving catalog. Fight the tendency to use too much "what we have for sale" product or service information.

New BMA Products

Listed below are the BMA products that will become available to BMA members within the next few months. If you are interested in receiving more information as the brochures become available, contact Linda Coleman at (312) 782-1442. For your assistance, when ordering for information, product codes have been placed next to each item listed below.

SELLING IN BANKING: TODAY'S REALITY, TOMORROW'S OPPORTUNITY (PC-1)

Sequel to "Bankers Who Sell." It's an update of the survey presented in "Bankers Who Sell." Included is a list of recommendations for bank executives interested in moving ahead in personal selling for their institutions.

SAFETY & SOUNDNESS COMMUNICATIONS KIT (PC-2)

The book is designed to assist you in communicating the facts of the FSLIC crisis and your institution's position in your marketplace. Material includes: employee overview on FSLIC, questions and answers, communication tips, speech, guide to FDIC insurance, communication resources, letters, communications plan and employee communication tips.

MARKETING TO THE MATURE BANK CUSTOMER (PC-3)

Topics cover: Understanding the market, research, segmenting, and communicating with 50+ customer, packaging and pricing, developing a membership program, tracking results, staffing, employee sensitivity, seminars and social activities.

EFT AND THE MATURE MARKET (PC-4)

(Research program conducted by the Gallop Organization for EFTA in conjunction with AARP.)

Results of research conducted to ascertain the degree of which individuals older than 50 years of age use EFT services and how these services are perceived. It also includes marketing strategy recommendations for this key market segment. (Study sponsorship available now through your BMA membership.)

BUILDING A FINANCIAL SERVICES PLAN (PC-5)

Marketing plans and prototype marketing plans for various products and services from the BMA's School of Bank Marketing papers.

SALARIES OF MARKETING PROFESSIONALS IN BANKS (PC-6)

(Research with Abt Associates Inc.) Salary information for bank marketing professionals. Various demographic factors (asset size of bank, region of country, community type, etc.) will be included. Survey is expected to be conducted annually. (Available in September.)

USE OF TECHNOLOGY TO SUPPORT MARKETING STRATEGIES (PC-7)

(Joint venture with Andersen Consulting Research Report.)

This research cites how banks are using technology to respond to a variety of marketing strategy issues.

Included: Combined information about customers across different banking business units; identifying customers and understanding the full set of each customer's relationships within the organization; using information about customers more intelligently in areas such as planning, product development and pricing, credit and risk management.

WINNING STRATEGIES FOR CONSOLIDATION (PC-8)

(Forum and research report.) An in-depth "hands-on" analysis on the industry consolidation. Topics cover: How your institution is viewed, successful defense strategies, how to manage integration, how to maximize franchise value, and prospect for consolidation, plus five in-depth case study analyses.

HOT TOPIC PACKAGES (PC-9)

The best 10-15 articles on a current subject, case study, executive summary, FINIS bibliography, and a list of other products relating to the "hot" topic. "Hot" topics are identified and produced regularly. (Always available.)

Selling in Banking: Today's Reality, Tomorrow's Opportunity

Dr. Leonard Berry's new book, **Selling in Banking: Today's Reality, Tomorrow's Opportunity** reveals the results of a recent updated survey from the findings presented in his earlier best seller, **Bankers Who Sell**.

In 1983, Dr. Berry conducted a study to find out the status of personal selling within American banks. The study provided data for measuring the banking industry's progress in the years ahead, and was published in his earlier book **Bankers Who Sell**.

In 1988 Berry teamed up with associate Donna Kantak to measure how the banking industry had progressed since his last study.

Berry and Kantac replicated Berry's original study five years later. The results can be found in **Today's Reality, Tomorrow's Opportunity**, which offers an up-to-date portrait of the state of retail and wholesale personal selling, in U.S. banking.

Retail price is $40, but BMA/ABA member price is $30. To place your order, see the information listed in the New BMA Products section.

Figure 5-18. The "new products" column blends well with the marketing mix and has the proper tone of newsletter conciseness.

94

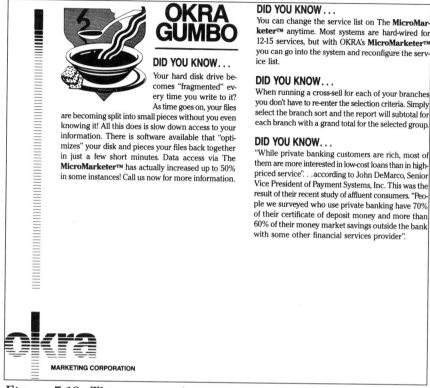

Figure 5-19. This is a good example of how you can integrate a "Did you know" column with promotional copy.

In fact the way it's done—the new products column isn't hard-sell, it doesn't have to be—by featuring new products in the newsletter, these products sell themselves more profoundly than they could in ponderous hyper-promotional text.

6. **F.Y.I. columns and articles.** "F.Y.I" (For Your Information), "Did You Know" columns, and checklists—if done right—are highly valuable to your client or customer and can benefit you as well if they interweave information with what you're trying to accomplish.

Take a look at how the sponsor newsletter in figure 5-19 integrates a "Did you know" column and promotional copy.

This approach is painless...parallel to hiding a dose of castor oil in a chocolate soda. "Did you know" is just one way of presenting this type of information. Another is the straightforward approach: stating the problems which happen with computers when trying to do a certain job, relating what the company does to confront and conquer those problems, and then having a conclusive statement such as a call to action.

7. **Business or news brief columns.** Business or news briefs can work effectively for promotional editorial content by writing the briefs in a

Business briefs

It's in the cards
The definition of money has been evolving ever since the days of barter. The standard has gone from coin to cash to check to plastic — and now beyond.

The newest form of plastic money is the "chip" or "smart" card. An extension of present-day ATM

Some estimates project widespread smart card usage worldwide by the late 1990s.

cards, these cards will perform almost all your banking and non-banking transactions.

Smart cards will hold computer memory that stores certain types of information. For example, one section of memory will debit your bank account each time you make a

retail purchase. Another will act like an electronic key, unlocking your home and starting your car. Still another will hold your medical history and insurance information.

The possibilities are endless. And the increasing need for better, more efficient service is making the card a reality.

Wire delays are opening lines of communication
The Federally imposed 15% cap on intra-day overdrafts, instituted in January 1988, has some banks experiencing overdraft pile-ups. The resulting delays are creating increased float time. And that's generating concern among banks.

To discourage the pile-ups, some banks may charge hourly interest on overdrafts. Another possibility is increasing the price of wire transfers during peak hours.

All of this talk has opened lines of communication between many businesses and their banks. Some companies have reached agreements on individual overdraft caps. Still others have agreed to pay overnight interest on their negative account balances.

Corporations that haven't done so already should contact their banks to

discuss overdraft agreements. Because while few banks have actually implemented wire-transfer or overdraft-interest charges, it's clear changes will have to be instituted to cope with lower overdraft caps.

Dueling tactics
The debate still rages. Some say "Tastes great," while others opt for "Less filling."

But this time it's bankers, not ex big-leaguers, engaging in the playful repartee. And the bone of contention is controlled disbursement services.

It's easy to understand the fuss, since the number of banks offering controlled disbursement services has increased by 57% since 1984. That's according to a survey by Phoenix-Hecht, which also isolated two bank strategies for selling controlled disbursement services.

One is the "Tastes Great" strategy — selling the services based on float gains. Another approach is the "Less Filling" strategy, which sells disbursement services based on low per-item charges.

According to the survey, the "Tastes Great" strategy is the favorite among banks' corporate clients.

Figure 5-20

manner which is newsworthy *and* promotional for your company or organization.

The ''Business Briefs'' column shown in figure 5-20, integrates ''news'' with the Association's own products. Actually, news and products overlap, because this is a trade association.

One possible criticism: ''Smart cards'' aren't new...especially within the world of electronic cash management. The thrust of this ''brief'' isn't relevant to the newsletter's readership. The problem of matching text to reader is often the result of failure to analyze the key to pertinence:

Who is my target?

The ability to answer that question is in direct ratio to the writer's immersion in the field the newsletter represents.

Is the Boom Moving Toward a Job Bust?

THE U.S. WORK FORCE GREW 0.5 PERCENT BETWEEN DECEMBER 1989 and December 1990, slower than the population, as we moved into a recession. And with the middle-aging of the baby boom, unemployment isn't just for kids anymore.

The total civilian labor force averaged 124.8 million adults aged 16 or older in 1990, according to annual figures from the Bureau of Labor Statistics. The unemployment rate for the year averaged 5.5 percent. The workplace treats women equally in this respect; their unemployment rate was 5.4 percent, compared with 5.6 percent for men.

Men's work force participation peaks in their 30s, women's in their early 40s. In combination with the baby boom's current concentration in these groups, this means that fully 40 percent of workers are now aged 30 to 44. This share crept up during the 1980s as baby boomers got older and women continued to increase their labor force participation even through the family-raising years.

If we thought we had problems with a middle-management squeeze before, they may only get worse. The number of people aged 30 to 44 in the general population will peak in 1996, according to Census Bureau projections. The current recession isn't helping matters, either, as unemployment rates rise. Although older adults are much less likely than teens and young adults to be unemployed, a much greater number of them want or need jobs. Half of unemployed workers in 1990 were under the age of 30, but another third were aged 30 to 44.

During the recession of 1982, the overall unemployment rate was almost 10 percent. At that time, 58 percent of the unemployed were under the age of 30, and only 26 percent were aged 30 to 44. Baby boomers were aged 18 to 36 that year. We can expect the age distribution of both the employed and the unemployed to shift upward as the boom ages.

THE MID-(WORK)LIFE SQUEEZE

(civilian labor force and participation rate by sex and age, 1990; numbers in thousands)

	total number	total rate	men number	men rate	women number	women rate
total, 16 or older ...	124,787	66.4%	68,234	76.1%	56,554	57.5%
16-19	7,410	53.7	3,866	55.7	3,544	51.8
20-24	13,843	77.8	7,291	84.3	3,544	51.8
25-29	17,421	83.6	9,583	93.8	7,836	73.8
30-34	18,362	83.9	10,230	94.6	8,152	73.4
35-39	16,902	85.0	9,262	94.9	7,640	75.5
40-44	14,942	85.5	8,007	93.9	6,936	77.6
45-49	11,576	83.3	6,237	92.3	5,339	74.8
50-54	8,916	77.5	4,940	88.8	3,977	66.9
55-59	7,073	67.0	4,014	79.8	3,059	55.3
60-64	4,788	44.9	2,771	55.5	2,016	35.5
65 or older	3,535	11.9	2,033	16.4	1,502	8.7

Source: Bureau of Labor Statistics.

Reprinted from The Numbers News, ©1991 American Demographics, Inc.

HEARING THE VOICE OF THE MARKET
Competitive Advantage Through Creative Use of Market Information
by Vincent P. Barabba and Gerald Zaltman

Perhaps no person is better qualified to write about understanding market information than Vincent Barabba. Currently executive director of market research and planning at General Motors, he has held similar positions at Eastman Kodak Company and the Xerox Corporation, he has served twice as director of the U.S. Bureau of the Census, and is currently president of the American Statistical Association. Along with distinguished marketing professor Gerald Zaltman, he maintains that competitive advantage results more from how information is used than from who does or doesn't have it. Market research alone does not guarantee success; intelligent use of market research is the key to business achievement. Based on the premise that inadequate information cannot be used well, and sound information is wasted if it is used poorly, this book prescribes the organizational framework of an Inquiry Center to manage the problem of information overload. In this model, Competent Curiosity will drive you to ask the questions that will allow you to hear the voice of the market, and Competent Wisdom will allow you to interpret data correctly, develop appropriate action plans, and execute them skillfully. (ISBN 0-87584-241-0; 1991) Book #464 $29.95

> ### Much more than you could ever hope to learn in a costly 3-day seminar!

CREATIVE STRATEGY IN DIRECT MARKETING
by Susan K. Jones

Direct marketers enjoy the best of both worlds: the freedom to express creativity balanced by the discipline of measured response—the excitement of striving for breakthrough ideas and the satisfaction of measuring the value of those ideas in absolute dollar terms. To become a good direct marketer, it is essential to fuel and tend your creative fires—to move beyond the predictable formula and format toward fresh words and images that move consumers to buy your products. Yet even direct marketers who call themselves "creatives"—copywriters and art directors—need a firm grounding in the scientific side of the business. This book will help you develop a winning creative strategy for any medium. In space ads and catalogs, for back-end marketing and telemarketing, for broadcast and TV shopping, you will learn how to keep your messages sharp and inviting. (ISBN 0-8442-3179-7; 1991) Book #465 $39.95

THE COMPLETE DATABASE MARKETER
Tapping Your Customer Base to Maximize Sales and Increase Profits
by Arthur M. Hughes

Never before has such a thorough guide been compiled to assist marketing managers, advertising and sales executives, brand managers, and consultants. Expert Arthur M. Hughes shares the secrets of how to return to the days of more personalized service and stronger relationships with customers. Although the ultimate aim of marketing is making a sale, the more fine-tuned marketing function, database marketing, begins with the sale and aims at establishing a lifetime selling relationship with customers. Database marketing allows you to analyze customers' past buying patterns and compare them with demographic and psychographic data; it is a phenomenal tool for determining future purchase behavior. You'll learn how to gain incremental sales through repeat purchases and improved communication, dealer support, telemarketing techniques, even renting your customer list—truly a comprehensive sourcebook on building profits through customer loyalty. (ISBN 1-55738-192-5; 1991)   Book #474 $39.95

© For fast, friendly service call 800-828-1133

Figure 5-21

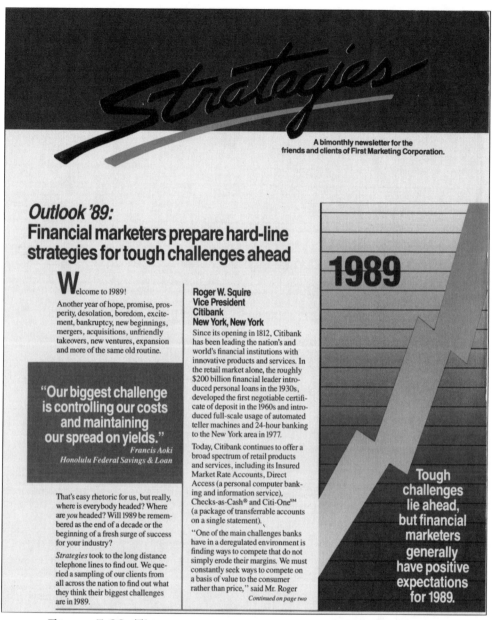

Strategies

A bimonthly newsletter for the friends and clients of First Marketing Corporation.

Outlook '89:
Financial marketers prepare hard-line strategies for tough challenges ahead

Welcome to 1989!

Another year of hope, promise, prosperity, desolation, boredom, excitement, bankruptcy, new beginnings, mergers, acquisitions, unfriendly takeovers, new ventures, expansion and more of the same old routine.

> "Our biggest challenge is controlling our costs and maintaining our spread on yields."
>
> *Francis Aoki*
> *Honolulu Federal Savings & Loan*

That's easy rhetoric for us, but really, where is everybody headed? Where are *you* headed? Will 1989 be remembered as the end of a decade or the beginning of a fresh surge of success for your industry?

Strategies took to the long distance telephone lines to find out. We queried a sampling of our clients from all across the nation to find out what they think their biggest challenges are in 1989.

Roger W. Squire
Vice President
Citibank
New York, New York

Since its opening in 1812, Citibank has been leading the nation's and world's financial institutions with innovative products and services. In the retail market alone, the roughly $200 billion financial leader introduced personal loans in the 1930s, developed the first negotiable certificate of deposit in the 1960s and introduced full-scale usage of automated teller machines and 24-hour banking to the New York area in 1977.

Today, Citibank continues to offer a broad spectrum of retail products and services, including its Insured Market Rate Accounts, Direct Access (a personal computer banking and information service), Checks-as-Cash® and Citi-One℠ (a package of transferrable accounts on a single statement).

"One of the main challenges banks have in a deregulated environment is finding ways to compete that do not simply erode their margins. We must constantly seek ways to compete on a basis of value to the consumer rather than price," said Mr. Roger

Continued on page two

1989

Tough challenges lie ahead, but financial marketers generally have positive expectations for 1989.

Figure 5-22. This sponsor-promoting newsletter features a number of experts' opinions on trends for that upcoming year in the organization's targeted industry. This is definitely a hard-hitting article which keeps the readers interested and keeps you in their minds.

Editorial Slants

Effective sponsor-promoting newsletters blend promotional editorial seamlessly with feature articles of straight editorial. For instance, your *promotional* editorial could be columns you use in every issue. The *straight* editorial would change from issue to issue and would depend on your chosen appeal or specific product or service highlighted in the issue.

But to make your newsletter into a publication your readers look forward to receiving, some genuinely newsworthy information has to be integrated into each issue. A few ideas for straight editorial slants.

1. Trends or Predictions in the Industry

For business-to-business promotional newsletters this might be market trends; for business-to-consumer newsletters it can mean including health trends, investment trends, economic trends, sociological trends. The key to trend-inclusion: These should be trends which pertain to and/ or affect your customers, donors, or prospects.

The article shown in figure 5-21 is predicting hard times for baby boomers, yet this newsletter is aimed at marketers. A mismatch? By no means. It's a bulls-eye.

If you don't see why marketers would be interested in the future unemployment rate for baby boomers, you aren't placing yourself in a *marketer* position. Marketers immediately see the relevance: A "job bust" among baby boomers will affect how businesses will target their markets in the future. Will readers want to find out more about this prediction? You bet. (What does this company sell? Books about marketing which are promoted in other areas of the newsletter.)

2. Guest Articles Written by Someone Respected in the Field

Guest features project the aura of a seemingly unbiased attitude toward the company sending the newsletter. Articles such as these can add credibility—and these articles aren't *directly* selling your product, service, or appeal.

Guest articles shouldn't get off on tangents or tirades which have absolutely nothing to do with the aim of your newsletter. They shouldn't talk about how to grow a vegetable garden when your readers live in condominiums. That's an obvious error; some are less obvious, and it's the editor's job to tailor not only the content of guest articles, but the original instructions from which guest writers prepare their articles.

Take a look at figure 5-23. This newsletter pitches newsletter publishing to a variety of industries. The guest article featured in this newsletter is about writing sales letters and is written by Herschell Gordon Lewis (the guru of direct response advertising copy).

Why put this article in the newsletter? Because the newsletter is built around marketing and advertising, and a showing of expertise strengthens the image of the newsletter itself. An article written by Mr. Lewis adds credibility to the company publishing the newsletter.

If the newsletter contained 100 percent promotional copy touting this company, it would be less effective than adding other types of information helpful to the readers of this newsletter. The "Five rules" article doesn't even mention newsletters; yet it still pertains to the readers...and helps the newsletter be perceived as beneficial.

3. Feature Articles Which Affect Your Client, Customer or Donor, but Aren't Directly Related to Your Organization.

Figure 5-24 is an example of what I mean by features which don't directly relate to your organization. This feature article is about how to stay healthy while traveling. The newsletter is from a pharmaceutical company, its target is seniors, and its goal is to keep people using prescription drugs for certain ailments. Travel is a good feature article for this newsletter because most retired seniors travel. Ensure your newsletter has something of interest which directly affects your readers.

4. Checklists and Helpful Columns Feeding Your Readers Information Indirectly Related to Your Organization.

Figure 5-25, "GOING ON A TRIP?" gives solid advice to people when they're leaving home. How does this checklist pertain to the newsletter issued by a savings bank? It doesn't pertain directly to what the organization is trying to sell (consumer loans), but it does pertain directly to a usual interest of its readers. For the bank, it's an image builder—a "We care about you" reinforcer.

5. Industry News

What's new in the industry? How are different organizations using what's new in the industry? What industry-affecting announcements have come from government or authoritative sources?

Behind the scenes

… from page three

ber of colors, a given job could require anywhere from four to 15 separate stripping flats.

The stripping flats, in turn, must fit together into a final, perfectly calibrated package. Otherwise, the printed newsletter will be "out of register" — which occurs when the various colors don't line up together.

After the negatives are stripped into place, technicians prepare the "blue-line." The blueline is used to check the position of all elements of the newsletter before the printing plates are made. Your editor, art director, production traffic manager, and pre-press supervisor all review the blue-line, checking for anything out of place or out of register.

Printing plates are produced only after the blueline has been approved. Then, the newsletter is ready to go to the press room.

Those afterthoughts

What happens if you require a change in copy content at the last minute? The entire process begins again. Your newsletter goes back to the editor, the artist, the typesetter, the camera operator, the stripper — and finally, the blueline technician again. The process can take days — and is best avoided.

And what would happen without the internal organization that puts each step in precise order … or without the perfectionistic determination of each specialist? Yes, you might get a printed piece — but without the crispness one expects of truly professional production that elicits reader response.

First Marketing invites you to tour our new, showcase plant, if the mechanical and electronic wonders of the production process interest you. You can easily arrange this by calling Ms. Shelly Schiff, Workshop Coordinator, at 305-979-0700. We'll have you speaking "printese" in no time!

Five rules for better sales letters

by Herschell Gordon Lewis
President, Communicomp
Fort Lauderdale, Florida

Everybody writes letters.

Maybe that's why *everybody* is an expert. A businessperson will hire consultants for advice on every facet of business operation from color of washrooms to width of parking spaces. But letter writing? That same executive not only won't hire an expert, he or she *is* one.

As one expert to another, I don't object to this. The person whose signature is on the letter is who should make the decisions.

But here, in a pressure-free forum, I'll offer some opinions that might — not tampering with the decision-making process — result in better-looking, better-read business letters.

Rule 1: Keep your first sentence short.

What an easy rule to implement! The first sentence is your indicator to the reader. It's an early warning, and your target forms a quick impression: The letter is going to be hard slogging.

Rule 2: No paragraphs longer than seven lines.

Oh, you can bet you'll run afoul of a preconceived prejudice. I brought this up in a workshop for a group of professional writers, and sure enough, one fellow asked, "But what if a paragraph has to be longer than seven lines?"

My answer, there and here: Insert a period and start a new paragraph. No paragraph has to be longer than seven lines.

Rule 3: Vary paragraph length.

Reader fatigue is a genuine threat to the letter-writer. We can fight off that fatigue by having an occasional paragraph of one line or less.

Whatever you do, don't have a solid string of four-line paragraphs. That violates another rule: Neatness is boring.

Rule 4: Single space the letter. Double space between paragraphs.

A double-spaced letter takes about twice as much space as a single-spaced letter. A two-page letter becomes a four-page letter, and a four-page letter — well, don't even think about it.

Manuscripts call for double-spacing; that's to enable an editor to write chicken-scratch comments into the text. Letters aren't supposed to subject themselves to editing by the people who get them.

(A suggestion, if you disagree on grounds of tradition rather than reader attention: Type out your next letter both ways. Ask 50 people which one is easier to read.)

Rule 5: In a letter longer than one page, don't end a paragraph at the bottom of any page except the last.

Newspapers have known this for a hundred years. Readers demand completeness. If you've ended a paragraph at the bottom of the page, the reader has a reason to read on only if he or she already has a firm interest in what you're selling.

If you leave the reader in mid-sentence you, as letter-writer, are in command. The letter-reader is your captive until the end of the sentence — on the next page.

How much difference will adherence to these mini-rules make in the effectiveness of your letters? One-tenth of one percent? Then why not use them?

4

Figure 5-23. Why bother with an article about how to write better sales letters? Because even though the article doesn't tout the services of the company, it is still in direct interest with this company's target market and is indirectly tied to the interest of the company itself.

Figure 5-24. Be sure your newsletter contains something of interest which directly affects your readers.

Experts Cautious About Mortgage and Housing Outlook

The national housing market in 1988 has been characterized by booming sales, sharply rising prices in selected regions, and the spectre of rising interest rates for the balance of the year. But from this industry-wide profile one trend has clearly emerged. Housing starts and home sales both have reflected a move from financial assets to real estate, and more specifically, toward single family housing—a trend touched off by the October 1987 stock market crash.

Although multi-family housing has remained depressed and commercial construction has dropped off somewhat, single family housing starts are expected to pass the one million mark for the sixth consecutive year.

So far this year, housing starts in general have suffered through bad weather in January and February, but recovered strongly in March and April. Most experts express caution, however, that rising interest rates could mean a weakened housing market for the balance of '88. They point to April single family housing starts, which showed a six percent decline from March. Total housing starts are expected to remain below last year's levels by five to 10 percent.

In California, a potential slowdown in housing starts could exacerbate a current shortage of homes for sale, in part due to the decreased mobility of home owners and local slow growth initiatives. But despite sharply rising prices, home sales in California rose at an annual rate of nearly 12 percent during the first quarter, while many states experienced declines.

The sales boom in California can be traced to several other factors as well. One, as mentioned at the outset of this article, is the flight from financial assets. And for roughly five years, stocks and bonds have enjoyed an unprecedented up cycle, while real assets stood in the background.

Interest rates also have played an important part in spurring demand. Before the October crash, fixed rate mortgages stood at 12 percent. By March 1988, they had bottomed out at just under 10 percent. Since March, however, fixed rates have climbed to 10.75 percent. The net impact . . . lower rates have increased overall demand, while the probability of higher rates has compacted demand into a shorter time period.

The general outlook for the remainder of 1988 is for higher interest and fewer housing starts, and a slow down in home sales as skyrocketing prices and higher mortgage rates eliminate more potential home buyers.

The current forecast calls for 30-year fixed mortgage rates to peak this summer in the 11 percent range, while ARM rates should simultaneously tip 9 percent. Look for the possibility of declining rates some time toward the end of the year. ▲

GOING ON A TRIP?

BEFORE YOU GO, protect your home . . .

☑ STOP DELIVERY of newspapers, laundry, mail, etc.

☑ Leave a "LIVED IN" look
- Lights on timers
- Shades up
- Volume of phone bell turned down
- Arrange for garden and lawn tending.

☑ Have POLICE and CLOSE NEIGHBORS keep an eye on your house or apartment.

☑ DON'T DISCUSS YOUR TRIP IN PUBLIC before you go.

ON THE WAY, have fun but . . .

☑ Use caution at AIRPORTS and BUS TERMINALS.
- Keep luggage locked, carefully watched.
- Leave identification inside luggage.
- Carry travelers' checks and credit cards instead of cash.

☑ Be alert at your HOTEL/MOTEL.
- Keep room keys at all times.
- Keep room locked, luggage inside.
- Leave valuables in an office safe.

8

Figure 5-25

Turn-key customer retention from MasterCard

MasterCard's "Mastering Retention" reflects an increasing emphasis by banks on direct marketing tactics but it fails to build individualized relationships with cardholders.

It isn't getting any easier to compete in the credit card business these days, and bank credit card issuers have a special disadvantage. While American Express and Discover represent unified, centralized marketing efforts, MasterCard and Visa operate as umbrella brands whose central marketing budgets are contributed by the hundreds of member banks, all of which issue both cards and each of which pursues its own separate set of local, regional and, in some cases, national marketing objectives. That is, many issuers must compete against each other as well as against American Express and Discover.

To make matters worse, the business has reached near saturation levels, with the average American holding 9.2 credit cards as of year-end 1990. (The *Nilson Report*, July 1991, Issue No. 503) In addition, cultural trends are pointing toward a reduced emphasis on debt-creating consumption. With so much competition, the marketing focus is shifting heavily toward customer retention and activation

— a battle for share of wallet and to hold on to customers bombarded with competitive offers. This shift is reflected with an increasing emphasis on direct marketing tactics that attempt to create the feel of frequency marketing (FM), without going all of the way.

MasterCard's "Mastering Retention" is a good example — a series of targeted incentive offers. While most banks hold more information about their customers than almost any other business, few banks centralize and strategically apply that information to grow their business. This is especially true of local and regional banks, where small and unsophisticated marketing departments are often content to buy pre-packaged marketing programs.

Enter mastering retention...

Rather than building a dynamic database of cardholder information and creating a flow of individualized customer benefits, most banks prefer a turn-key program delivered for them. They look for programs requiring a minimum of their own marketing staffs' involvement and that are priced on a per cardholder basis, preferably with a flexible menu of options.

MasterCard recognizes this, and has appropriately responded with Mastering Retention. It is comprised of six promotional modules including: the Reactivation program, the Transactional Goal program, the Cash Advance program, the Convenience Check program, the Incremental Usage program, and the Portfolio program. "Each of the six programs is a turn-key operation that offers fully developed creative packages; customized artwork; printing and mailing; database set-up; customer service; and tracking and program analysis reports," says Susan Klieman, a consultant for MasterCard.

Each program is designed to reward cardholders with incentive premiums or gifts, based on the frequency and dollar amount of their transactions. For example, as a way of enticing cardholders to take cash advances against their credit,

6

Figure 5-26

Industry features are directly beneficial to your readers and should, indirectly or directly, pertain to your organization.

The newsletter in figure 5-26 takes a totally different approach to sponsor-promoting newsletters (which I'll expand later on in this chapter). This company is a frequency marketing organization. It uses this particular issue to explain how other companies are using frequency marketing programs. The feature uses no promotional copy—but by assuming the mantle of commentator, it positions the company as the "expert" in the field of frequency marketing.

6. News Flashes

Late-breaking news which pertains to the industry or which will affect your readers is a logical component of any newsletter.

Depending on the frequency of issue, "late-breaking" may be a euphemism. If you newsletter is a quarterly, don't label this component "Hot News"; rather, call it a "Summary" or "Roundup."

7. Book Reviews

If your organization is selling the books you're reviewing, a book review won't have the same effect on your readership as it would if you're not directly involved with the publication, *unless* you adopt the image of providing books as a service to your readers.

What's wrong with selling books? Nothing...if you understand the difference between "selling" and "hawking." It's normal, expected, and good business practice to extol the virtues of books written by your staff members; it's unacceptable to try to make book sales a profit center in a newsletter whose goals are oblique to book sales.

8. Profiles

Especially in fund-raising, finance, advertising, and service industries, profiles about people who have made a difference in the area of your appeal or field of activity is a logical inclusion.

9. Interviews

Interviews with well-known experts (provided they don't flagrantly push your products, services or appeals) can have a positive effect...especially if you can create the impression that these experts either respect your organization or are available to you as consultants.

The better-known these experts are, the more valuable photographs of them with your corporate officers will be.

Should You Include Advertisements in Your Newsletter?

If you handle your promotional copy properly (i.e., by inserting at the end of an informational article whom to call, where to write, and what you can do for the person inquiring...or a bio if the article is written by one of your sales people), you shouldn't have to place in obtrusive advertising copy everywhere in your newsletter. (Response devices should be able to carry out the rest of your promotional copy.)

If you want to add an advertisement about your organization, I would suggest a quarter-page ad or a $1/6$-page ad. "House" advertising shouldn't take up a lot of space in the newsletter. You could even include a bound-in insert within the newsletter, recognizing the huge lift that bind-ins give to response of any type.

Conflicts in Editorial/Promotional Mixes

Three viewpoints appear to co-exist, not so peacefully, regarding the degree of promotional and editorial mix for newsletters:

1. The newsletter should contain no promotional copy.
2. Promotional and editorial copy should blend together for the perfect mix.
3. The publication is actually one hundred percent promotional copy, disguised as a newsletter.

Which of these types of sponsor-promoting newsletters do you think would be most effective?

No contest. If your answer is number two, you have a chance of making the best success of your newsletter program. You're using your newsletter as a promotional medium, not as an exercise in statesmanship that probably won't pay off nor as a disguise.

These philosophies defeat the purpose. You want to overcome skepticism, not instill more doubts. You're creating customer loyalty, instilling customer confidence, interacting with your readers, and positioning your organization as an experienced, knowledgeable professional source.

Strictly Editorial?

Organizations who use their newsletter strictly as a straight editorial publication, containing no promotional copy, need to have a strong sales force behind them because their most natural and logical sales weapon, the newsletter, has been emasculated.

If you have no sales force behind you, or a minimal sales force I wouldn't tread the waters. There's a good chance the newsletter could backfire on you. It's not the fault of the newsletter medium; rather, it's in the way in which you use the medium...or, rather, *haven't* used the medium.

106

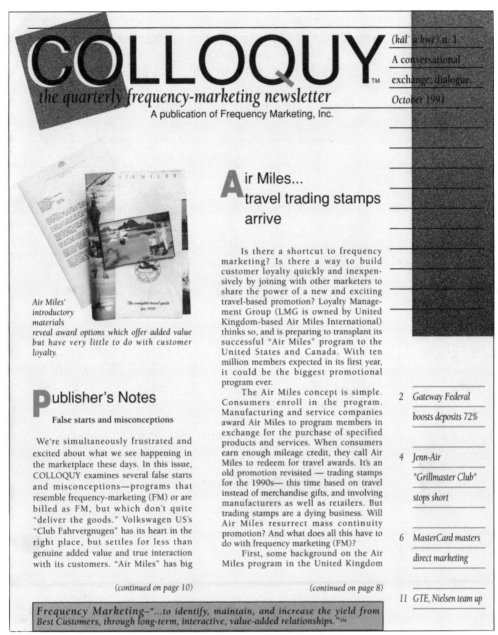

Figure 5-27

Again, the sponsor-promoting newsletter in figure 5-27 uses straight editorial in its newsletter. In fact, I wouldn't put this publication in the same category as a sponsor-promoting newsletter.

The newsletter is positioned as a publication for marketing professionals. It positions itself as a "trade publication." And that's what it is. One would expect to pay a subscription fee, because the promotional purpose of this publication is so thoroughly masked. The company's name is mentioned only once, in the name plate.

Why would a company bother integrating this type of newsletter publication into their marketing mix? They don't even sell it by subscription. But they could. This organization uses the publication to get their foot in the door: "Oh, you're the people who publish 'Colloquy'." Does it work? Maybe. In this instance, a bind-in card does make a solid move toward reader-response.

Questions to ask yourself when determining the amount of self-promotion to include:

> 1. Will people think of the true organization as the same publishing firm which writes this particular newsletter when the sales person mentions the name? (They should.)
> 2. If the sales people do get the chance to mention that they work for the same organization which publishes the periodical—how many business or donor prospects will actually have read the newsletter and take an amiable view of speaking with someone from the organization issuing the publication? (It should be all of them.)
> 3. Will the readers feel misled if the publication generates leads *for itself as a publication*, but the sales force follows up on behalf of the company? (A hard-boiled viewpoint: So what?)
> 4. Is a co-existing strong sales program in effect? (It had better be.)

Hard-sell vs. Soft-sell

Hard-sell copy can be devastating in this medium. If you come on too strong, you may be defeating the whole purpose of why newsletters are read in the first place.

You have to be good at your craft to achieve a hard-sell "harmony" in newsletters. But you can do it—and it can work to your benefit. Writing hard-sell copy without the reader becoming aware that this *is* hard-sell copy is the height of the art!

CHAPTER *6*

Effective
Newsletter Copy
Tactics

Let's start this chapter with...

Congratulations! You've come this far (hopefully with little difficulty). The formula for a successful sponsor-promoting newsletter is just about in your hands. But hold it for a moment; there's still more road to travel.

Once your promotional and editorial mix is in perfect sync, you still need *the right words* to convince your readers to take notice...and for that matter, to keep reading.

The style and slant you adopt in each article and column are the factors determining how your readers respond. Will they respond favorably? Will they respond at all? Will your newsletter be read? If so, will it be read sympathetically or with hostility? *Are you generating the reaction you're supposed to generate?*

Here's a checklist to keep in front of you while you write. (NOTE: "Copy" is the generic term for the wording of a message.)

Copy guideline checklist

☐ Does the newsletter copy grab your readers in one to three seconds? (Never forget: Sponsored newsletters are unsolicited. Competition from *solicited* media—television, radio, newspapers, mailed material, a person's stomach, and time itself—is brutal.)

☐ Does the newsletter copy lead your readers where you want them to go, forming the conclusions you want them to form?

☐ Is your newsletter copy both brief and interesting?

☐ Does your newsletter copy strike a match under your readers? (To light a motivational fire under the reader's casual interest, two sub-questions: 1. Does the copy zoom in on the emotional appeal of your readers? 2. Does the copy give solutions to the problems you've posed?)

☐ Is your newsletter copy informative and pertinent?

☐ Does your newsletter copy offer the reader an easy way to respond?

☐ Does your newsletter copy convey reliability and engender trust in your company or organization?

☐ Does your newsletter copy integrate the entire piece into a coherent whole?

Okay, how do you know whether your newsletter copy has accomplished all this and more?

Communication: The Key to Successful Writing

What do I mean by communication?

Don't write above (or for that matter below, although *below is better than above*) the experiential background of your readers.

Fact: If your message matches the *background* of your target readership, you've hurdled the biggest obstacle in the path of determining whether your newsletter will be a failure or a success.

This may seem easy to you, but sometimes it's like attempting to make gold from silver. It's especially difficult when a writer's ego blocks the communication frequency because he or she would rather spit 6 syllable words onto the paper instead of communicating a message others will understand.

Fact: No one will respond to your written piece if it reads as if it's in code. Your readers don't have the time nor the inclination to try to decipher an obfuscatory newsletter.

Writing vs. Communicating

Does the need for clarity + a motivational message answer your question about *who* should write your newsletter copy? I hope so.

Anyone can write. But not everyone can communicate. Written communication isn't easy. Words may flow easily and steadily from the fingers to the paper—but only from someone who's honed his or her craft well.

Even a skilled writer may have to do re-writes until he or she grasps the right editorial style of your company or organization.

Editorial style. How about a "style sheet," which enables any writer to conform with the editorial style you've chosen?

Putting together a style sheet isn't easy, but does it save time and frustration down the line when articles you yourself haven't written start coming in! You won't encounter big problems if your organization has thoroughly considered what type of editorial style your newsletter should be written and if that style is consistent with the image you're establishing. If your writing style is totally out of context with the targets to whom you're writing, go back and rethink your decision. It's not the writer's fault if you're too vague or don't have the time to sit down with your editor (even if *you're* the editor) and define your editorial policy.

A word of advice: Everyone believes he or she is a copywriter. But few actually are. And if you aren't a career writer, for heaven's sake don't try to rewrite your copywriter's words. You're paying good money for a skilled job. Don't think automatically, "I can do it better." If you're convinced you can do it better, and if you have the time, by all means write it on your own. Then ask somebody who isn't dependent on you for income to give you a dispassionate opinion before you invite your target-public in to read.

Professional courage calls for changing the concept if the concept is wrong. But the professional copywriter *usually* knows how to get inside the reader's head and motivate the reader into action.

The good copywriter can get your newsletter read, get the reader involved, make you credible, increase customer retention, and get response soaring.

The Importance of Consistency in Newsletter Tone

Whichever "tone" you decide best fits your targeted reader, be sure you maintain that voice throughout your newsletter issue.

What do I mean by the *tone* of the newsletter? I'm referring to the dynamics of force-communication. The greatest power isn't necessarily the most effective power, any more than constant screaming is more effective than constant calm speech.

For example, your tone can be intimidating, straightforward, humorous, conservative, personal and friendly, urgent, heroic, or tragic. The tone you choose will depend upon your intended relationship with your target reader. Here are a few guidelines to help you:

1. In cases of fund-raising, religious groups, institutions and political tracts you may want to take the heroic (idealistic) tone or tragic/desperate (fund-raising) tone; for more extreme religious groups you may want a tone which is intimidating.
2. For financial services, high-ticket items, or business-to-business newsletters, your tone would probably take a straightforward, well-reasoned attitude. (Note: You can use this tone and still strike with emotional motivators.)
3. The tone which works best for readers of health care, self-help products, or insurance services would probably be personal and friendly...even breezy, if your relationship is fraternal or equivalent ("Fellow member," for example).
4. Travel services, customer services, or club newsletters might take on a quietly conversational tone.

The tone you use in your newsletter will directly affect reader perception of your message and your organization or company. You're in control. Different tones for the same subject matter can set a totally different ambience and convince (or leave unconvinced) your readership in totally different directions.

Tone inconsistency in the same issue can be detrimental to your objectives. If your tone is straightforward, don't change in midstream and become sentimental.

EXCEPTION! You can present facts in a straightforward manner, then switch tones *within a specific message from the president or executive director*, to an impassioned cry for action.

But what makes a good "news" story? What should you avoid and what should you elaborate on as you're writing your newsletter? In these pages I've given you a few tips about what to do and what not to do as you write your newsletter; but for a comprehensive book about direct response copy writing, I recommend a book called *Copywriting Secrets and Tactics*, by Herschell Gordon Lewis. This is an in-depth book about "power communication."

Six Key Components for the Professional Story

The six keys to professionalism in writing: Unity, Consistency, Accent, Brevity, Clarity and Conciseness.

Let's take a look at the first three keys:

Unity

Newsletter articles that contain a strong sense of unity will keep your readers on the same track as your rhetorical engine. This means you, as a writer, create the theme for your readers to follow without either of you straying off track.

Consistency

Consistency glues the structure of your newsletter articles together, so your words, sentences, and paragraphs flow smoothly from idea to idea and tie together.

Accent

Accent stresses those ideas you want to stand out as key elements of your story.

Figure 6-1 is an example of non-unity. The writer exhibits no consistency to create an even flow of ideas throughout the story. The report begins in the middle, describing solution before problem. It reads as if each sentence was an individual thought, unconnected to what goes before or after.

The next three components—brevity, clarity, and conciseness—are essential to *newsletter articles* because these types of articles are meant to be read fast, leaving no room for misunderstanding. You don't have time for long and involved storylines and you don't have the time to tease your reader into the article. It all has to happen fast, and it has to happen clearly.

Brevity

Be brief. You don't have to forsake flair for the sake of brevity. This just gives you a better challenge to make the story interesting without getting florid.

Clarity

The easiest road to clarity is to write the way people talk. Don't get out your high school grammar book and follow rules such as a taboo on ending sentences with a preposition. I'm not saying you should omit apos-

unicef 🌐 IN ACTION

REPORT FROM THE FIELD

A Newsletter from the U.S. Committee for UNICEF   Fall 1991

UNICEF Responds to Bangladesh Cyclone

The generosity of friends like you enabled UNICEF to respond quickly to the devastating cyclone that killed nearly 140,000 people in April. With funds raised through its appeal, UNICEF was able to provide emergency supplies and immediate relief to the children and mothers in the worst-hit areas.

Immediately after the cyclone struck, UNICEF and the government of Bangladesh, with broad international support, were able to react quickly and efficiently to the disaster. UNICEF redirected supplies and resources from its ongoing programs to meet the urgent needs of surviving children and mothers.

The cyclone of April 30 destroyed or damaged over 600 health centers and 5,000 schools, along with crops, livestock, and homes. Because it hit during the harvest season, the winter rice crop was seriously damaged. Agricultural land and water sources have been ruined by debris and salt water, and the survivors are facing disease and starvation. Once again, the most seriously affected are the most vulnerable—women and children.

Bleaching powder was purchased for disinfecting polluted tube-wells. Emergency hygiene kits, containing flashlights, plastic jerry cans, drinking cups, laundry soap, plastic sheeting, nylon rope, hurricane lamps, candles, and batteries, were sent to relief camps scattered along the worst-hit coastal areas.

UNICEF was able to purchase locally 4 million ORS (oral rehydration salts) packets for immediate distribution, with 5 millon more under production. To meet the present demand and ensure future supplies, UNICEF is also importing the raw ingredients to produce locally 15 million more packets. In addition, UNICEF is providing vaccines, syringes, needles, and cold storage boxes for transporting the vaccines. Vaccination teams are also distributing vitamin A capsules and water-purification tablets to mothers and children.

UNICEF has been focusing on the rebuilding and long-term maintenance of the

Continued on page 2

Children on Kutubdia Island, Bangladesh, were among the many saved by UNICEF's quick response.

Major Milestone Reached Globally in Immunization

This is the story of a major success—and a global one at that. Eighty percent of the world's children are now immunized against the six diseases responsible for the most child deaths. The achievement of this level of coverage has been called one of the "biggest collaborative peacetime efforts in history, stretching from the Amazon to the Himalayas and from megacities to remote hamlets unreached by even the postal service."

Why is this achievement so important? Current levels of immunization are saving the lives of nearly 3 million children each year—lives that would have been lost without the global immunization campaign.

The story began in 1974 when the World

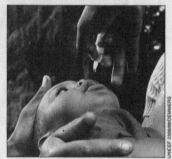

The oral polio vaccine is widely used in Africa.

Continued on page 4

Figure 6-1. Here's a good example of non-unity in a newsletter article.

trophes or run two sentences together, but we need to communicate clearly.

When in doubt—spell it out. Choose strong words to lead the reader.

Conciseness

Please, please try not to overwrite. Your copy has to be tight. Needless words don't belong in your copy. We all have the inclination to make a point over and over again, because we believe in that point or fear we haven't been emphatic enough. Stifle that impulse.

How Long Should an Article Be?

Think of article length this way: Can your article be divided into littler stories? If so, do it. Attracting the reader with many short, snappy articles breaks monotony and reader-fatigue and makes it easier for the readers to read everything in your newsletter *at a faster pace*.

Obviously this procedure isn't possible for certain subjects. For instance, if you're explaining a complex computer program, naturally copy could take considerably more than a few paragraphs to expand on the program...and you don't want to break up the text into sub-components.

But think about this: If you find you need more space for an important *philosophical* or *historical* article, divide the article into parts and use it in your upcoming issues. This way the reader will look forward to your next issue.

The general rule: Shorter copy is easier to read.

How to Cut Copy Without Losing Your Story

If you find you have to cut your copy, be sure you don't cut out key elements of the article. An easy way to deal with trimming copy is to write in the pyramid style.

Here's how: Begin your article with the most important facts, reducing the most newsworthy fact to a single sentence if you can. As you progress down the factual pyramid, first expand on the most crucial points, then tackle the lesser points. If your articles are set up in this fashion it's easier to cut copy.

Tricks for Long Copy

Eight little tricks for reducing long copy without damaging clarity.

1. If you list points in your article, don't hit and run. Integrate them into the story.

2. If you have a sidebar, place it where there's dead space within the format.

3. Reread every sentence. If you don't need it—even if it's good—take it out.

4. Condense wordy sentences to make them shorter.

5. Don't repeat yourself to death with redundancies.

6. Rid yourself of lesser points the reader will regard as inconsequential.

7. If your article begins to go off on a tangent, stop, edit fiercely, and decide whether the tangent is worth another article.

8. If you have art, consider reducing its size or eliminating non-pertinent peripheral details.

Tricks for Short Copy

Six little tricks for expanding short copy without adding ''fat.''

1. Check the article for incomplete descriptions and make them more complete.

2. Whatever you do, don't add ''fluff.''

3. Add callouts to any illustrations or art.

4. Include a ''deck'' (one element of the story, repeated and set larger within its own border inside the story), or a sidebar.

5. Make your artwork bigger.

6. Include a ''teaser'' or a call-to-action box.

Tips for Good Leads

You have the power to win or lose your reader with your lead. What does a good lead include? What's entailed in writing a good lead?

The first item to remember when you're writing your lead is that newsletters are meant to be read fast. You don't have time to build anticipation in any article...and this rule is doubled in whatever appears on page one.

Different types of lead models exist: Explanatory, benefit-oriented, questions, scenarios, punchy, outrageous statistics, or raising a problem issue. Try them, as an exercise. When you look at a lead you've written and it seems flat or verbose, replace it with a different type.

Here's a checklist for lead effectiveness. Use it and readability of your newsletter will leap.

1. Give your readers a benefit.
2. Make the reader feel you're talking to him or her.
3. Remember to be clear.
4. Don't promise something you don't deliver later.
5. Make the lead short, snappy and exciting.
6. Use emotional motivators.

> *The CAN'T MISS technique for newsletter leads:* Ask yourself: What's the most important newsworthy component of this article? What's the crux? Then reduce that element to a sentence. That's your lead.

Let's take a look at figures 6-2 through 6-4 for a few examples of effective and ineffective leads and see why one works and one doesn't.

This lead raises a problem-issue. But it's so jumbled with mismatched percentages it tires the reader out before the writer gets to the point of what he or she is talking about. Note the "deck," beginning, "We do not believe...." This saves fragments of clarity.

Problem: Common to most writers is the problem of beginning the story. Many times a writer will begin a story and ramble along until finding the right flow for the article.

If you sense rambling, usually you can take out the first paragraph and the crisper second-paragraph lead will take the reader where the writer had intended.

Perhaps this writer could have begun with the last sentence of the first paragraph, to read something like this:

"Today's recent volatility won't warrant a major repositioning of your assets."

The lead in figure 6.3 brings the reader into the article with a short, compelling question. It's not too wordy, it's provocative, and it flows smoothly, leading the reader directly into the story.

The lead in figure 6.4 gives the reader some compelling (shock is always compelling) facts about surgical procedures. It transmits an emotional motivator which works well with the target—FEAR.

Guidelines for Headline Grabbers

What do your readers see when they lay their eyes on your newsletter? The overall design, sure, but if your headline is catchy (the type style has to be a grabber too) your readers will be drawn to your lead article.

What is it about a headline that grabs the readers? What is it that makes a headline work or fail, makes your readers stop and notice your article or toss it aside, entices them to read further or induces a ho-hum passivity?

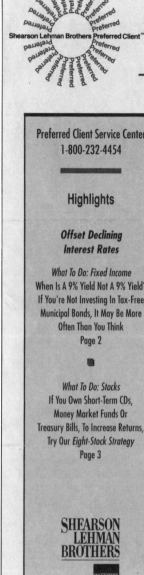

DECEMBER 2, 1991

THE **INNER** CIRCLE

Preferred Client Service Center
1-800-232-4454

Highlights

Offset Declining Interest Rates

What To Do: Fixed Income
When Is A 9% Yield Not A 9% Yield?
If You're Not Investing In Tax-Free
Municipal Bonds, It May Be More
Often Than You Think
Page 2

What To Do: Stocks
If You Own Short-Term CDs,
Money Market Funds Or
Treasury Bills, To Increase Returns,
Try Our *Eight-Stock Strategy*
Page 3

**SHEARSON
LEHMAN
BROTHERS**

AMERICAN
EXPRESS ®

You can get there
from here℠

Despite Recent Stock Market Volatility, Our Message Remains The Same – *Stay The Course*

We expect that the recent volatility in the stock market — a reaction to such events as the government's attempt to cut credit card interest rates from 19% to 14%, unemployment claims increasing, slumping automobile sales and the rumor of dividend cuts — was a reminder that investors should never be complacent in a time of economic malaise. However, while we do

*Michael H. Sherman
Chief Investment Strategist*

We do not believe that this recent volatility warrants a major repositioning of your assets

see a 10% correction in the stock market sometime in the next six months — from higher levels than exist today — we do not believe that this recent volatility is going to go far enough to warrant a major repositioning of your assets.

It's a fact that in post-war recession bull markets, significant market corrections usually occur only after the economy has turned up vigorously and short-term interest rates rise from their lows. While we had a faint recovery last spring and summer, the slowdown since then has prompted a further decline in short-term rates. What the economy now needs to create a vigorous upturn is lower long-term rates (especially lower mortgage rates) to revitalize construction.

If inflation continues to move downward and government policies remain supportive of the goal of lower inflation, we could get lower long-term rates over the next three to four months, setting the stage for a vigorous recovery next spring. In that period, the market could suffer a 10% correction of the type seen in late 1975 and early 1984. These corrections have normally been great buying opportunities, but they don't last long. Subsequently, interest rates usually hit new lows and stock prices set record highs ■

Happy Holidays!

Health and Prosperity for the New Year and Beyond

Figure 6-2. The lead is so jumbled with mismatched percentages it tires the reader before the writer gets to the point.

118

Now more than ever it's...
Time to Light a Fire Under Your Accountant

...and make him more aggressive in cutting your taxes

QUESTION: How often in the past year has your accountant come to you with a list of creative ideas on how to cut your taxes?

Rarely? Not once? *Never since you've known him?*

Actually, it is not common practice for accountants to come to you with creative tax-reduction ideas, and this is exactly why *you* need to urge him to do so. You see, accountants have *hundreds* of clients, and so much paperwork on each, they have all they can do to handle *routine* tax preparation.

So that's the type of service you wind up getting —*routine.* There is just no time in your accountant's busy day to research every single area of your personal and business life... and then spend more hours on creative daydreaming about new and interesting ways to cut your taxes. *Yet that's precisely how the biggest tax savings can be uncovered!*

And its especially important now and for the next several years, as Congress and the IRS start to come after your wealth fang and claw in their all-out effort to reduce the federal budget deficit.

There's an Easy Way to Help Yourself... and Make Your Accountant More Aggressive

The blunt truth is, *no one cares about cutting your taxes as much as you do.* You must be involved in the process. Yet you don't want to become an accountant yourself... or waste time poring over tax journals.

Here's a suggestion... the easiest way ever invented to be sure you're taking advantage of every single tax break that can possibly apply to both your business and personal life. You can do it in just minutes each week, once you receive your copy of the bonus report, *"Declare Your Own Tax Freeze"* (yours free with a no-risk trial subscription to the weekly *Research Recommendations*).

All you do is quickly scan this bonus report, plus your regular issues of *Research Recommendations,* which are chock-full of tax-reduction and wealth-building ideas every week. Whenever you come across a tax-cutting strategy that may apply to you, put a checkmark next to it.

Then, as soon as you see your accountant, pull out your file and ask him if any of these tax-reduction strategies can apply to you.

Simple, right?

But look at the marvelous benefits this brings you.

First, by your actions, you show your accountant that you don't want to be a "tax patsy." You are aggressively looking for every legitimate tax cut you can find, and you expect him to do the same.

Second, in several cases, he is likely to tell you, "Yes, I think you *can* benefit from this," and you will have lowered your taxes, perhaps by thousands of dollars.

Third, in a subtle, non-threatening way, you start to light a fire under your accountant. It can be embarrassing for him if you point out tax-reduction ideas he's overlooked, and he won't want that. When he sees you taking an active interest, bringing him ideas, he will work all the harder to stay on his toes to think of strategies *before* you bring them up.

This is a universal law of managing any supplier effectively, including accountants—the more you know, the more demanding you can be, the greater respect he will have for you, and the more likely he will be to give you his best work.

You'll get more value for every dollar you're paying in accountant's fees. You will encourage your accountant to think more aggressively and almost certainly lower your taxes as a result. *All from a simple process that takes you about 4 minutes a week!*

From now on, every meeting you have with your accountant will be an exploration of new ways to cut your taxes. And why not! This is the main reason you're paying him—*to cut your taxes*—not just file forms!

Figure 6-3

Avoid passive headlines.

Passive headlines = inactive readers.

Scream benefits.

What are your readers going to get from your article?

Use emotional motivators.

Whenever possible tickle or punch your readers' emotions.

Tie your headlines into your graphics.

This can be a powerful double-whammy as long as the graphic matches your message.

Treatments That Are More Lethal Than The Diseases They Treat

Has your doctor ever told you that nobody—not the government, not even the American Medical Association—is responsible to determine if a new surgical procedure is safe and effective BEFORE it's used on you?

Shocking, but true. To approve new drugs for use, the Food and Drug Administration requires testing that takes about 12 years and costs on average $231 million. But new surgical procedures can be rushed into practice before any meaningful studies are done at all!

This is particularly bizarre because all major surgical procedures are far more dangerous than the most dangerous drug imaginable. Here are just four examples:

Angiograms are special X-ray procedures that require a catheter to be threaded into the heart and its arteries. A dye is then injected and an X-ray picture is taken. This picture supposedly shows blockages in the heart's arteries.

A million angiograms are done in this country every year, and 90% of them are unnecessary. Of those, between .1% and .5% result in the death of the patient. In other words, cardiologists are killing up to 4,500 patients a year with unnecessary angiograms.

To add insult to injury, the angiogram is one of the most inaccurate tests used in modern medicine. Comparisons of angiogram readings and actual measurements of blood flow through the arteries have proven that the angiogram is so inaccurate as to be virtually useless.

Balloon Angioplasty is a procedure cardiologists use to compress fatty deposits inside the heart arteries—supposedly to eliminate blockages and head off a heart attack. Nearly 300,000 people have the $15,000 angioplasty procedure every year, generating a windfall of over $4 billion to hospitals and doctors every single year.

Only two problems: First, about 2% to 4% of all angioplasty patients die during the procedure or within a year afterwards. Since there are about 20 million candidates for angioplasty alive today, as many as 800,000 people could eventually be killed by angioplasty (only about 500,000 people die from heart attacks each year!).

Secondly, there's never been a study that indicates angioplasty extends life expectancy at all! There's not a shred of evidence that indicates this dangerous procedure does any good whatsoever! To the contrary—studies have shown that about 35% of all blockages return within six months, and that angioplasty can actually create

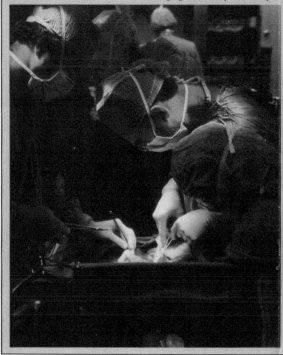

Figure 6-4

Match your headline with your storyline.

Nothing is more aggravating than a headline that doesn't have anything to do with what's written in the body copy. It could be a powerful grabber but if it doesn't match the story you've lost the readers. They're looking for something that isn't going to materialize.

Make a promise.

Headlines can promise your readers an answer to a specific problem. Be sure to follow through on what you promise.

Figures 6-5 through 6-8 have examples of interest-grabbing headlines. Some of them work and some don't work.

6 Painless Ways To Eat Less Without Feeling Hungry

1. Always eat breakfast. It gets your metabolism going at the beginning of the day.
2. Eat a mini-meal every three to four hours throughout the day. You'll speed up your metabolism, and stay full all the time.
3. Drink 96 ounces of water every day—your stomach will stay fuller.
4. When you eat, choose more complex carbohydrates like fruit, vegetables, or pasta. They make you feel fuller.
5. High water content foods also make you feel fuller.
6. Plan activities that aren't compatible with eating for times of the day when you're most likely to "blow it."

Another idea: When you're tempted to pig out, put on some tight clothes.

Figure 6-5

"6 Painless Ways To Eat Less Without Feeling Hungry" (figure 6-5).

This headline gives the reader an implicit benefit, and the text follows through with brevity, clarity, and conciseness.

"Message from the President" (figure 6-6).

A personal prejudice I really hope you share: I can't tolerate this type of feature. A message from the president can be robust if the president gives the readers something to use, rather than just touting inconsequential events and what "is going to be addressed" later. That's exactly what this nondescript boiler-plate headline warns me the president is going to do. (And it's what he does.) Instead, why not create a headline that will

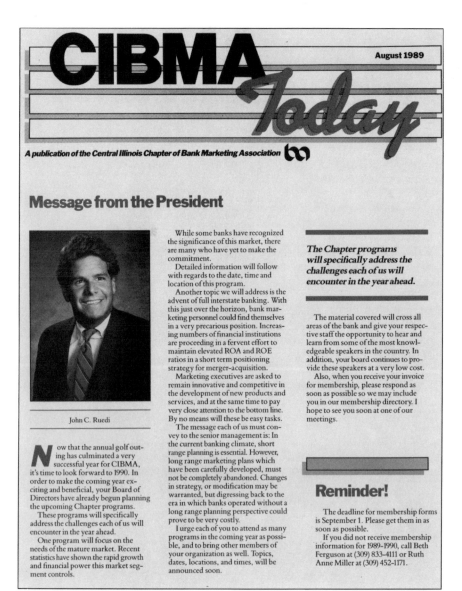

Figure 6-6

get the reader to read the message? Such a headline might even inspire a useful message instead of space-filler.

"63 Very Profitable Ways to Boost Your Direct Marketing Response" (figure 6-7).

This headline screams benefits. Anybody in the field of marketing would want to read not just this article but the entire newsletter.

"Recognizing and overcoming the procrastinator in you" (figure 6-8).

This headline is passive. Why not write something like this:

How to Shake, Rattle, and Roll the Procrastinator in You"

Winning Marketing Strategies

130 Garden Street • Santa Barbara, CA 93101 • (805) 563-0937 FAX (805) 563-9706

63 Very Profitable Ways to Boost Your Direct Marketing Response!

President: Geoff Hasler

TEST YOUR DIRECT MARKETING KNOWLEDGE!
Discover the answers to these — and EVEN MORE — important direct marketing questions inside!

1. Name the 10 best "test" cities in America? (see # 45)
2. How can you use selectivity as a direct marketing appeal? (see # 52)
3. When should you add a color flyer to your DM package? (see # 56)
4. When should you use copy-packed outer envelopes? (see # 54)
5. Do courtesy envelopes depress response? (see # 59)
6. Should you use illustrations or photos? (see # 55)
7. When should you use postcards? (see # 1)
8. Are colors important in marketing? (see # 6)
9. Should you use a time limit? (see # 31)
10. Should you use Early Bird Offers? (see # 29)
11. How can you boost high ticket buyer response? (see # 60)
12. How do you structure a winning Guarantee? (see # 41)
13. What size reply envelope to use? (see # 42)
14. Why promote your product on TV Game Shows? (see # 7)
15. How to use personalized birthday greetings in direct marketing? (see # 25)
16. What makes a good direct marketing product? (see # 19)
17. What are the hottest TV markets right now? (see # 24)
18. How can you enhance reply envelopes to boost response? (see # 28)
19. Specify a highly successful response booster used by auto clubs and insurance companies? (see # 32)
20. Name an effective response builder if you mail similar looking direct mail packages to the same list regularly? (see # 23)
21. How many premiums should you use? (see # 27)
22. Are brand-name premiums cost efficient? (see # 33)
23. Name an almost guaranteed response builder for mass consumer mailings? (see # 30)
24. Specify one great technique to get your carrier envelope opened? (see # 34)
25. How can you use your staff to increase response? (see # 35)
26. When should you admit that your product has shortcomings? (see # 39)
27. Why is the senior citizen market so important to direct marketers? (see # 20)
28. Should you specify name or job title in executive mailings? (see # 37)
29. Why should you use a "pass-along" slip? (see # 36)
30. In space advertising, should you use a right hand or left hand page position? (see # 40)
31. What are the best days of the week to advertise? (see # 44)

OPEN PLEASE

Figure 6-7

Wait a minute...

Recognizing and overcoming the procrastinator in you

 hy do today what you can put off until tomorrow? It's the credo of one species of investor — *financial plannis procrastinus*.

These investors are characterized by their good intentions. They recognize the importance of sound financial strategies and have every intention of implementing their plans . . . someday. But like a plane with too much cargo, the procrastinating investor's plans just never seem to get off the ground.

I'll do it tomorrow

All of us have, at one time or another, put something off. Maybe we didn't have time to get to it or maybe we just plain forgot. But neither of these instances constitute true procrastination.

By contrast, the procrastinating investor puts off his responsibilities for *no good reason*. A procrastinator's delays may be a result of confusion or, in today's busy world, lack of time. Or the problem may stem from some form of fear — fear of failing, fear of success or fear of losing control. For this investor, procrastination is a protective buffer.

By putting off the creation or implementation of a financial plan, the procrastinating investor avoids having to cope with potential investing mistakes. The reverse is also true — some investors aren't ready to cope with the responsibilities of a *successful* financial plan. Fear of loss of control can be equally paralyzing. For some, the thought of putting their money in someone else's hands is unnerving. Though they know it's counterproductive, for the time being, it's less stressful to do nothing.

Another reason some people put off planning for their financial future is that they are forever looking for a "good deal" or the "perfect" investment. What they fail to

Financial plannis procrastinus are characterized by always putting off financial responsibilities.

realize is that no one investment can have everything. There is no perfect investment — only investments that may or may not help you reach your specific goals. No investment is "right" for you unless it helps you meet your objectives.

Recognizing the procrastinator in us is a big step, but it's only the first step. Changing procrastinating tendencies isn't easy. It starts with convincing yourself that it makes a difference to change. Make a list of all the benefits you are missing out on by not putting a financial plan to work, such as minimizing taxes and providing the financial means to fulfill your future needs. When you become convinced of all the opportunities passing you by, you'll want to change.

Do it now!

Your Waddell & Reed representative can help. Once we have completed our analysis and reviewed appropriate strategies, we recommend a specific plan of action. We will look at the total picture and help turn your doubts and questions into a recommended series of actions. We're always ready to handle your concerns or questions — which makes executing your financial plan easier. And the easier your financial plan is to implement, the greater the chance you won't procrastinate.

Finally, remember that it isn't easy to shed the mantle of a *financial plannis procrastinus*. Steel your determination to overcome your procrastinating ways. Keep in mind all the benefits of a successful financial plan as you look at the task ahead.

And, most importantly, do it today.

Financial planning

. . . from page one

Each aspect of your plan, such as providing for your children's college education, will outline a specific action to be completed within a given time frame.

Together with your Waddell and Reed representative, you can develop realistic strategies and time frames to ultimately reach your goals.

Taking action

This next step is both the easiest and the hardest. Easiest, because all the mental legwork has been done — you now know what to do, all that remains is to do it. Hardest, because until now your financial plan was only a plan. Now you must implement the plan.

After completing the analysis and reviewing appropriate strategies, we will review with you a recommended plan of action. You may be apprehensive as you prepare to take these big steps. To combat this natural reaction, remember that you and your Waddell & Reed representative have carefully evaluated your present financial status; determined a set of realistic goals; and chosen a reasonable course of action to achieve those objectives.

Also remember that your financial plan is flexible. It is not cast in stone. The plan is a framework that you can and should adjust as your personal situation or the economic climate changes. That's why it's important to monitor your program. Periodically you should meet with your Waddell & Reed representative to review your progress and make any adjustments.

At Waddell & Reed, we believe that financial planning is important for everyone, regardless of income. There is simply no better way to plan for your future. You owe it to yourself . . . and those you care about. To implement a financial plan or review your current plan, call your Waddell & Reed representative today.

Figure 6-8

Captivating Subheads, Captions and Callouts

Subheads, captions, and callouts instead of transitions are sharper, speedier, and more likely to attract the attention of your readers if they're merely skimming the newsletter. These devices easily break the monotony of straight body copy . . . plus they add to your promotional selling copy. So why not make them work hard? Take a look at figures 6-9 through 6-12.

unicef ⊛ IN ACTION
REPORT FROM THE FIELD

A Newsletter from the U.S. Committee for UNICEF   Fall 1991

UNICEF Responds to Bangladesh Cyclone

The generosity of friends like you enabled UNICEF to respond quickly to the devastating cyclone that killed nearly 140,000 people in April. With funds raised through its appeal, UNICEF was able to provide emergency supplies and immediate relief to the children and mothers in the worst-hit areas.

Immediately after the cyclone struck, UNICEF and the government of Bangladesh, with broad international support, were able to react quickly and efficiently to the disaster. UNICEF redirected supplies and resources from its ongoing programs to meet the urgent needs of surviving children and mothers.

The cyclone of April 30 destroyed or damaged over 600 health centers and 5,000 schools, along with crops, livestock, and homes. Because it hit during the harvest season, the winter rice crop was seriously damaged. Agricultural land and water sources have been ruined by debris and salt water, and the survivors are facing disease and starvation. Once again, the most seriously affected are the most vulnerable—women and children.

Bleaching powder was purchased for disinfecting polluted tube-wells. Emergency hygiene kits, containing flashlights, plastic jerry cans, drinking cups, laundry soap, plastic sheeting, nylon rope, hurricane lamps, candles, and batteries, were sent to relief camps scattered along the worst-hit coastal areas.

UNICEF was able to purchase locally 4 million ORS (oral rehydration salts) packets for immediate distribution, with 5 million more under production. To meet the present demand and ensure future supplies, UNICEF is also importing the raw ingredients to produce locally 15 million more packets. In addition, UNICEF is providing vaccines, syringes, needles, and cold storage boxes for transporting the vaccines. Vaccination teams are also distributing vitamin A capsules and water-purification tablets to mothers and children.

UNICEF has been focusing on the rebuilding and long-term maintenance of the

Continued on page 2

Children on Kutubdia Island, Bangladesh, were among the many saved by UNICEF's quick response.

Major Milestone Reached Globally in Immunization

This is the story of a major success—and a global one at that. Eighty percent of the world's children are now immunized against the six diseases responsible for the most child deaths. The achievement of this level of coverage has been called one of the "biggest collaborative peacetime efforts in history, stretching from the Amazon to the Himalayas and from megacities to remote hamlets unreached by even the postal service."

Why is this achievement so important? Current levels of immunization are saving the lives of nearly 3 million children each year—lives that would have been lost without the global immunization campaign.

The story began in 1974 when the World

The oral polio vaccine is widely used in Africa.

Continued on page 4

Figure 6-9. Unrelieved, forbidding text here. No subheads are used throughout the entire newsletter. The newsletter does use some photo captions but the captions don't inspire. The copy could have been helped by the use of subheads to break the monotony and to give the articles some kind of semblance of direction.

IMPRIMIS

Because Ideas Have Consequences

HILLSDALE COLLEGE

20th year

360,000 subscribers

Hillsdale College, Hillsdale, Michigan 49242

April 1992   Volume 21, No. 4

"Slouching Toward Catastrophe: 1914-1939"
by George H. Nash, Author, Presidential Biographer

Preview: The year 1992 marks the 50th anniversary of America's entry into World War II, the most titanic struggle in human history. Nearly every nation and every people were involved. When it was over, more than 50 million soldiers and civilians were dead, as were whole nations whose borders would be redrawn in the succeeding era. It came, ironically enough, on the heels of another war, the one that was to be "the war to end all wars." In reality, however, World War I was only a dress rehearsal for a far more cataclysmic event. Here, historian George Nash explains why. His remarks were delivered during the Center for Constructive Alternatives seminar, "America's Entry into World War II," in November 1991.

Seventy-three years ago, the First World War ended in Europe. The armistice took effect at eleven o'clock in the morning—the eleventh hour of the eleventh day of the eleventh month: a symbolic acknowledgement that European civilization had come close to irreversible ruin.

The Great War, as men and women then called it, had been a conflict like none other in history. It had begun in the summer of 1914, when 20,000,000 European men had put on their uniforms, boarded trains, and headed off to preassigned battle stations. At the time, the British foreign secretary had remarked, "The lamps are going out all over Europe; we shall not see them lit again in our lifetime." The men who marched believed, as the German Kaiser and others promised, that they would be home "before the leaves fell." Instead, *they* fell, in dark, unimaginable encounters like the battle of Verdun, which lasted for ten months and took 850,000 French and German lives. They fell in battles like that of the Somme, on whose very first day (July 1, 1916) the British army

suffered 60,000 casualties, including 20,000 dead. By the time "the war to end wars" ceased, 10,000,000 people had died. In its final months a great pandemic of Spanish influenza swept over much of an exhausted globe. By the time the scourge subsided, 20,000,000 more people had died, including half a million in the United States.

embarked upon a second and even more titanic struggle, rightly described as "the largest single event in human history." Fifty million people died before it ended; nearly half of them were civilians. In the United States alone, more than 12,000,000 men and women wore uniforms.

In duration, scale of combat, the expanse of theaters of operations, the number of casualties, and physical damage, the Second World War clearly dwarfed the First. But the *psychic* wounds of the earlier war, it seems to me, went deeper, and it is this dimension that I wish to explore this afternoon. It is not my purpose today to chronicle the diplomatic maneuvering that culminated in the German assault on Poland in 1939 or the Japanese attack on Pearl Harbor two years later. Still less is it my purpose systematically to analyze the immediate origins, both great and small, of those events. I propose instead to examine some of the ways in which the experience of the *First* World War affected the coming of the Second. You may ask why I do so. Because, in the words of the British historian A.J.P. Taylor: "The first war explains the second and, in fact, caused it, in so far as one event causes another." We cannot

> "By the time 'the war to end wars' ceased, 10,000,000 people had died. In its final months a great pandemic of Spanish influenza swept over much of an exhausted globe. By the time the scourge subsided, 20,000,000 more people had died, including half a million in the United States."

Less than a quarter of a century later, the Great War had its name changed. Now a numeral—number I—was affixed, as nations

fully understand the horrific conflagration of 1939-1945 unless we fathom some of the psychological and intellectual impulses that the

Figure 6-10. This newsletter is exactly what the title says: "Because Ideas Have Consequences." In other words it's one continuous story. Because of this the text cries for subheads, captions, and callouts to add accent to transitions within the storyline. Visualize subheads here. Wouldn't they relieve reader-fatigue?

Figure 6-11. Here's a perfect example of breaking up what could have been one big block of gray copy. On the first page the writer leads the reader into the story with a photograph caption that ties directly with the headline. But as we continue with the story it turns into photos and captions. This adds a dramatic visual twist to the storyline and breaks up the monotony.

127

IDS **Update**

IDS Financial Services Inc.

Winter 1989

In this issue:

The new president's $150 billion roadblock

Candidates for the presidency will spend millions of dollars, travel thousands of miles and give hundreds of speeches in their efforts to differentiate themselves from each other and win the election.

Yet, from the standpoint of post-election economic policy, it may not make much difference who wins. Republican or Democrat, liberal or conservative, the new president will come into office already bearing a tremendous burden — the $150 billion-plus federal budget deficit. Until the deficit is brought under control, any major policy initiatives by the new president will be put on hold.

"The deficit basically serves as a policy straightjacket," says William Melton, vice president and chief economist for IDS Financial Corporation. "The new president can do anything he wants, as long as it doesn't cost any money."

Breathing room

The first step for the new president and new Congress will be to begin reducing the deficit, to get some breathing room for intiatives that cost money. The blueprint for deficit reduction is likely to come from the bipartisan National Economic Commission (NEC), established last December to study the deficit problem. While the commission has maintained a low profile, and will continue to do so throughout the campaign, it should have a program ready by spring 1989.

According to Melton, that program is likely to consist of three parts:

• A revenue raiser, probably in the form of a surcharge on both personal and corporate income taxes. The percentage will have to be negotiated. But, for example, if it were 10 percent, you would multiply your tax bracket by the surcharge (28 percent x 10 percent) and add the result to your tax bracket. In this case, your new tax bracket would be 30.8 percent.

Melton says the surcharge is the only way to raise significant revenues ($40 billion to $50 billion) quickly and easily. It took the government two years to develop the 1,800 page Tax Reform Act of 1986. The government no longer has that kind of time to deal with the deficits, he says. While there will be changes to the law (there are more than 200 bills in Congress dealing with "technical corrections" to the tax law), the basic structure of tax reform is here to stay.

• Changes to such entitlements as Social Security and Medicare. For the first time in years, government officials are looking at entitlements as a place to help reduce the deficit. Whatever the NEC comes up with, whether it's skipping one cost-of-living adjustment (COLA), changing the COLA formula or something else, the changes will probably reflect a growing sense that everyone must contribute to the task of deficit reduction.

• Spending cuts in such non-entitlement areas as defense and agriculture. This probably won't be too significant, as most non-entitlement areas have already experienced budget cuts.

While other issues will crop up during the first months of the new administration, none is likely

Roadblock
continued on page 4

Confirmation change

Beginning Oct.1, 1988, you will no longer receive a separate confirmation if you have such regularly scheduled transactions as directed dividends, bank authorizations or payroll deductions. Instead, this information will appear on your quarterly consolidated statement.

How your mutual fund dividends are taxed

If you are like many mutual fund shareholders, you've probably been perplexed by the information on the Form 1099-DIV that you receive for tax return preparation purposes. Jim Jarvis, manager in IDS Tax Services, a division of IDS Financial Corporation, explains the taxation of mutual fund dividends for the 1988 tax year. The dividends you receive depend on the type of fund you invest in and its performance.

Mutual funds pay shareholders five kinds of dividends:

Ordinary dividends — These consist of income from a mutual fund's investment in corporate stocks and other securities, including bonds. Included here are short-term capital gains representing the fund's sale of investments held for less than a year. Ordinary dividends from a mutual fund are fully taxable to individuals.

Capital gains dividends — These are proceeds from the mutual fund's sale of securities held for more than one year. Capital gains dividends are reported as long-term capital gains, regardless of how long the investor held the mutual fund shares.

Exempt-interest dividends — These are proceeds from the fund's interest income from tax-exempt securities. Although this income is tax-exempt interest, taxpayers must show on their tax return the amount of tax-exempt interest they received or accrued during the tax year. This is an information-reporting requirement and does not convert tax-exempt interest into taxable interest.

Nontaxable distributions — These represent a return of capital or proceeds from the receipt by the mutual fund of corporation distributions that were not out of earnings. The mutual fund will designate on Form 1099-DIV, or a similar written form, the amounts representing return of capital. They reduce the cost basis of the fund shares. A return of capital is not taxed unless the distribution (when added to other such distributions received in the past from the fund) exceeds the shareholder's investment in the fund. Generally, funds in the IDS MUTUAL FUND GROUP do not make nontaxable distributions.

Income from foreign corporations — Income from the fund's investments in foreign companies may be taxable in foreign countries. Generally, the mutual fund pays the foreign taxes. If any special tax treatment is required, the shareholder will receive instructions from the fund company.

Calendar-year-end dividends — Under the Tax Reform Act of 1986, all mutual funds are now required to pay out dividends by Dec. 31 of each year. You may receive an extra dividend as a result of this law. For example, if you receive a distribution in July and the fund earns income between July and December, you will receive a dividend and will be taxed for the income the fund earns from the end of July to the end of December.

When filling out your tax return, make sure that all 1099s have been included and that entries are in the correct sections of the tax return. A common mistake, for example, involves the taxpayer incorrectly listing dividend income in the interest income section of Form 1040, Schedule B. If you have questions, be sure to check with your tax preparer or accountant. ☐

> A common mistake involves the taxpayer incorrectly listing dividend income in the interest income section of Form 1040, Schedule B.

Plug in to new utilities fund

Given today's volatile economy, many investors are looking for reasonable return without a lot of risk. If you're one of those investors, IDS Utilities Income Fund may be the right investment for you. The Fund's main objective is to provide a high level of current income to investors. In addition, the Fund offers the potential for long-term growth and appreciation, while pursuing lower volatility in both up and down markets.

The Fund invests primarily in higher quality common stocks of leading public utility companies. These companies provide electricity, natural gas, water and telephone services around the country. ☐

Figure 6-12. This is a good example of callout usage. The writer took information which otherwise might have been overlooked and used callouts to call more attention to each chunk of information.

Copy Tactics

1. Active voice vs. passive voice.

Use the active voice. No exceptions. Passive writing leads to passivity in the reader.

2. Make your paragraphs shorter.

If your paragraphs are more than seven lines long begin a new paragraph. Long paragraphs are uninviting.

3. Humor.

Humor in a newsletter can be disastrous. You may be alienating your prospective customer and existing customers (figure 6-13).

Okay, okay, I know years ago divers were regarded in the same context as beer-guzzling fools. But not any more. Diving is every water-lover's favorite pastime...and it's expensive, which means it's an upscale sport ...which means this newsletter isn't targeted right and just the title itself will definitely offend a lot its readers.

4. Don't use a lot of qualifiers.

Qualifiers, such as *mostly, sometimes,* and *if,* weaken your copy. If there isn't a need for them don't use them.

5. You is stronger than we.

The little word ''you'' gets your readers involved and can automatically gives your readers a feeling of belonging. Especially in a fund-raising newsletter, you want the donor or prospective donor to feel he or she is part of what's making the difference in your appeals.

Most often larger organizations and companies prefer to use the ''we/ us'' instead of the ''you.'' Big mistake. It makes no difference whether your tone is conservative or friendly—''you'' is much stronger than ''we/ us'' when it comes to getting the attention of your audience. The ''we/ us'' stance sounds pompous, impersonal, and stuffy.

If you'd like to keep an arm's-length distance from the very people you're trying so hard to reach, then go ahead and use the ''we/us'' stance. But if you felt that way you wouldn't be reading this.

6. The use of contractions in newsletter copy.

I know many technical writers don't like to use contractions. They believe in order to sound professional they shouldn't use contractions. But this is the newsletter world. What do you want to achieve? Friendlier, closer relationships? Or a twenty-foot cool distance?

Unless you're aiming your newsletter at the Queen of England, I'd use contractions. Newsletters are supposed to be writing to a friend. Don't distance your readers.

"Writer's Block": Tips for the Copywriter

If a writer ever tells you he or she has never gotten ''writer's block'' don't believe that writer. Every writer at one time or another has faced a

130

The Official Newsletter of Maui Sun Divers

Bobby Baker's
Bubbles 'n Bullshit
Volume 2, Number 1 Spring 1992

Maui Sun Divers Secedes From The United States

By El Presidente Generalissimo Roberto Baker

I've recently heard so much gloom about the recession on the mainland (thank you Ronald, George, and Mr. Moto), that I borrowed an idea from the USSR and declared Maui Sun Divers an independent republic. Luckily, we are maintaining friendly relations with both the United States and Canada, and no passport or visa is required for entry.

I call this new country "Club Bob," population two. That's me and my pet lobster, Larry. He's a Hawaiian spiny lobster, about fourteen inches long who lives just off-shore. I've trained him to eat Snicker's Bars out of my hand. He's a great friend and pet, but more on Larry later.

Club Bob is located right on the beach in Kihei on Maui, where we have one of the best views on one of the best beaches anywhere. My tiny

Freedom! Life, Liberty and the pursuit of Lobster!

Photos by Matias.

country, after two years of water and TLC, looks great. We're surrounded by papayas, bananas, mangoes, lemons, limes, tangerines, tangelos, coconuts and the best grapefruit I've ever tasted. Lots of plumerias, pikake, ginger, hibiscus and too many other tropical flowers, vines, trees, and plants to even start naming.

Yes my friends, you could be here!

Just think...if you were staying here, you'd be home by now.

Larry the Lobster enjoys the company of a svelte Blonde at Club Bob.

Figure 6-13

blank page, fingers literally frozen. It's frightening, especially when you know you have to meet a deadline. It can be even more frightening when the project seems too big to handle.

What can you do about writer's block? Good question!

1. Find the best time of day when your mind is the freshest for writing. I find that 5 a.m. is the best time for me, but others prefer to work late in the day or evening. When you're working on a deadline you may not be able to just write at the time of day most comfortable for you. So what? Self-discipline is what professionalism is all about.

If you're hung in the belief that you can only write under a specific set of conditions, use your less-productive time to do your research.

2. When you're on a roll—don't stop. I've done just that—stopped when I was hot at it—and regretted it. It never rolls along quite the same later.

3. When you're really stuck—go on to something else. I'm doing that as I write this piece of this chapter. If you can brainstorm with someone or move over for an hour or so to a similar project, it may help get you back on track.

4. Give yourself plenty of time to meet your deadlines. Don't expect yourself to have your articles researched and outlined in an afternoon and then write the articles during the night for delivery the next morning. Be realistic in the time you allot yourself to each newsletter step.

Wow, do I know this from experience! I've set unrealistic goals for getting a newsletter out the door because a client wants the newsletter and wants it now. Believe me, shifting into overdrive when you're out of gas is unrealistic and the newsletter will show its haphazard creation. So don't promise an unrealistic deadline you can't keep.

The Seven "Deadly Deadline" Busters

As an editor and writer for a sponsor-promoting newsletter you know the importance of constant, consistent communication between you and the customers, donors, or prospects. Do you ever feel as though it's not as important to others? Other people can hold you up and ultimately if the newsletter is late it's your fault. Here are seven tips to keep the newsletter ball rolling.

1. If you have to rely on someone else to give you information for an article and that person hasn't kept the agreed deadline, go ahead and write what you can without the information.

Keep calling the person you've requested the information from and ask simply for any notes that individual may have. Don't stop dead in the water; begin writing the rest of your articles.

2. If your supervisor insists on putting the newsletter on hold for a specific new product, service or appeal, offer a few alternate suggestions: A special issue when more details are available or a teaser in the issue you're holding.

3. If marketing decides to cut back on expenses and hold off on the newsletter issue see what you can do to help reduce production costs without eliminating the issue.

4. Input for the newsletter is most important. If you can't seem to get everyone involved to get final input or okays, set up a monthly task force meeting.

5. When the newsletter isn't a priority because other marketing plans are being rehashed, use the task force meeting again. Different heads of departments should be named to the task force so they know ahead of time it's part of their job description.

6. What happens when it takes too long to get final approval on your copy? Start earlier. Build the time in. After a while you should know how long it takes people in your company or organization to get certain tasks done. Build your schedule not only around your other duties, but theirs as well.

7. What about if *you* don't manage your time wisely? Ask for help! But get the newsletter out on time.

Conclusion

Logic is as valuable as writing talent in newsletter writing. If you didn't have some writing talent, you wouldn't be editing a newsletter to start with.

The writer Samuel Clemens (Mark Twain) once was asked: ''Can you teach people to write?'' His answer: ''I can teach writers to write.''

You're a writer. Enough said.

CHAPTER *7*

Helpful Hints for Fund-Raising Newsletters

The 1990s have brought a whole new set of problems for those in the field of fund raising. Until recently, the words "sales and marketing" were foreign to this universe. Today they're implicit in any successful fund raising campaign.

Yes, I said *sales and marketing*. Fund raising is a business too, and professionals in this field are as different from their forebears of the 1960s and 1970s as a supersonic airplane is from a DC-3. In the 1990s, personal speculation about what you think will work must be tossed out the window and replaced by a more scientific approach.

The road to successful fund-raising needs to be clearly defined. My definition:

> You're competitive with every other nonprofit activity, whether that activity is remotely comparable to your own or not. Donors have a finite amount of money to contribute to *all* causes. Compete or die.

What does it take to compete? Nonprofits that survived well on stuffy traditions in the first six or seven decades of the twentieth century now had better break that crusty mold and become daring, innovative marketers.

Planning + Courage = Success

When I think of most nonprofit organizations the visual my mind conjures up is 10 million different department heads running into each other backwards, crashing heads, then never turning around to see whom they bumped into. Each one is rushing to get some project out the door—a project unintegrated with other projects from this same organization—and no one has taken the time to plan or think about what they're doing or why they're doing it.

Some worst case scenarios, actually in place for an astonishing number of nonprofit institutions:

• Thirty years ago donor lists were put into place. Today, whether those donors are alive or not, they still receive fund-raising appeals. (Fund raiser: When was the last time you cleaned *your* mailing list?)

• If a donor donated $500 last quarter or last year—that same donor receives an appeal for a donation of $20.

• Worse yet, the same appeal that didn't work on one group of people for the last seven mailings is mailed again for an eighth time, ninth time and tenth time.

The biggest crime of all is the invisible stodgy bureaucracy (which thinks it's aristocracy) preaching from the sidelines ''This is the way we've always done it, this is the way we'll continue to do it...'' (NOTE: ''This is the way we do it'' is *worse* than ''This is the way we've always done it.'')

Who are these people that preach such fund-raising tactics? They're ghosts from a bygone time—ghosts who sometimes manage to keep the rest of us in line by their haunting nature. It's time to exorcise those ghosts.

Oh, I'm not saying every organization mirrors this image. For one thing, most fund-raising organizations are too small to drown in bureaucracy. But the smaller organizations reap their own set of problems and chaos. Volunteer staffs aren't usually trained in sales and marketing.

Overcoming these typical inside problems isn't easy, because triumph over tradition requires a victory over dogged folklore. But on the outside, separate donor problems exist:

1. Donor skepticism
2. Scandalous rumors
3. Government tightening of tax deductions

4. Overuse of the ''same old pitches''
5. Too many organizations vying for attention

The Highest Hurdle in Fund Raising

Fund raising has *always* faced a huge generic problem which differentiates itself from regular business-to-business or business-to-consumer marketing: How do you convince someone of the need to donate money?

Granted, in every business a classic problem exists—which is: finding the perfect (or at least profitable) strategy to convince the public to buy. But in the field of fund raising, you also have to convince the public to donate to a cause from which they possibly won't benefit from in their own lifetime. They may not see tangible results. They might not get something concrete to show for their efforts. They may never know if they've made a difference.

So what do we do?

Two Target Groups of Fund Raising

In my world, centering on fund-raising newsletters, I divide potential donors into two general target groups.

Indirect Targets in Fund Raising

This is targeting a group of people who aren't directly affected by the appeal. They have an ''If I can't see it, it doesn't exist, and if it won't affect me in my lifetime, I don't care'' attitude. This includes organizations who raise funds for starving children, animals, the environment, the arts, loathsome diseases, and public welfare.

The problems: Making prospective donors realize how once-removed, unrelated circumstances can affect them at home. Creating a sense of urgency. Giving your donor base a reason to keep contributing their money after the first guilt-driven or ego-driven response.

Direct Targets in Fund Raising

This is targeting a group of people who are directly affected by the donation of these funds. The direct target approach of fund raising would include organizations such as health care (contributions from prior patients and their families), chambers of commerce, law, alumni groups, governmental reform, political campaigns, and special interest clubs. It's easier to target people when your organization directly involves them—or, if you're a shrewd fund raiser, *appears to* directly involve these people. They see how it will benefit and enrich their own lives, which makes you super-competitive against other nonprofits who can't create such benefits and enrichments.

Problems: Membership acquisition. Donor attrition. Changing sets of values. Burnout.

Why is it easier to appeal to the second group? Because more than likely, the targeted people for whom the organization is raising funds have "logical" money to donate. The targets in the first group aren't usually directly involved. In fact, in that first group, those who are directly involved don't have the money to donate. They are the ones in need. These types of fund-raising organizations have to create an awareness and an urgency that suggests to their targets the activities actually move the cause into the second group. *That's* professionalism! And *that's* a direct argument in favor of the newsletter.

How Would Your Organization Use a Fund-Raising Newsletter?

Some general rules apply to both types of targeted fund raising. The only differences would be: a) the technique of dramatizing the cause and b) what emotional appeal to use.

First of all, your fund-raising newsletter should complement your other fund-raising strategies. The newsletter should augment, not hinder your ultimate goal—increasing revenue.

But how do you integrate a newsletter positively into your other marketing efforts?

I keep hearing about "stuffy nonprofit" newsletters: "Why bother, people don't read them." "What are they for?" "What a waste of money."

Why do you think people call them "stuffy"?

For one reason, some nonprofit organizations believe they should be. I had one nonprofit organization literally tell me that the "stuffiness" and the incomprehensible writing in their newsletter is what their donors expect.

Get with the program! Do you mean to tell me your donors look forward to misleading, incomprehensible reading material? Do you mean to tell me they sit and wait for a dull newsletter to read? Should you maintain an air of superiority? Should you appear to be talking down to your donors and prospective donors? If so, you're on a different planet from your donors. You're the victim of "in-group" thinking, and you're really publishing your newsletter for yourself, not for outsiders you'd like to draw into your orbit.

The counter-argument: "We don't want to risk losing our existing donor base by changing the tone of our newsletter." It's your call, but an ingrown newsletter invariably shrinks the universe of donors. Why? Because sooner or later, your donors will feel left out—exactly the reverse of the receptive climate you should be generating.

I don't think you really want to waste the time, effort, and money it take to create a newsletter that absolutely won't get read or saved.

Please don't waste the organization's money. Money that many donors believe comes from the very hands of the people you're sending the newsletter to—for a confusing, misbegotten message just because newsletters are the "thing" to do for your donors. For a perfect example, take a look at figure 7-1.

The recipient of this two-page newsletter sent it on to me with a note:

"The newsletter was addressed to me. Reading page one, I hadn't the foggiest notion of what this organization does or why they sent this to me. On page two is a passing reference to AIDS, so I *guess* that's what this is all about. They want me to give merchandise or take an ad in their program book. Why? What do they do? What does this have to do with me? Who *are* these people?"

Who, indeed? Save some of your organization's money by following this little rule:

> If you're aiming your newsletter at insiders, don't mail it
> to outsiders.

Why should you create a donor newsletter at all?

The main purposes behind a donor newsletter are any or all of these: to educate, reinforce donations, reinforce donor loyalty, reinforce donor retention, combat donor attrition, maintain integrity of the organization, instill confidence, use as a donor special membership benefit, and/or to be a public relations/direct response vehicle. Ultimately the purpose is more primitive than most of us admit—to add that extra oomph of power for generating increased donations.

Getting the Most Mileage from Your Newsletter

You already have my suggestions for blending editorial and promotional slants. But in this chapter, let's concentrate on the relationship newsletters can have, positively or negatively, with fund raising and its unique communications problems.

Because so much fund raising seems to have the stigma of being stodgy, conservative, and downright impersonal at times, let's take a look

Think Life

LifeLines

A publication of Think Life, Inc.   Spring '92

PRESIDENT'S MESSAGE

Another year is almost here as we plan our annual major fund raiser to benefit Think Life. Our Celebrity Dinner Auction will be held on July 18, 1992, at The Westin Hotel, Cypress Creek.

We already have auction items donated by Chris Everett, the Jungle Queen, the Coconut Grove Playhouse, the Hyatt Regency Coral Gables, and a seafood splash party for four by Commissioner Poitier.

We have contacted Elizabeth Taylor, Sophia Loren, Magic Johnson, Dionne Warwick and a few more in the hope that one or more will be our guest speaker. We now know that Magic will be in Barcelona and therefore will be unable to participate.

If you know any celebrities you think might be interested in participating in our benefit evening or donating auction items, do call Bob MacKilligan, at 527-4260.

Please note that the Friends of Think Life, our volunteers, meet at Eduardo's Restaurant, at 2400 East Las Olas Blvd, the third Wednesday of each month at 7:00 p.m. It looks like those of us helping with the Celebrity Dinner & Auction will be there every Wednesday evening between now and the event. We would certainly appreciate all the help we can get!

Some people are curious as to why we are raising money when we received a grant from the County. The grant we were awarded has enabled us to provide rent-free housing to residents in our first seven apartments. But to expand and serve more people in need in our community, we need to raise a great deal more money. Also our grant does not cover operational expenses, nor do the payments always coincide with our monthly lease payments. Needless to say, we require a steady cash flow to maintain the apartments for our residents.

Think Life hoped to have an office at our first property, which was zoned for commercial and residential use. However, because some influential neighbors did not want "Those People" in their neighborhood, we chose not to take the property and instead selected one in another area. This section is zoned only for residential use, so we've had to forego having an on-site office.

We continue to grow by leaps and bounds, and do need to centralize what we are doing closer to our residents and our volunteers. At the present time our operational office is in North Miami, while the program and all our activities are in Fort Lauderdale. If you have any suggestions, we are certainly open to them.

For those of you who aren't aware, we hosted a "Night at the Races" at Pompano Harness Race Track, with almost 250 participants. It was a lot of fun for all of us, even though admittedly some of us didn't know the first thing about horse racing. We also were involved with other non-profit organizations in the "Ultimate Garage Sale" sponsored by The Miami Herald.

SHARING HOLIDAYS

For Thanksgiving last year we had a pot luck dinner at the facility, where each of the Board members and each resident brought a dish. It was delicious! Some of us who had other places to go for later dinners enjoyed ourselves so much that we didn't want to leave!

For Christmas we requested a wish list from each resident. Most of them got exactly what they had asked, which they did not expect. Gifts included a trip to Disney World, a microwave oven, a color television, and lots of clothes!

RESIDENTS MONTHLY MEETINGS

We hold monthly meetings with the residents at the apartment where we discuss such topics as their responsibility to themselves, to each other and to Think Life.

We've talked about death and dying, especially since some of our people have died since the program's inception. This discussion allowed the residents to explore their own personal feelings about immortality.

Think Life, Inc.

P.O. Box 17352
Fort Lauderdale, FL 33318
Dade   (305) 653-6164
Broward   (305) 475-0793

THINK LIFE'S CELEBRITY DINNER & AUCTION

A benefit to provide housing, support and education for members
of our community diagnosed HIV positive or living with AIDS.

Saturday, July 18, 1992
The Westin Hotel, Cypress Creek

Yes, I am interested in supporting Think Life's Celebrity Dinner & Auction
with a donation of:

_____ Merchandise: _____

_____

_____

_____ Gift Certificate worth $_____

_____ Contribution of $_____

I would like to advertise in the evening's Program Book:

_____ Business Card or Booster Ad $25.00

_____ Half Page Ad (5" w X 4" h) $50.00

_____ Full Page Ad (5" w X 8" h) $75.00

Enclosed is $_____ for a _____ ad.

(Please supply camera ready art work no later than June 20, 1992.)

NAME _____   DATE _____

BUSINESS/ORGANIZATION _____

ADDRESS_____   PHONE _____

Figure 7-1

141

at how to *communicate* effectively and therefore sell your appeals effectively to your donors through newsletters.

Fund-Raising Strategies for Newsletters

Too many times the newsletter is thrown into the company public relations tactic pile as an afterthought. You have your mailings, you have your television ads, you have your public relations, you have your fund drives—and oh, yes, let's throw in a newsletter because donors need to know how their money is being spent.

Terrible approach. This kind of attitude *will* make your newsletter dull and stodgy. An effective newsletter enforces and *re*inforces what you are trying to accomplish in other areas.

Integrate the newsletter into your fund-raising programs. Don't make it a separate entity which has nothing to do with your long-term and short term objectives. You have a result-driven medium: Use it to your best advantage.

This approach means serious targeting for each of the two different categories of fund-raising newsletters.

Strategies for Indirect Targeting in Fund-Raising Newsletters

What can you put into your newsletter to get an indirect target in fund raising to take action?

—Report the facts, even harsh ones. In fact, harsh facts can drag contributions from some whose cynicism rejects success stories.

—Play on emotions.

—Show how a certain problem can affect the readers.

—Be sure to point out how what you do provides a solution to that problem.

—Give a means to respond.

Strategies for Direct Targeting in Fund-Raising Newsletters

What can you put into your newsletter to get a direct target in fund raising to take action?

—Include articles which show different ways you might, properly funded, help prevent catastrophes.

—Illustrate urgency.

—Appeal to the reader's sense of importance. Boost egos.

—Use reader-involvement devices.

—Show the readers progress they have helped achieve.

Scare Tactics: Do They Work?

One question is often raised for fund-raising campaigns for people in need, for the environment. and for endangered animals: Do fear and scare tactics work?

Some argue that if fear and scare tactics are used to the hilt, people will be too devastated to read on. People who feel they're indirectly involved don't want to know about seemingly unreconcilable problems. So how do you get people to stand up and pay attention if they want to hide their heads in the sand?

Balance these two unlike factors: 1. The very word "newsletter" means just that—news...a medium to bring information to your donors. 2. Emotion outsells logic.

In my opinion, if you're going to get people to rise and take action, you must play on or instill an emotional reaction that will cause them to take this action. Logic and the "everything is just peachy" attitude won't inspire a need of *urgency* in your readers. If there is no urgency in your newsletter it doesn't help to back up your appeal. You must convince these targets that they are directly involved.

Using the Newsletter to Create Awareness of a Need

A newsletter is the perfect medium to educate and build an awareness among your readers, motivating them to take action. Awareness of how a certain problem could affect them and how its now affecting others is the emotional precursor to logical reasoning that "something needs to be done and I'm involved in doing it."

The first priority to build awareness is: Don't sugar-coat the issues.

Once the newsletter creates awareness, the second priority of business is to show the readers something *can* be done. But it can't be done if they aren't willing to help: "Only you...''; "It's in your power to...'' "Will you...'' (never "Can you...'').

I said awareness of how a problem affects the reader is the emotional precursor to logical reasoning. Logic alone won't work. If the newsletter merely lists the needs of someone or something and expects donors to fork over the money, you're in for an unhappy surprise. We're in the hyper-competitive, self-centered 1990s. Save pure logic for the classroom.

How can you integrate a feeling of urgency into your newsletter?

143

Figure 7-2. I view this environmental newsletter as an example of indirect fund raising because it takes a lot of work, even today, to convince non-dedicated recipients of the message that the problem of environmental disaster is knocking on everybody's door.

Looking at figure 7-2, how does this newsletter try to convince the readers of this? The article "Creating A New Atmosphere" asks people to quit accepting situations in which the earth is being destroyed. The scare tactic is used quite properly: "When people begin to understand that the ozone crisis will permanently impact their lives and health, and that of their children, they will be outraged..."

The organization is trying to instill a sense of urgency but it falls short of maximum effectiveness because this article misses one key strategy for indirect targeting: By using dispassionate *third person* ("people") instead of passionate *second person* ("you") the message dilutes its emotional content.

The first paragraph is directed inward instead of outward. Tactical error? For dedicated Greenpeace contributors, no; they're involved, which makes the message, for them, *directly* targeted. For prospective contributors, "we" excludes them. The message becomes a report rather than a call to action.

In a dynamic fund-raising message, you can't go wrong by getting the readers involved right away...by speaking directly to them. Referring to readers as "they" can alienate as many as it attracts.

At the end of the first paragraph:

> "Yet the battle to save the ozone layer will require imme-
> diate action for results neither instantaneous nor tangible.
> How do we mobilize people under these circumstances?"

This typifies the apparently self-aimed message in this article. Note, please: The article *isn't* self-aimed...but too many readers will interpret it that way.

How do you avoid *any* accusation of being self-stroking? An easy rule:

> Let your donors and prospective donors feel they're part
> of your family—working toward the solution. (After all,
> they are, or they're worthless prospects.)

Another strategy to incorporate into indirect target newsletters is to make the prospective donors or donors feel they already play an active part in your organization. Give them a way to interact with the group. Mild quizzes, ballots, "Don't you agree?" and "Aren't you outraged?" stories—all contribute to this effect.

Care World Report uses a "Donors Ask" column dedicated entirely to questions and answers from donors to the organization. What better way to instill a feeling of having a voice in what the organization is doing?

Take a look at figure 7.3 to see another way *Care World Report* gets its donors to feel active.

Some Strategies for Reaching Both Indirect and Direct Targets

Here are a few suggestions you may want to incorporate into your newsletter. But remember the promotional and editorial mix: Don't get too carried away with the promotional side of the newsletter, or your donors won't find the newsletter beneficial.

Membership

If your nonprofit organization depends on membership for a lot of its donations (such as the chamber of commerce), your newsletter can play an important role in maintaining and strengthening each membership. You can even include the newsletter as a benefit of membership, exploiting the exclusivity of belonging.

Incorporate a membership column. Use benefits of belonging, free of-

We Care What You Think

CARE is interested in the opinions, thoughts and suggestions of our donors and friends. Please tell us what you think by completing the following survey and returning it to CARE at the address below.

■ Do you think CARE should undertake programs in the following areas of the world, and if so, what type of program?

○ Republics of the former Soviet Union
    ○ Emergency relief only
    ○ Emergency relief and long-term development*
○ Eastern Europe
    ○ Emergency relief only
    ○ Emergency relief and long-term development*

Long-term development means helping people improve their lives and become self-sufficient through programs in agriculture, health and small-business support.

■ Do you believe CARE should help people wherever there is great need, regardless of their government's political or religious philosophy?

○ Yes   ○ No

■ Would you be more likely to buy a product from your grocery or department store if you knew a percentage of the price was a donation to CARE?

○ Yes
○ No, it would not influence my purchasing decision
○ Not sure

■ Some donors want to play a more active role in supporting CARE's work. Indicate below if you would be interested in participating in activities that require specific actions such as a letter-writing campaign or a grassroots event.

○ Yes, I would like to become more involved in CARE's work
○ No, I prefer to limit my involvement to making contributions
○ See my comments below

■ Please use the space below to tell us any thoughts, opinions or suggestions you may have about CARE's work in general or about specific questions raised in this survey. *(use additional paper if needed)*

_____
_____
_____

Name _____

Address _____

City _____ State _____ Zip _____

Please mail this survey *in your own envelope* to:

Scott Swinton, Donor Services Department,
CARE, 660 First Avenue, New York, NY 10016

Figure 7-3. "We Care What You Think": A brilliant inclusion. A survey which apparently enables donors to have a say in the direction the organization will follow not gets the readers involved, but it makes them believe they're an integral part of the process. Beyond that, if you actually pay attention to such a survey you'll get invaluable information. An absolute mandate: Respond to every survey transmitting a firm opinion. You'll transform many borderliners or even detractors into lifelong contributors.

fers, discounts, easy payment terms, premiums for members by members, and response devices. You can check effectiveness with a specific offer only inside your newsletter.

The newsletter in figure 7-4 is newsier and chattier than most fine arts newsletters would be. Filling your newsletter with social notes about donor members is great. . .if you're one of the donors getting the recognition. But too much of this can backfire. If this is all the newsletter is going to focus on, too many members may feel left out of this ''in'' circle. They'll get tired of looking to see if they've made headlines.

Create an exclusive ''members only'' program through your newsletter, if your organization has been relying on donations with no membership overtone. The simplest way: Put together a special membership package for those who donate so much money a year or a month, complete with recognition in the newsletter and a reinforcing *dated* (expiration date, please) certificate. This special membership package can only help you, but there must be apparent benefits to the package or it won't be sought after. Take a look at figures 7-5 through 7-7.

Another problem is weakness of motivators. This appeal to join the monthly pledge program doesn't give the donor any emotional satisfaction, the key reason one might join. It begins:

> We would like to invite you to join a select group of caring people who have agreed to participate in a bold new program that will enable UNICEF to help save thousands of lives.

Why should they join? Because they too, are caring people? Nice try. This may work if you're staring face-to-face with the person you're targeting, but once removed your target doesn't have to look you in the eyes and tell you, ''I'm sorry, but I don't care.'' Altruism isn't going to work. Trying to appeal to an altruistic sense, especially through the mail, will end with a blind eye and a deaf ear. They don't have to face you; guilt doesn't exist because you haven't generated any.

Compare the blandness of this assumptive copy with the powerful line on the response device:

> We can't let children become blind and die for lack of a vitamin supplement that costs three cents. . . .

Recognition Awards

A surefire donor-holder: Give certificate awards for donations over a certain amount, or for outstanding support. Then give these people recognition in your newsletter. Others will want to follow suit.

Fort Lauderdale
Philharmonic Society
Philharmonic Notes

May, 1992

Vol. 16, No. 9

President's Message

DID YOU KNOW that April 26 - May 2, 1992 is National Volunteer Week? Well, it is, and I think we deserve a round of applause for another good year! I certainly want to thank all of you hardworking members of the Philharmonic Society for your many hours of volunteer time, and the services and resources you have donated to make our fundraising events successful. Without you, there would be no us.

As we come to a close of this fiscal year, I have to admit that we did not quite make our budget (who did?). We did, however, accomplish one goal--we raised approximately $154,000 for the Orchestra and we had fun doing it.

We began the year by doing something different with the Community Calendar. The Sun Sentinel made us an offer we couldn't refuse--to print, free of charge, quarterly updates of the Calendar for their entire distribution.

The Luncheon Fashion Show with Oleg Cassini and the presentation of the Ten Best Dressed Women of Style and Substance was a smashing success. The Deck the Halls Holiday Games Party was a lot of fun and the 43rd Annual Philharmonic Ball was an elegant, fun event. The Sixteenth Annual Plant Affair had beautiful weather both days, drawing huge crowds, and the Living Legend Golf & Tennis Invitational was a full, fun day with our Living Legend, the first International Tennis Star, Fred Perry.

Every one of the Membership Meetings (so far) have been lovely, elegant events. I am confident that the Annual Meeting on May 12th will be one to remember. Nell Lewis has a beautiful day planned for you and the Officers to be installed. I hope you can attend to show them your support.

As I pass the gavel at our May 12th Membership Meeting, my personal wish for the incoming Officers is a better economy and the continued dedication of the Society members. You will be there for them, won't you?

Sincerely,

Shirley

Shirley Herreid

INSTALLATION LUNCHEON

An extraordinary Installation Luncheon is being planned by Nell Lewis and Helen Isley on May 12, 1992 at Paesano's Restaurant. The mood will be set by the beautiful and talented Marcia Maze Thieme as she plays the grand piano during the cocktail hour. To highlight the event, Dr Anthony James Catanese, President of Florida Atlantic University, will install the new officers.

Let's show our gratitude to the retiring officers and pledge our support to the incoming Executive board by attending this significant meeting.

COMMUNITY CALENDAR
OUR NEW GOAL

It may read May on your calendar but it is time for the Philharmonic to begin preparation of next year's COMMUNITY CALENDAR.

This year the calendar will be a REAL Community Calendar. In response to requests by the entire community, voiced through the President's Council, the Philharmonic will expand the scope of the Calendar.

The goal of expansion and betterment of the Calendar will be reached by contacting many more non-profit groups within the county -- by setting our listing fees at a lower rate -- by making our date clearing and listing service more accessible and thus much more of a service to the entire community.

Service to the Community has always been the goal of our calendar. It will be a reality this year. Without a doubt, the calendar sales will increase appropriately.

The Calendar Committee is just getting underway. At this point Ande Bellevue, Dottie Kone, Diana Metcalf, Jeanne Burlew, Valerie DeBianchi, Ginny Miller, Sarah Rivoir and Joan Forester are calling a few more good workers to join them. You ladies who take off for parts unknown for the summer - relax - the Calendar Presentation Party will be waiting for you when you return in late September.

CALENDAR OF EVENTS

Celebrity Concerts . . . . May 5-6
Installation of Officers . . . . May 12

148

WAYS AND MEANS

This will be my final message to Society members as your Ways and Means Vice President.

I would like to take this opportunity to thank those individuals who have gone out of their way to assist me this year. In a recession (or worse) year, it hasn't been easy beating the bushes to raise money, especially for the arts. But, we did it and I am proud to have been associated with such hard working committees that "made it happen" for us.

Incidentally our final overall figure has been submitted by our Treasurer to me for the Forty-Third Annual Philharmonic Ball. I am pleased to report that we were able to make nearly $57,000.00! Our Meet the Musicians series of three afternoon concerts and was netted over $2,600.00. The figures are not yet tallied for the Plant Affair but it is expected to have brought in approximately 20,000.00. We are still computing debits and credits for the Living Legends Golf and Tennis Tournament. The first newsletter of the 1992/1993 season will have my Final Ways and Means Report and will advise you of the figure.

Thank you again for your enthusiasm and support this year.

Valerie DeBianchi
Vice President Ways & Means

MEMBERSHIP MATTERS

Currently, we have a total membership of 865, with the fiscal year ending May 31st. As I began the year June 1, 1991, my goal was to reach 900. However, with necessary deletions (deaths, life members who asked to be removed from the active file and unreachables) we will fall short of the goal. There are many persons who have promised to become members but have not as yet done so. The receipt of these memberships could change matters. If you know any of these potential members please persuade them to join. Many of you have given me referrals throughout the year, and I sincerely thank you.

Sue Gencsoy and her committee did a fabulous presentation of a "Sophisticated Afternoon Tea." It was well attended, and we were delighted to hear Bob Goldner at the piano and the selections of the 4 piece ensemble of the Florida Philharmonic Orchestra. I hope you saw the special table of a "perfect tea", which Sue displayed along the north wall of the Tower Club. It was truly elegant. Thanks Sue and your whole committee for a delightful afternoon.

Membership renewals were bulk mailed to all members except new ones) on April 8th. Returns are coming in very nicely. Those of you who have yet to respond, please do so now.

Heartfelt thanks and love to all - until Fall - have a great Summer!

Dottie Kone, V.P. Membership

"Meet the Musicians" at Jessups home on March 15th. To be continued in the Fall.

ABOVE: Kathryn Hyde, Pete Forester, Jeanne Sneath
TO RIGHT: June Valassis, Joan Morden, Joan Forester, Sherly Day

OUR NEWEST AND YOUNGEST MEMBER

Miss Samantha Dydo is a new "Supporting" member of the Philharmonic. So? Well, Samantha is only 3 years old.

Samantha is starting early in the family tradition of supporting the arts and particularly the Philharmonic. She is the daughter of Mr. & Mrs. Glenn J. Dydo and the niece of Mr. & Mrs. Michael Biennes. We all are indebted to them for their extraordinary contribution to the Orchestra. Welcome Samantha! Now some committee - put her to work.

FRAN GOODWIN DOES IT AGAIN

Fran Goodwin has an uncanny knack of knowing when you need her most. She has come through again when we needed her and the Leo Goodwin Foundation to help us come closer to making our budget. We have received another $10,000 donation from the Foundation, and it will be included in the $70,000 we will (by the time you receive this newsletter) have turned over to the Orchestra at our April 14th Membership Meeting.

Fran, many thanks for being our friend and supporter. By supporting us, you support the Orchestra we all love and you help to guarantee that their music will still be there for our children and future children to come.

OFFICERS 1991-1992

President
Mrs. Ernest Herreid (Shirley)

Vice Presidents

Ways & Means	Personnel
Mrs. Paul DeBianchi	**Mrs. Rudolph Frei**
(Valerie)	**(Carol)**
Membership	Public Relations
Mrs. Kenneth Kone	**Mrs. William Rivoir, Jr.**
(Dottie)	**(Sarah)**

Recording Secretary
Mrs. Edward Michaelson (Susan)

Corresponding Secretary
Mrs. James Schulke (Lynn)

Treasurer
Mrs. Don Ascione (Andrea)

Figure 7-4

News From: the Digit Fund

For Mountain Gorillas

JUNE 1992   THE DIGIT FUND NEWSLETTER

GORILLAS OF THE MONTH – Inshuti and Izuba

Inshuti

(from a field report by Martha Robbins, November 1991)

Inshuti (meaning "friend" in Kinyarwandan) is a 3 ½ year-old male in Group 5, a large gorilla group currently consisting of 30 individuals. His mother is Simba and his father is probably either Ziz or Pablo. Inshuti is a very boisterous, energetic and lively juvenile who seems to get along well with everyone in the group.

Inshuti
(photo: Pascale Sicotte)

Inshuti is also a very lucky gorilla. In April 1990, he had the misfortune of becoming trapped in an illegal snare, a thick wire that

dug deep into his right wrist. It took 3 days for the Volcano Veterinary Center veterinarian and researchers and trackers from Karisoke to find the appropriate opportunity to dart him with anesthesia, remove the snare, and treat the wound. He had a 4 to 6 inch long, ½ inch deep cut on the inside of his wrist and his hand had swollen to twice its normal size. He was in obvious pain and looked as though he was tiring from lack of sleep. Simba was very caring of Inshuti during this time, as always.

Once the snare was removed, Inshuti was known as the "miracle gorilla" because of his amazingly rapid recovery. Within days he was seen briefly putting pressure on his hand and within 2 to 3 weeks he was back climbing and playing with other infants and juveniles. It was surprising to see him quickly reintegrate himself among his peers. It took several months for the hair to grow back on his wrist and this served as the only reminder of his traumatic experience.

Figure 7-5. "Gorillas of the Month" may cause some smirking among outsiders, but this breezy newsletter quickly wipes the smirk off the skeptical reader's face through its exceptionally talented writing. Gorillas become persons . . . and this is the historical thrust of the Digit Fund, named for a gorilla brutally murdered some years ago. This newsletter assumes reader participation. Sent to prior donors, it's a potent reminder of the organization's dedication.

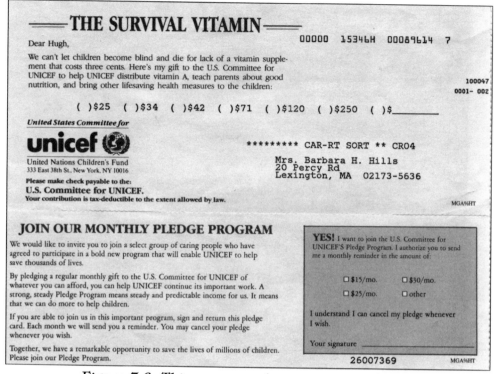

Figure 7-6. This response device comes with this organization's newsletter. But nowhere inside the newsletter does any article or column mention the monthly pledge program.

Case Studies

Personal case studies from someone in the field or a famous spokesperson about how they benefitted from service and/or found personal satisfaction from donating time and money to an appeal can help response.

Case studies, celebrity participation, and "How I saw the light" articles make sense in a newsletter when they appear arrogant, egocentric, or ridiculous in other fund raising media. Explore this avenue!

Points to Consider

Let's go over some important points to consider as you create your fund raising newsletter:

How Safe Is Bottled Water?

Bottled water is increasingly the choice of the American consumer, with one out of every six households buying it as a source of drinking water. But recent events, such as the 1990 recall of 170 million bottles of benzene-contaminated Perrier, have caused many to question its safety.

FDA Regulation

The U.S. Food and Drug Administration (FDA) regulates bottled water as a "food" and therefore it must be produced in compliance with FDA Good Manufactur-

You can check your favorite brand.

ing Practices. The FDA has developed standards that set a minimal acceptance level of quality for bottled water, including adoption of the Environmental Protection Agency's (EPA) public drinking water standards. Domestic bottlers are also subject to periodic, unannounced inspections by the FDA. Because bottled water is classified as a very low-risk product, domestic bottling plants are inspected an average of every five years. The FDA supplements this infrequency by requiring bottlers to periodically self-test their water. Foreign bottling plants are not under FDA jurisdiction; however, imported waters may be tested at their point of entry into the United States.

Filling in the Gaps

Does this infrequency of testing by the FDA mean that bottled water is unsafe? Not necessarily. Domestic bottled water producers are subject to inspection by state health officials and must comply with all applicable state laws and regulations. State authorities have their own standards, which differ considerably among states. Several states, including New York, New Jersey, Florida, Pennsylvania, and California, have bottled water safety standards that are higher than those of the federal government.

The bottled water industry also has a program of self-regulation through the International Bottled Water Association (IBWA). The IBWA requires its members –

which include both foreign and domestic bottlers – to test for 200 possible contaminants and undergo an annual inspection. Members are evaluated on their compliance with both the association's requirements and FDA regulations. A passing score is mandatory if bottlers want to retain IBWA membership. There are 852 domestic and 149 foreign members, accounting for about 85 percent of total U.S. bottled water sales.

Making Sure

If a bottler is in full compliance with the above regulations, its water is safe to drink. To check out your favorite brand:

- Find out your state's bottled water laws and regulations.
- Check to see if the bottler is a member of the IBWA.
- Contact the bottler for information on their required chemical analysis.

For more information, call the EPA's Safe Drinking Water Hotline at 1-800-426-4791 from 8:30 a.m. to 5:00 p.m. eastern standard time.

☞ Collect the "AICR Guide to Beverages" for nutritional information on over 150 different beverages. Check box 4 on the Free Information Request Card or write AICR national headquarters.

A Special Invitation to You

from

Marilyn Gentry

The American Institute for Cancer Research invites you to join a special group of donors who play a vital role in support of our cancer research and education programs.

Our Monthly Donors are Leaders in Supporting Cancer Research – Join Today!

We thank the many members of this important program and invite all of our Newsletter readers to join. Included in the benefits you will enjoy are:

- Tasty, lowfat recipes in their own convenient recipe box
- "Members Only" updates on AICR's education and research programs
- Discounts on AICR cookbooks and special publications

Please RSVP using the enclosed envelope.

Figure 7-7. This exhibit shows how one non-profit organization interjects the membership drive inside their newsletter. Along with the invitation and newsletter is a response device telling the reader what to do. This is a benefit-oriented membership package and also appeals—although in a way so generalized as to water down the impact—to the impression of exclusivity of membership.

1. Care for and feed your donor lists.

Your first priority is a strong, clean list. Collect data on your prospects and donors. Rework your list and turn it into a powerful marketable member database. Find out not only how old, which sex, and what income bracket they occupy, but what their interests are, and what appeals to them. Within your newsletter, you'll probably wind up using a number of these motivational factors by weaving information and appeals aimed at donor demographics into your articles and columns.

All the mailings, offers, and appeals in the world won't do you any good if you don't have a way to keep your lists clean, track responses, and keep tabs on comments and criticism. This should be your first priority before you set any fund-raising programs in place. If you can't take the time to do this, you'll never know what you can improve and what you can throw away.

2. Beyond public relations.

Don't limit your thinking to public relations *as public relations*.

Stop right there for a moment. Take your public relations beyond the obvious publicity-gathering point to public relations with a direct response benefit.

For example, the American Heart Association issues a publication about how to reduce heart disease. The media gets wind of it, the public gets wind of it, and the organization gets free public relations. Great. Now what? Ahhh—along with public relations as public relations come qualified leads; and qualified leads turn into donors.

3. Use powerful motivators.

Emotion outsells logic. (Refer back to chapter two for a discussion of this point.)

To apply this point: First of all, what type of fund-raising organization are you? Are you raising funds for children in third world countries? For heart disease, lung disease, cancer? For your local chamber of commerce, a church affiliation, your library?

What your organization is raising funds for will influence what type of emotional motivation you can use effectively. Guilt works on alumni; it doesn't work so well on people who never heard of you before.

If you're raising funds for an organization which doesn't *directly* affect your donors, will exclusivity and greed be better motivating factors to use on your donors? Probably.

If you're raising funds for an organization which directly affects your donor base, fear (assuming you can find a way to make it apply) is a major motivating factor. So is anger, provided you're absolutely positive of your database.

4. Bridge the gap between your organization and your donors.

It makes perfect sense that expanding the donation amounts within your existing donor base costs less than bringing in new donors. Take advantage of this truth. Once you've taken the time to find out more about your donors, you can make great strides in building a lasting, bonding relationship with them.

Don't alienate your donors, even when a year or more has gone by between contributions. Make them feel a part of the organization. Let them know they have a voice. Let them know you feel they're on the bandwagon. You're generating guilt every time you *don't* say to them, "You're guilty of overlooking us."

What better way to do this than in your newsletter? That's the beauty of this medium. Not only can you educate your donors and prospects, but if you edit it with targeting in mind, the newsletter is your vehicle to better customer relations. It's the voice of your donors, and it's the vehicle to help those increased donations come across the desk.

5. Altruism vs donations: Altruism loses.

It's time for you to put on your business and marketing hat and forget about altruistic attitudes and methods. Granted, the world would be a better place to live if everyone did good things out of the kindness of their hearts. But then again, if everyone did—think about it—you wouldn't be having to work so hard raising funds for worthy and needy causes.

So what does this tell you?

It tells you that to raise the most possible funds, nonprofits must start thinking with more than a little business savvy. You aren't living in a world all your own. You have big competition for those donated funds. Either you get them or someone else will.

6. Donor skepticism: Feed on it!

Today, the world thrives on scandal. And the best scandals are always about the organizations or people who appear to be beyond reproach (i.e., ministers, politicians, and yes—fund-raising organizations that take people's money for one purpose and use it for another). Even if your organization hasn't been the butt of a scandal, suspicions bleed over onto you. People are naturally suspicious today.

A sponsored newsletter can overcome donor skepticism by keeping the lines of constant communication open and presenting your most deserving, most honorable, most lovable face.

"United We Stand, Divided We Fall"

Get your readers involved. Create articles which will make them feel as though they are a part of a united effort sewn together by one single interest. . . and play mercilessly on this idea. Don't use "we did this"; instead use "you." Get your readers involved in your efforts. Don't ever let them feel they're standing on the outside looking in.

154

Don't Think of Your Fund-Raising Tactics as Sensationalism

The reason your fund-raising organization came into existence is more than likely because of some overpowering need, some overpowering wrong, or desperation which calls for people to unite and correct the problem. *Raising funds with ho-hum tactics gets ho-hum results.*

Convince your readers of the overpowering necessity to stand up and take action. To do this effectively, adapt your approaches. Generate different tactics for different targeted audiences. You can't do this with cold, unemotional facts and statistics.

No, I'm not saying omit facts and statistics; but you have to light the match before a fire can start inside the reader's mind. Your newsletter can be the match that starts the fire and keeps it burning brightly.

CHAPTER *8*

A Closer Look at Tangible and Intangible Products and Services Newsletters: Is There a Difference?

A definition of sponsored newsletters:

> The art of integrated advertising and relationship marketing in one medium.

What a conceptual breakthrough for those who haven't sampled the power of a properly produced sponsored newsletter!

But can newsletters stand alone without integrating themselves into a total promotional program which includes other forms of image advertising and sales programs? A true but unsatisfactory answer: Maybe.

Think of the newsletter as the glue keeping you and your customers together for a lifetime. Today, that's the most valuable function. Why? Because now, when consumers demand a personal relationship with a company—even a company selling packaged goods—or for that matter, with *any* organization wanting a relationship—newsletters are implicitly personal.

Except for one-to-one letters, whose cost can be ten to one hundred times that of newsletters, no communication is as personal.

Another peculiarity of today's marketplace: It seems the company or organization selling tangible items must also be "politically correct" as well as delivering merchandise, ego satisfaction, or both.

Can the newsletter medium work as well for tangible products as it can for intangible services? You bet it can. Newsletters are *main line* relationship-holders.

A new tone has been set in the 1990s in both general advertising and direct response, which is to give primary attention to extending lifetime customer value. *Customer relations*. Companies now recognize the commercial value of customer loyalty (together with ongoing generation of sales leads and measuring results).

This is where, after all these years, we've found we can make the most money—not just *getting* the customer but *keeping* the customer.

Tangible and Intangible Products and Services

Many people argue the marketing of tangible and intangible products and services are on opposite ends of the sphere in marketing.

Stop and think about it. Though wide mechanical and descriptive differences do exist, when it comes to relationship marketing (a 1990s buzzword that does have teeth in it) you must sell yourself and the company or organization to attain a true personal relationship with your existing customers and to attract the attention of your prospective customers.

Similarities of Product Marketing and Service Marketing

As we all know, a tangible product is something the consumer can, to a certain point, experience. Consumers can see, touch, smell, or taste the product. The can *own* it. Prospective customers often can test or use a product before buying it and taking it home. But what happens after this consumer buys the product and takes it home?

The company worries about whether the product will be used correctly . . . whether or not the instructions are clear . . . whether or not the product is faulty or the person using the product isn't using it properly.

This set of circumstances is complex—and increasingly so, since vendors are increasingly isolated from their customers. But as complex as they are, they don't yet touch intangibles and services that may accompany or even be generic to the product and its uses. They may not apply to moderate-to-low priced consumer goods which can't be pre-tested.

In the case of intangibles and services, prospective consumers rely heavily on reputation, current users, or a shot in the dark. These prospective customers can't experience service—or lack of it—until they buy.

In all respectable business transactions, tangibles and intangibles alike are bought on a promise of reliability.

In this age of skeptical consumers, the need for the promise of liability leaves both packaged-good marketers and the marketers of services in the same predicament. Both face the same set of problems:

1. Getting comparative or competitive attention
2. Getting your message across
3. Achieving and maintaining customer loyalty
4. Transforming the customer buying your product or service into an advocate for your product or service... and in many cases, cross-selling services which complement the tangible product (examples: computers; appliances; automobiles)

Marketing Tangible Products with Newsletters

Tangible products have always been built around general "brand image" advertising. As recently as the mid-1980s, tactics for selling packaged goods were much different from those which work effectively today.

Three general goals still apply:

1. To create broad awareness of a company's packaged goods.
2. To create a package or advertising the consumer easily recalls.
3. To keep the consumer buying with frequency.

Packaged goods marketers have realized they need to walk the extra mile. For competitive survival they must add an additional goal:

4. To create the climate for long-term relationships.

Marketers of packaged goods realize they have to compete to keep customer loyalty. They know they have to generate and build on sales... and have the ability to measure results. What caused what? What worked and what didn't? What's cost-effective and what's wasteful?

Much of this requires more targeted messages to those consumers who fit the product-use profile.

So to business!

What types of attention grabbing articles could you incorporate in your newsletter if you're selling tangible products?

Let's take a look at how some packaged goods marketers are overcoming marketing problems with their new weapon: the newsletter.

The example in figure 8-1 targets a very specific audience: British car owners. General advertising dollars would be wasted on a lot of deaf ears and blind eyes because the universe of appeal is specific—ergo, implicitly limited. (The rule: The more specific the target, the more limited the target.)

The company sells tangibles—British car products.

Before you read on, take a look at the at the front page. What do you see that you would do differently, now that you've read much of this book?

Right! The front page attacks the reader with ''company puffery'' the second you look at the first column.

What would *you* do?

Sure. You'd grab the reader's attention with an article treating something unusual about British cars...for example, some tidbit about the history of a specific model of British car.

The page does have a sidebar article, ''Thank God For British Sports Cars!'' But this is both secondary and trivial.

(WARNING! Avoid trivial topics on page 1.)

The column telling the reader what's inside the newsletter is in my opinion a wonderful idea. Except for the coupon reference, however, what the column contains doesn't move the reader to open the newsletter.

So what might this include instead of self-puffery and car clubs? They might list some important ''inside'' information British car owners need or want to know about and then insert it adjacent to the coupon insert. Mentioning ''freebies'' is always safe in a tangibles newsletter.

The overall concept is valid because the newsletter gives the reader a feeling of belonging to an exclusive club...but doesn't carry this concept as far as it should.

Let's use this newsletter as an unwitting guinea-pig. (Before continuing: Look at the reproduction and list what you regard as both professional procedures and correctable shortcomings.)

My analysis: The newsletter could have achieved a better effect through the following points.

1. Article blending.

The headlines scream company sales pitches and self-backpatting rather than customer benefits or customer-interest articles, which is too bad because hard information in the newsletter is, for the most part, customer oriented.

2. Promotions.

The company decided to make over 50 percent of the copy in its articles promotional, rather than giving the newsletter an even editorial mix. If

The Roadster Factory

Thank God For British Sports Cars!

British sports cars have been a part of my life since I was ten, when I first fell in love with an MG-TD that was parked in a neighbor's drive. A lot of things have changed in the world since the 1950's, and I guess that is part of the appeal of the old sports cars to me.

High-technology, complication, emission, pollution, recession, ergometrics, bionics, avionics, computerization, capitalization, digitalized instrumentation, graphs, charts, human resources, genetic engineering, AIDS, cancer, heart disease. Lord! Give me a can of Castrol, a tweed jacket, and my old TR2. I'm out of here!

Against the backdrop of The Nineties, isn't it refreshing to drive a car that was designed to be infinitely rebuildable and to last for hundreds of thousands of miles—that can be worked on by anyone who cares with a monkey wrench, that can be tuned with a piece of rubber tubing and a twelve-volt light bulb. I could drive a sports car for everyday transportation. I did it for years in The Sixties and Seventies. I could go back to having only one car and working on it every Sunday. I could! I could! Couldn't you?

The Roadster Factory Wants You As A Customer!

The Roadster Factory is dependent upon British car enthusiasts for its business, and we put a lot back into the hobby. Most importantly, we produce hundreds of components which would not be available otherwise, and we reinvest most of our earnings in inventory so that we have the parts you need on the shelf. We also provide considerable support to club activities across the nation by sponsoring trophies, providing door prizes, and by traveling in person to local and national car shows, meets, and conventions everywhere. We attend as many as one-hundred British car events every year, and to the largest conventions, we bring a store-full of products which we set up in hotel display rooms. To smaller outdoor events, we may only bring catalogues and give-aways in one of our own sports cars, but we do try to have a presence at as many car events as possible during each year. One of The Roadster Factory's most important contributions to the British car hobby is the information which we publish. Catalogues, newsletters, technical information, car club information, etc. Most of this is provided for free to anyone who needs it, including our unique technical service telephone line which is staffed throughout the week.

Those of us who work at TRF believe that we offer the best overall parts service available, and we work very hard every day to maintain the level of our service. We are located further than some suppliers from the large number of potential customers on the West Coast, yet we have been extremely successful in getting and keeping West Coast customers. We concentrate on getting every order out quickly, almost always within twenty-four hours and usually the same day; on keeping inventory in stock to avoid delays, and on handling only the best parts so that our customers everywhere in the country can depend on our service.

This publication is sent out to MG and Triumph enthusiasts whose names we have acquired from clubs, vehicle registrations, and other sources. We want you to try our service, and we puzzled over the best way to attract your interest. In the end, we chose to give you the set of coupons included in this publication. These can save you quite a lot of money on some of our most popular parts. If you purchase any of the items using the coupons, you will be buying parts at prices which are lower than those paid by most dealers. We are providing these parts to you, often at less than cost prices, so that you will give our service a try. We hope that, once you have tried us, you will want to become a permanent customer. When you place an order for parts, please also request catalogues for the car models which you own, and don't forget that our Winter Parts Sale runs through the end of March.

If you are interested in becoming a TRF customer, we welcome you, and if you have sold your car or if you are not interested in buying parts for some other reason, we thank you for the time you spend in reading this publication.

The Roadster Factory

The Roadster Factory will be completing its fifteenth year of business in June 1992. We have been selling Triumph sports car components longer than any major supplier in the U.S., and we added MGB and MGB-GT to our range in 1988. When TRF was founded in 1978, many original parts for earlier Triumph models were still available from the factory, and we stocked up, giving us the world's largest inventory of original-equipment components. Over the years, we have also become major manufacturers in our own right, producing hundreds of components which would not be available otherwise.

TRF added over $1-million to our stock of components to handle the MGB models back in 1988, and today our inventory fills a warehouse complex measuring over 35,000 square feet. The total value of our inventory is over $12-million now, and it includes every imaginable part from chassis frames to body shells; from nuts and bolts to engines, gearboxes, and rear axles rebuilt in our own factory; interior, chrome, badges, wheels, tires, suspension, brakes, sheet metal, exhausts, clutches, and regalia. We especially pride ourselves in not only stocking the major parts themselves but also all of the related hardware. Much of this is available in unique kits which make it simpler to order and to have everything you need on hand when you start to work.

The Roadster Factory still offers old-fashioned personal service. We do what we do here in the mountains of Western Pennsylvania not because it is a job but because it is what we like to do. We take the time to help you through a problem on the telephone, and we like to share the knowledge that we have built up over the years. We like to sell the best possible parts, and we do not like to sell junk. We pride ourselves in selling the right parts at the right prices. That means that we sell good parts at competitive prices. We also stand behind what we sell. If you have a problem with anything you buy from us, we will find a way to solve it. In fact, we have even flown our technicians out to repair minor problems with major mechanical units.

TRF is housed in a warehouse complex located in The Laurel Mountains of Western Pennsylvania. We design and build our own buildings in a style that we like. We have also designed and built most of our furniture. Our operation wouldn't look at home in most modern cities today, but it would have looked quite at home in Coventry or Abingdon during the time that our cars were made. We try to run clean and efficiently. We insulate well and heat with electricity. If it gets cold, we wear sweaters. We recycle everything we can, and we contribute very little to landfills. Our neighbors are the wild turkeys and the white-tailed deer which graze unharmed in our fields. We employ sixty local people here in Indiana County, and we make British sports cars a part of our lives.

Inside:

Details of Our Annual Famous Winter Parts Sale. Over the past fourteen years, it has become the premier sales event in the British car industry, and this year's sale offers the best values ever! Call our toll free telephone number to receive your copy of our sale booklet!

Valuable Product Coupons. We want you to try our spare parts service, so we have provided these valuable coupon discounts as incentive. Great savings!

Join a British Car Club. Every British car owner should belong to at least one national club. See inside for a listing of major clubs, as well as the locations of national-level car events.

The Roadster Factory • Post Office Box 332 • Armagh, Pennsylvania 15920 • Telephone (800) 678-8764

Figure 8-1

Who Are TRF's Customers?

The Roadster Factory has tens of thousands of customers in every state in the U.S., all of the Canadian provinces, in Australia, New Zealand, Japan, South America, and most Western European countries. We supply individual enthusiasts, clubs, shops, garages, parts stores, and SCCA and vintage racers. We also pride ourselves that nearly all concours winners at local, regional, and national club events are our customers. TRF has a racing car sponsorship program which includes most Triumphs and MGB's which compete successfully in SCCA racing and many cars which compete in vintage racing and autocrossing. Who are our *most important* customers? People just like you, people who work on their cars and use them for every purpose from out-and-out racing, to concours events, to daily transportation. We cannot do what we do without you, and your business means everything to us at TRF.

The Roadster Factory Winter Parts Sale

The Roadster Factory is holding its Fourteenth Annual Winter Parts Sale from January 13th through March 31st, 1992. This sale is the premier sales event in the British car trade, and it is not too late for you to participate this year.

The Winter Parts Sale is a unique concept which has intrigued British car owners since 1979. Every part in The Roadster Factory's vast inventory of twenty-thousand part numbers is discounted. In addition, you may select items from a free premium list, which includes over one-thousand of TRF's most popular items, based on the size of your order. Additional discounts are available for fax and mail orders, and overall savings can go as high as twenty-five percent and more.

Famous WINTER PARTS SALE — The Roadster Factory

ENTIRE INVENTORY DISCOUNTED!

VALUABLE FREE PREMIUMS!

SAVE 20% OR MORE!

JANUARY 13th THROUGH MARCH 31st, 1992

You Won't Believe What You Can Get For Free!

The Winter Parts Sale includes free premiums based upon the size of the order which you place during the sale. The list of free premiums includes over one-thousand items, and it takes twenty-four pages in our Winter Parts Sale booklet to list them all.

The free premiums include far more than the usual can of brake fluid or a free oil filter. In fact, the items included are nearly all chosen from TRF's most popular inventory. There are four pages of listings which you can chose with an order valued at just $50.00. These include key fobs, owner's handbooks, touch-up paint, badges and emblems, window winder handles, body parts, rubber body seals, throttle cables, and many other items, almost two-hundred in all.

There are also separate lists of items which you can choose for free with orders valued at $100.00, $150.00, $250.00, $350.00, $500.00, $750.00, $1,000.00, and so on right up to $5,000.00. Even at the $500.00 level, you can choose free dash crash pads, major body panels,

road springs, etc. At $2,500.00, you can have free TR6 fenders and free MGB fenders. Free chromed wire wheels and TR7 cylinder heads with a $5,000.00 order. There really is something for everyone, and you can choose several items from a lower category rather than one item from a higher value category if you wish. You can also combine small orders during the entire sale period to choose one large premium at the end. Our computer will keep track of your total order value.

To Receive Your Copy Of Our 32-Page Famous Winter Parts Sale Booklet, As Well As A Free Parts Catalogue For Your Specific Car Model, Call The Roadster Factory Toll Free At (800) 678-8764, 24 Hours Per Day From 7:00 A.M. Monday Through 6:00 P.M. Saturday!

Simplified Packing, Shipping Charges During The Sale

During The Winter Parts Sale, we are using a simplified shipping chart which provides one low cost for packing and shipping your order, including any backordered items, to anywhere in continental U.S. by UPS ground service. Rush service is available, when required, at no extra charge. This means that any order received here by 1:00 P.M. will be shipped the same day. In fact, TRF ships every order very quickly, and you may very well receive an order from TRF days sooner than an order placed with a closer supplier. The Roadster Factory also provides Federal Express, Emery Air Freight, truck freight, one-day air, two-day air, Saturday delivery, or anything else which we can make available to you on a custom basis at the exact cost to us for the service you want. We aim to please!

Figure 8-1 (cont.)

Super Rebuilt Engines, Gearboxes, Axles, Hubs, Steering Racks

*T*he Roadster Factory has its own rebuilding factory for engines, gearboxes, differential units, carburettors, IRS rear hubs for TR4A, TR250, and TR6, MGB front suspension components, and steering racks. We realize that many enthusiasts do a great job of maintaining their cars until something major breaks. When they have to entrust their cars to local garages without British sports car expertise, things sometimes go wrong.

The goal at C.A.R. Components, TRF's rebuilding factory, is perfection. We want every component which we supply to look and function as if it were brand new or better than brand new. In fact, Frank Stoddard, former BL Manager now employed by TRF, states that our components have a better failure rate than the factory ever achieved. We replace more parts than any of our competitors in the world market, and we balance every engine that we sell. When we are satisfied that a unit has been rebuilt to our specifications, we apply a good-looking and long-lasting finish which is designed to match the appearance of the unit to what was originally supplied. We even paint aluminium gearbox castings with a beautiful coat of protective silver enamel which protects the units from oxidation.

Using a rebuilt engine, gearbox, or other mechanical unit from C.A.R. Components, any enthusiast who is experienced in car maintenance can replace a faulty unit, restoring his or her car to original reliability and performance, using only basic hand tools, an engine lift if applicable, and a good workshop manual. Our rebuilt units are supplied on an exchange basis, and if possible, you should keep your old unit until the new unit is received. This way, you won't make the mistake of sending anything along with the old unit which is required for installing the rebuilt unit. TRF will also arrange to rebuild the customer's old unit if desired in order to retain original serial numbers on engines, gearboxes, and rear axles. TRF units are covered by a limited warranty for a period of twelve-thousand miles or one full year, provided that the unit is properly installed and maintained and provided that the car is not used for racing or other high performance competition.

A fuller discussion and prices of the rebuilt components supplied by TRF through C.A.R. Components is included in our Winter Parts Sale Booklet. You may receive this booklet, along with any of our catalogues and price lists, upon request, by calling us toll free or by sending in a copy of the request form included in this brochure.

Precision and cleanliness are scrupulously maintained during the rebuilding process at C.A.R. Components, Ltd. At left, Derek Hodge uses the proper Churchill tool to disassemble a Triumph hub prior to rebuilding. Below, Rick Tascarisks monitors crankshaft endfloat as part of the engine assembly process.

Please Order Now! Special Coupon Offers End March 31, 1992.

1 Validate the coupon or coupons that you wish to use by writing the Customer I.D. No. in the space provided on the coupons. Also record this number in the proper space on the order form at right. This I.D. number registers the special coupon discounts in your name, and your name only. You will find your special Customer I.D. No. in the upper right-hand corner of the address label on this mailer.

MS. TAMMY SKUBIC
ROUTE 1
BOX 191
SEWARD, PA 15954

2 Record the part numbers for the items you wish to order on the order form at right, along with the quantity desired and the *List Price* for each item. The *List Prices* are the prices listed on the coupons, before the coupon discount is subtracted.

3 Add up the *List Prices* of the items you have chosen and enter the total in the *Parts Total* area on the order form.

4 Find the correct Packing and Shipping charge from the chart below based upon the *Parts Total* of your order. Enter that amount in the *Shipping* area on the form.

Shipping Chart—UPS Ground or Parcel Post

Order Parts Total	Packing/Shipping Charge
Up to $20.00	$3.70
$20.00 to $50.00	$6.05
$50.01 to $100.00	$8.75
$100.01 to $150.00	$12.50
$150.01 to $250.00	$15.75
$250.01 to $600.00	$19.25
Over $600.00	$39.00

5 *Subtract* any coupon discounts that apply to your order from the parts list price and packing and shipping total.

6 Pennsylvania residents only must add 6% State Sales Tax to their order total. Residents of other states are not required to pay sales tax on their orders. Total your order.

7 Enter *Method of Payment* information in the area provided. TRF accepts MasterCard, Visa, Discover Card, American Express, personal check, cashier's check or money order, or C.O.D. for cash or cashier's check.

Orders may be placed by mail, or by toll free telephone at (800) 678-8764, 24 hours a day from 7:00 A.M. Monday through 6:00 P.M. Saturday!

The Roadster Factory

POST OFFICE BOX 332, ARMAGH, PENNSYLVANIA 15920   TOLL FREE ORDERING (800) 678-8764   FAX (814) 446-6775

INVOICE NO.

CUSTOMER I.D. NO.	NAME

MAILING ADDRESS / SHIPPING ADDRESS

HOME PHONE

BUSINESS PHONE

CAR YEAR/MODEL	COMMISSION/SERIAL NUMBER		ORDER DATE

PART NUMBER	QTY.	DESCRIPTION	PRICE EA.	PRICE

7 METHOD OF PAYMENT:
☐ CASHIER'S CHECK OR MONEY ORDER   ☐ PERSONAL CHECK—ALLOW 14 DAYS
☐ C.O.D. FOR CASH OR CASHIER'S CHECK
☐ VISA   ☐ MASTERCARD   ☐ DISCOVER CARD   ☐ AMERICAN EXPRESS
CREDIT CARD NUMBER
CARDHOLDER NAME
EXPIRATION DATE

Parts Total	
Shipping (See Chart)	
Subtract Coupon Values	
6% Sales Tax Pa. Residents	
ORDER TOTAL	

Figure 8-1 (cont.)

Car Clubs Are Important To The Long Term Survival Of British Sports Cars

Sports car owners have always enjoyed participating in events which allow them to test themselves and their cars against other cars and drivers, and many of us also like to get together with other sports car owners to compare notes, to socialize, and to have a good time.

The national and local car clubs provide one of the best ways to find other sports car enthusiasts. Clubs usually have a social and business meeting every month, and they get together for other events on a frequent basis. Many clubs hold road tours, tune-up clinics, autocrosses, picnics, rallys, etc. They also have car shows where you can see how your car stacks up against other cars in your area. Local clubs are usually part of some national organization, and the national organizations mostly hold a national meet or convention on an annual basis. This gives you a chance to see more sports cars than you've ever seen in one place before, and it gives you a chance to see some very special cars indeed. If you are into competition of any type, be it rallying, autocrossing, or concours, you will find it at a high level at most national conventions.

Since the Triumph and MG factories have closed, the car clubs are really the only organizations to provide a focus on these two marques. They provide historical continuity and standards for maintaining a car in the future. We at The Roadster Factory heartily recommend club membership to any Triumph or MG owner who wants to own and maintain a car over a long period.

U.S. NATIONAL TRIUMPH AND MG CAR CLUBS—ADDRESSES AND INFORMATION:

The Vintage Triumph Register
VTR Membership, Dept. T, 15218 West Warren Avenue, Dearborn, Michigan 48126

For enthusiasts of all models of Triumph cars.
Annual Dues: $20.00; free club brochure with S.A.S.E.
1992 National Show at Savannah, Georgia, July 23-26.
Contact Hal Doky: Days, (404) 972-3690;
Evenings, (404) 979-2311; Fax, (404) 972-4073.

The Triumph Register of America
5630 Brook Road, N.W., Lancaster, Ohio 43130
For enthusiasts of Triumph TR2 and TR3 models.
Annual Dues: $15.00
(Continued in next column.)

1992 National Show at Salt Fork State Park, Cambridge, Ohio, June 18-21.
Contact Bruce Clough: (513) 294-3792,
3207 Oakmont Avenue, Kettering, Ohio 45429.

6-PACK
11792 Thomas Spring Road, Monrovia, Maryland 21770
For enthusiasts of Triumph TR250 and TR6 models.
Annual Dues: $15.00

1992 National Show at Solomon's Island, Maryland, September 24-27.
Contact Andy Hundertmark: (301) 242-5870,
1300 Francis Avenue, Baltimore, Maryland 21227.

American MGB Register (AMGBA)
Post Office Box 11401, Chicago, Illinois 60611.

For enthusiasts of MGB, MGB-GT, Midget.
Annual Dues: $25.00

1992 National Show at Palo Alto, California, September 13.
Contact Frank Ochal: (800) 723-MGMG

North American MGB Register (NAMGBR)
Post Office Box MGB, Akin, Illinois 62805
Telephone (800) NAMGBR-1

For enthusiasts of MGB, MGB-GT, Midget.

1992 National Show at Peterborough, Ontario, Canada.
Contact MG Car Car Club of Toronto: Post Office Box 64, Station Road, Toronto M4G 3Z3, Canada.

MAJOR NON-CLUB EVENTS THIS SUMMER:

The Gold Coast Classic
San Luis Obispo, California, June 4-7, 1992.

For specifics, contact the organizer: British Car Magazine, Post Office Box 9099, Canoga Park, California 91309.
Telephone: (818) 710-1234. Fax: (818) 710-1877.

The Gold Coast Classic is a new event on the British car scene. The organizers want to develop the event into a major national event to be held on an annual basis, and the format is lavish with an automobile auction, a TSD rally through the wine country in Central California, and a major *concours d'élégance*. There will be social events such as cocktail parties, a banquet, and a barbecue. The overall winner of The Classic, based upon points accumulated from the rally

and the concours will receive a free trip for two to England as a prize. The Roadster Factory plans to participate in The Gold Coast Classic, and we shall look forward to seeing our West Coast friends in San Luis Obispo in June.

SVRA Vintage Race Weekend
Mid-Ohio Race Track, Lexington, Ohio, June 25-28, 1992.
For specifics, contact Jeannine Zimmer: (614) 876-3341, Mid-Ohio Sports Car Course, Post Office Box 3108, Lexington, Ohio 44904

Triumph is the featured marque at this year's vintage races. Cars will be coming from all over the country and all over the world. Also famous drivers and names associated with Triumph cars and Triumph racing. Jaguar and Morgan were featured marques in past years, and this year's event should materialize into something very special for enthusiasts of the Triumph marque. The vintage races are being held one week after The Triumph Register of America National Meet and in the same area of the country. The Roadster Factory will attend both events, and we will bring along several interesting cars from our collection.

The Roadster Factory Summer Party
Indiana County, Pennsylvania, August 7-9, 1992.

To register or to receive information as it is available, contact:
Dana P. Henry (Mr.), The Roadster Factory Ltd.,
Post Office Box 332, Armagh, Pennsylvania 15920.
Telephone: (814) 446-4423. Fax: (814) 446-6820.

The Roadster Factory Summer Party is open to all British car enthusiasts, whether or not they can bring cars. Events include: flea market, parties, racing, rallying, touring, *concours d'élégance*. This third annual party promises to be every bit as good as our previous parties. Cost of $45.00 per person includes admission to all events, including racing events, Saturday night party, and Sunday *concours*. Free camping is available for those who want to rough it, and special rates will be available at all of the area motels for those who don't. We expect more than five-hundred cars this year as well as a major flea market. We want you to come, and we guarantee that you will have a good time.

University Motors Summer Party
Grand Rapids, Michigan. August 21-23, 1992.

To register or to receive information, contact: John or Caroline Twist, University Motors, 614 Eastern Avenue, S.E., Grand Rapids, Michigan 49503, Telephone: (616) 245-2141, Fax (616) 245-6464.

The University Motors Summer Party is the largest gathering of MG enthusiasts in the U.S. John Twist of University Motors is a nationally known MG enthusiast, and this is the 16th annual summer party. Events include: flea market, tours of University Motors, rally, major *concours* event, and Saturday evening banquet. This writer attended two of the past three parties, and I have had a memorable time on both occasions. Great MG's.

You'll Like Our Free Catalogues and Newsletters!

The Roadster Factory publishes separate catalogues for each of the model ranges in which we deal. These models include Triumph TR2, TR3, TR4, TR4A, TR5, TR250, TR6, TR7, TR8, Triumph Spitfire and GT6, and MGB, MGB-GT. GT6 catalogues are currently in preparation. Catalogues for all other models are available for free upon request. TRF has developed a large catalogue format which has found great favor with our customers, and we are gradually rewriting some of our older catalogues into the new format. The new format provides listings for every component on the car no matter how large or how small, and our exploded diagrams provide better assembly information on many occasions than a workshop manual.

The Roadster Factory also publishes periodic newsletters which include technical information; background information on the cars, the car companies, and the country from which they came; and supplementary information on available parts and accessories. Everyone on TRF's active mailing list receives a free subscription to the newsletter. Our active mailing list includes everyone who has made a purchase in the past eighteen months.

Also sent out to every customer on TRF's active mailing list is our annual Christmas catalogue which is always very well received and our Winter Parts Sale Booklet which is the key to the premier sales event in the British car trade. You can put your name on TRF's active mailing list and receive all of our publications for free by sending in a completed Customer Data Form by mail or by fax or by calling us toll free.

CUSTOMER DATA UPDATE

NAME _____ CUSTOMER I.D. NO. _____

  Title   First Name   Middle Initial   Surname

MAILING ADDRESS: _____ SHIPPING ADDRESS: _____

HOME TELEPHONE: _____ OFFICE TELEPHONE: _____

MGB'S OR TRIUMPHS OWNED

Please be as complete as possible when you give your car information. Commission numbers (Car numbers, Serial numbers) are found on your title or state vehicle registration card as well as on a plate on the car itself. We can live without these numbers if you cannot supply them.

CAR MODEL/YEAR _____ COMMISSION NUMBER _____

CAR MODEL/YEAR _____ COMMISSION NUMBER _____

CAR MODEL/YEAR _____ COMMISSION NUMBER _____

CAR MODEL/YEAR _____ COMMISSION NUMBER _____

CAR MODEL/YEAR _____ COMMISSION NUMBER _____

To receive future mailings or to request a free parts catalogue for your car, please return completed Customer Data Update form to: The Roadster Factory Ltd., Post Office Box 332, Armagh, Pennsylvania 15920, or call toll free at (800) 678-8764 and provide the same information as requested above.

CATALOGUE REQUESTS:

Use this form to request personal copies of our catalogues; simply check the box next to the catalogue for your specific car model. Catalogues which have not yet been published are marked with projected date of publication. All of our parts catalogues are free of charge.

☐ **MGB, MGB-GT Preliminary Spare Parts Catalogue** (224 pages), published September 1989 (updated Third edition soon to be published); one of the nicest MGB catalogues anywhere!

☐ **Restoration Checklist** (112 pages), published 1988, covers the Triumph TR2 through TR4A range of cars in a quick reference format. Includes all of the most popular parts.

☐ **Triumph TR250 Spare Parts Catalogue and Engineering Assembly Manual** (248 pages, published February 1989). Lists and illustrates virtually every part on the TR250.

☐ **Triumph TR6 Spare Parts Catalogue and Engineering Assembly Manual, Vol. 1** (261 pages, published August 1990). Lists and illustrates all mechanical components of the TR6.

☐ **Triumph TR6 Spare Parts Catalogue and Engineering Assembly Manual, Vol. II,** to be published in 1992. Includes all electrical, body, and interior components not listed in Volume I above. Everything from nuts and bolts to major components!

☐ **Triumph TR7 & TR8 Spare Parts Catalogue** (144 pages), Second Edition published 1991, the best TR7/8 catalogue in the business!

☐ **Spitfire Mk.1, 2, 3 Spare Parts Catalogue** (68 pages), published November 1991. A thorough listing of popular early Spitfire components for the enthusiast.

☐ **Spitfire 1500 Spare Parts Catalogue** (96 pages), updated Third edition published May 1991. Also a valuable reference for the Spitfire mk.4 owner.

☐ **TRF Green Price List,** published January 1991 and still in effect! Our complete price listing for all Triumph and MGB components. Use with any of our catalogues.

You may request our free parts catalogues 24 hours a day from 7:00 A.M. Monday through 6:00 P.M. Saturday, by calling toll free (800) 678-8764!

Figure 8-1 (cont.)

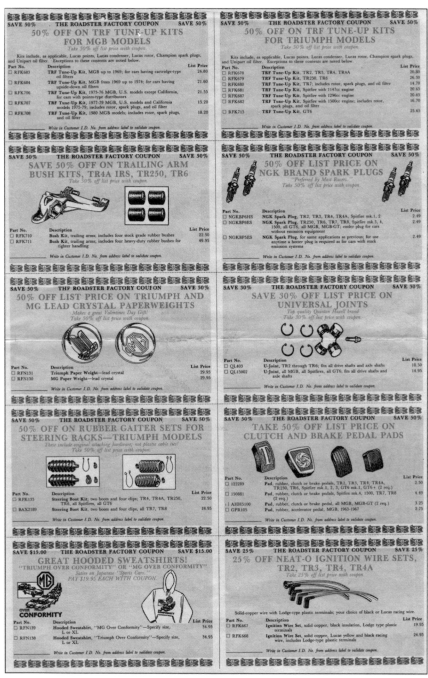

Figure 8-1 (cont.)

the newsletter contained more customer-interest articles this would have been a near-perfect advertising medium.

Straight promotional material includes a coupon insert and an order form for the sponsor's products, plus a way to order free catalogs and newsletters. Included in each article is a way to respond by writing or by phoning an 800 number.

Technical terms help rather than hinder in this newsletter's attempt to become close to customers and prospects. That's the benefit of specificity: speaking only to your specific target, with no need to speak in general terms.

The tone is personable and friendly, in a basically impersonal product market. Most car owners wouldn't think about where they went for car parts. They want convenience and assurance, and those qualities are here in abundance.

The newsletter doesn't talk down to its readers. Instead the tone is "You belong to a privileged group of people who love British cars." In this case, the company has an edge over a local car-parts source. They show class and superiority, so they're walking the extra mile it takes to capture the market.

As you can see, hard-goods marketers can have a hard time mastering the newsletter medium. This newsletter facade in figure 8-2 appears to contain valuable information inside. Take a closer look at *Today's Contents* on the back cover: "Heard On The Street" page 17. Uh-oh. When you turn to page 17 there is no story. The same thing happens with the rest of the stories listed.

The text copy reads like a catalog. In essence that's all it is, a catalog masquerading as a newsletter...which (opinion) damages the image of newsletters in general.

Does "getting attention" equate to "offering benefit"? This newsletter does get the attention of finance and business people because it uses a different approach. But it doesn't follow through, as you can see in figure 8-3.

The newsletter would be more effective selling the company's products if it gave the reader the information it promised on the front and back covers, instead of an obvious, naked sales pitch. If you're tempted to use the newsletter format as a facade for a sales pitch instead of as a sales weapon on its own, ask yourself:

What would a true newsletter do for your customers and prospects that a catalog can't?

Answer: It can combat consumer skepticism *and* sell your products. A catalog can only sell your products.

Take a look at the next exhibits in figure 8-4 and 8-5.

This is a good example of what the previous "phony" newsletter could have done. This company sells books. To be more specific, it sells books on marketing. Sure, when you're selling products you want to show the

(Story on Page 4)

(Story on Page 19)

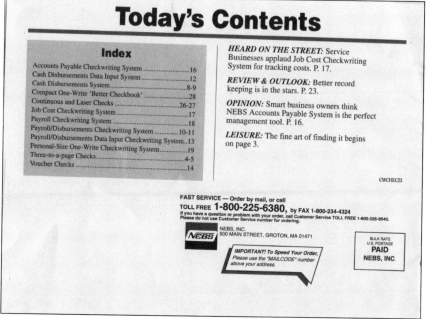

Figure 8-2

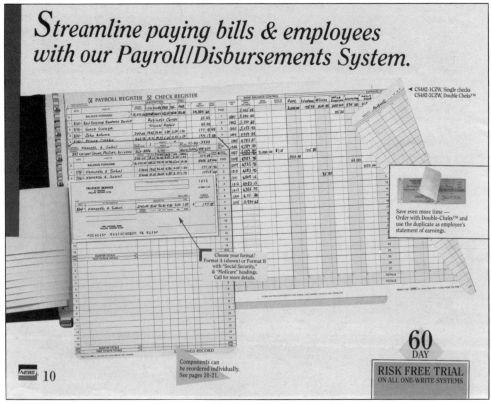

Figure 8-3

product. This company did just that; but instead of merely writing positive book reviews to help sell the books in its pages—which is what many people would do in a catalog which sells books—this company has improved on the catalog format.

Yes, every book seems to be a winner, in the mini-reviews; but the text injects a touch of statesmanship by extensive quotes from texts.

What better way to get marketers into the selling arena than to give them up-to-date material in their field?

What could have been done different on the first page?

The first page, except for the table of contents, is more catalog than newsletter. Why not have one of the news stories on the front page instead of only books the company sells?

I like the ''In This Issue'' column which lists what's inside in a manner piquing marketers' interest, sub-listing true newsletter columns: ''Every Day Shoppers,'' ''Women of the '90s,'' ''Energy Use in the U.S.,'' and ''Health-Care Markets.''

This newsletter-plus-catalog gives its readers pertinent information in

Figure 8-4

ONE OUT OF TEN AMERICANS SHOPS EVERY DAY

SHOPPING EXPERIENCES RUN THE GAMUT FROM PICKING up milk and bread on the way home to buying a car. The frequency with which people shop varies by sex, age, and marital status, among other things.

Nine percent of American adults shop every day, according to a poll conducted by Maritz Marketing Research for American Demographics; another 9 percent shop every other day. Twenty-seven percent shop two to three times a week, and 28 percent shop once a week. The remaining 25 percent shop less than once a week.

Men, unmarried people, and those under the age of 45 are more likely than average to shop every day. Frequent shopping would seem to be a hallmark of a younger and more impulsive lifestyle. But this shouldn't be confused with a single lifestyle. People who live alone don't shop that frequently, because many are older women. Among women who live alone, only 3 percent shop every day, compared with 11 percent of men who live alone.

Shopping frequency drops with age for women more than for men. With the exception of those under the age of 25, the share of women who shop every day falls—from 13 percent for those aged 25 to 34 to 4 percent for those aged 55 or older. For men over the age of 25, this share is never very high, and hovers between 8 and 11 percent.

Likewise, the share of women who shop less than once a week rises with age, from 20 percent of those aged 25 to 34 to 27 percent of those aged 65 or older. For men, the share shopping this infrequently drops somewhat, from 26 percent at age 25 to 34 to 20 percent of those aged 65 or older.

Because of the predominance of older women who concentrate their energies in fewer, more efficient shopping trips, people who live alone are particularly likely to shop less than once a week—32 percent. Men, those under the age of 25, and unmarried people are also more likely than average to shop infrequently—less than once a week. Middle-aged and older people, women, and those who are married are more likely to shop at least once a week, but not every day.

Reprinted from The Numbers News, ©1991 *American Demographics, Inc.*

Eleven percent of men shop every day, compared with 7 percent of women; this is a significant difference.

MEN ARE MORE FREQUENT SHOPPERS AT ALMOST ALL AGES

(percent of people who shop every day, by age and sex)

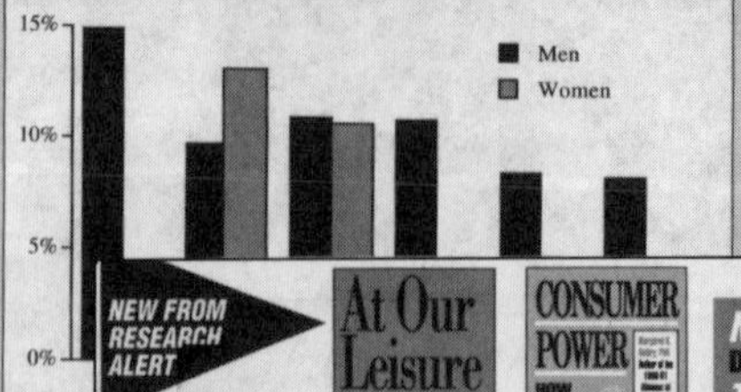

4 MARKETING TOOLS ALERT ◆ P.O. BOX 68, …

NEW FROM RESEARCH ALERT

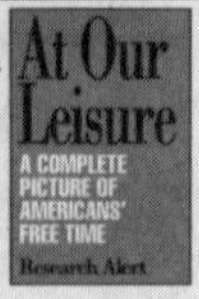

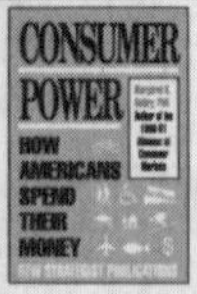

AT OUR LEISURE
A Complete Picture of Americans' Free Time
by Research Alert
Eric Miller and the editors of Research Alert detail the changing significance of free time in American life. Their report tracks a variety of trends that point to the growing importance of leisure in the life of the nation as a whole. This exclusive analysis is backed by hundreds of specific entries that factually, but readably, portray the major corners of free time. The report covers media use, entertainment, managing the home, sports and fitness, shopping, dining out, and more. It also presents hundreds of niches of leisure time such as: kids and chores, snacking, sex, who listens to which radio formats, who throws dinner parties, the latest (and the lasting) fitness crazes, hot menu items, the fate of mall-going, and the future of movie preferences. An authoritative presentation of the facts behind America's top priority. Special report #492 $120

CONSUMER POWER
How Americans Spend Their Money
by Margaret K. Ambry, Ph.D.
Are you targeting your most likely customers? Here is an easy-to-understand analysis of spending patterns and market opportunities that's guaranteed to help you find viable solutions to your marketing questions. *Consumer Power* is based on the Bureau of Labor Statistics' annual Consumer Expenditure Survey—one of the most reliable sources for information on what Americans do with their money. Because an individual's age, income, and type of household are all factors affecting buying decisions, data are given for 7 age brackets, 6 income groups, and 9 household categories. Replete with charts, tables, and fully indexed for quick reference, this groundbreaking reference, with projections through the year 2000, gives you the straightforward details about the dollar size of your markets that you need to make sound business decisions. (ISBN 0-9628092-0-9; 1991) Book #470 $69.95

MANAGING CONSUMER DIVERSITY
Editors of American Demographics *magazine*
To navigate the shoals of short-term economic upheaval, you need to understand long-term consumer trends. In an increasingly individualistic society, it's more important than ever to find the underlying characteristics that define markets. Experts from American Demographics magazine look at today's complex life-stages, the long-term shift from communal to individual values, and how these trends are changing the basic consumer unit: the household. Audio cassette #535 $17.95
Transcript #535-T $20

CONSUMER BEHAVIOR
Looking Backward to Look Forward
Watts Wacker, Executive Vice President, Yankelovich, Clancy, Shulman
After years of enthusiastic spending, the U.S. has entered into its first recession in over a decade. Now marketers need to develop strategic marketing plans that provide the basic benefits consumers seek in their search for products and services that will add value to their lives. This presentation explains the neotraditional values of the 1990s.
Audio cassette #541 $17.95
Transcript #541-T $20

HOW TO SURVIVE THE RETAILING REVOLUTION
If you need to know the demographic facts that will shape retailing in the 1990s, this special reprint package will help you get started. Topics include the evolution of retailing, why retailers must clearly define their markets, the demise of the department store, supermarket retailing, segmenting food customers, downscale buyers who spend billions on the basics, selling convenience, and riding local demographic waves.
American Demographics reprint package #347 $16

NEW! FROM AMERICAN DEMOGRAPHICS BOOKS
The first book to demystify psychographics

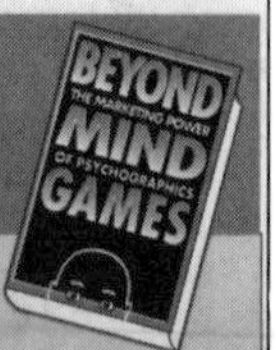

BEYOND MIND GAMES
The Marketing Power of Psychographics
by Rebecca Piirto
As consumers' spending choices increase, the advertising task of finding a selling hook becomes a search for nuances. Modern researchers continue to search for new ways to spot trends and determine how individuals select health-care products, make travel decisions, and choose grocery items. To accomplish this task, they use probing techniques such as Benefit Chains™, Emotional Lexicons™, word association, drawing exercises, and picture association. This is the first book that tells you what psychographics is all about, where it came from, and what you can do with it. It explains:

- The history and evolution of psychographic research
- How segmentation schemes were developed and how they are used
- Attitudes and feelings that cause consumers to bond to brands
- How information can be gathered through surveys, focus groups, observation, and psychological techniques
- Marketing implications for manufacturers, retailers, advertisers, local, national, and international marketers
- How to avoid the pitfalls of psychographic analysis
- How to combine psychographics with other information to gain a complete picture of consumers
- What lies on the frontier and in the future for psychographic research

Anecdotal examples of applied psychographic research make this one of the most interesting, revealing, and enjoyable books in the field of marketing. (ISBN 0-936889-08-X; 1991) Book #481 $29.50

SAVE *with this special pre-publication offer on a forthcoming selection from*
AMERICAN DEMOGRAPHICS BOOKS

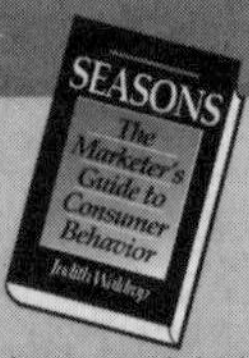

THE SEASONS OF BUSINESS
The Marketer's Guide to Consumer Behavior
by Judith Waldrop
Successful retailers know that when it comes to selling consumer products, timing is everything. For nearly five years, Judith Waldrop, research editor of *American Demographics* magazine, has observed how national events, weather patterns, agricultural cycles, the threat of natural disasters, hours of daylight, national holidays, and religious observances affect consumer behavior. In her unique guide to seasonal marketing, Ms. Waldrop examines, for every month, the primary marketing events, participation in sports and leisure activities, health-care issues, and personal attitudes. She explains which demographic groups are the principle players and which consumer concerns are most pressing. From travel to gardening, Seasonal Affective Disorder to allergies, tax time to tube time, romance to decadence, this guide will help you hit the right audience, with the right message, at the right time. *(Publication date: March 1992)* Book #487 ~~$29.95~~ ***Special pre-publication price $24.95***

Figure 8-5

their own field, and then backs it up by offering the books which will help the readers in their chosen field.

In this particular field of book marketing, the readers are definitely more targeted than they ever could be by simply placing a book on the shelf in a bookstore.

Integrated marketing! Product marketers who use newsletters and other informational material to keep in contact with their customers are *integrating* their marketing efforts.

For example: A mass marketing television advertisement for *Tampax Tampons* asks the viewer to call a toll free 800 number for a free newsletter issued by the company. Subject is how to care for the environment. This is an excellent way of a) measuring viewer response, b) finding out more about their targets, c) gaining credibility, and d) positioning the issuer as an environmental booster—a wonderful upgrade for a company which manufactures products that may be viewed as detrimental to the environment.

In a marketplace whose competing products often are indistinguishable except for *image*, whom do you think most people would rely on for these products? Right.

Turn on your television set (not now, please). See how many product marketers are doing this—and take their lead. These are archetypical examples of integrating promotional sales and advertising, image, and response in product marketing. But they're many times more expensive, and many times more likely to fail in their objectives, than properly edited, properly targeted newsletters.

Another avenue the product marketer has to trod is selling to the retailers. The next exhibit in figure 8-6 exemplifies a possible problem-solving approach you can use if you're vying for product placement in a retail outlet.

This is a "pure" newsletter whose ostensible purpose is to help the retailer with promotional ideas.

The typical retailer will keep the "An Idea A Day" page for the whole month. Beyond keeping it, the retailer will occasionally use it. If the retailer uses it successfully—and that depends on the validity of your suggestions—he'll be grateful.

On we go: If he's grateful, he "owes" you. If he owes you, he's more likely to do business with you. *That's* the triple-key to newsletter success:

> 1. Select topics of interest and value to your best reader-targets.
> 2. Write with authority, knowledge, and clarity.
> 3. Be sure you're the logical source of projected benefits.

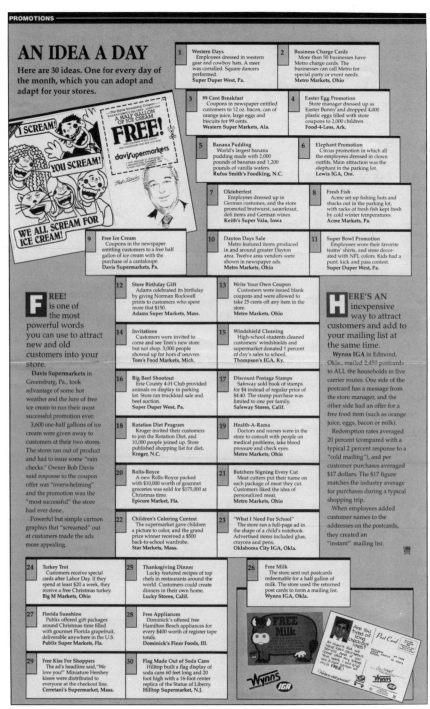

Figure 8-6

Marketing Intangible Services with Newsletters

The biggest problem in marketing intangible services is that those "consuming" these services don't realize what they're getting...until something goes wrong.

You can see why this would be a problem if your customer doesn't recognize the value of what you're giving him or her until a problem arises: You're automatically connected with a bad experience. The paradox: Consumers of services often don't know what they're getting until they don't have it any more. And in that consumer's mind it's your fault, making you the unhappy target for your competition's counter-promotions, moving in on your customers and swaying prospects from thinking of you as the logical, positive source.

Another problem is the consumer doesn't often think of the intricacies or varieties or options available within a number of services such as health care, banking services, telephone service, or energy. They don't think of these in terms of "repeat services."

Many consumers enlist a service and don't think about it again. Their eyes aren't open for "expanded services" types of advertising messages.

So how do you combat these negative forces?

The answer is easy but deceptive: interactive communication with your customers and prospects. But the road can get murky.

Here are some examples of how intangible service companies attempt to combat apathy and a take-it-for-granted attitude by effective newsletter use. Let's look at a couple shown in figures 8-7 through 8-12.

This company sells computerized mailing system services for direct marketers; the newsletter's purpose is to provide "Breakthroughs, ideas and strategies for direct marketers."

Ugh. First of all, that statement of intent is false. The purpose is obvious from the first word of text, the company's name. The text blatantly promotes its sponsor. The flagrant "puff" about the company on the first page is a turnoff to those who may have believed the overline.

Remember, for heaven's sake: If you decide to write a newsletter, don't make it a company brochure. This issue of the company's newsletter could benefit from articles of interest in direct marketing.

Now, another alternative:

Instead of "Breakthroughs, ideas and strategies for direct marketers," why not openly make your promotional point:

"Breakthroughs, ideas and strategies available at CMS, for direct marketers." The reader's attitude is on course from the first word.

BREAKTHROUGHS, IDEAS AND STRATEGIES FOR DIRECT MARKETERS FROM   CMS

The Listener

A Quarterly Newsletter from Computerized Mailing Systems • Volume V • June 1992
300 2nd Street NW Saint Paul, MN 55112-3242 • (612) 636-6265

GIVING BACK TO THE COMMUNITY

CMS employees have traditionally contributed their time and talents to a wide variety of charitable organizations in the New Brighton community. And to celebrate our 10th anniversary as a community leader, CMS will help to build the community the same way it's built its business— through dedication and hard work.

This summer, CMS employees will sweat it out with other volunteers for Twin Cities Habitat for Humanity (TCHFH), a non-profit organization that uses donated labor and supplies to build homes for disadvantaged families. Since its founding in 1986, TCHFH has built houses for 47 families in the Twin Cities metro area.

CMS employees volunteer their time for disadvantaged families.

HOW'S YOUR CATALOG MAILING? LET CMS TAKE YOUR PULSE!

CMS is taking the pulse of catalogers all over the country with *PulseCheck*— a free start-to-finish analysis of list processing methods that helps catalogers discover new cost-saving techniques. CMS brings you a fresh perspective on mailing and distribution, from the big picture to the smallest details.

Are you looking for ways to mail smarter? Why not invest a few minutes and receive expert advice from a 10-year list-processing veteran? For a free *PulseCheck*, fax a copy of your most recent list processing instructions to CMS at (612) 636-0879, or call Joe or Jami at (612) 636-6265.

PulseChecks find money-saving techniques for catalog mailers.

ADDRESS STANDARDIZATION: WHAT IS IT AND WHY?

In keeping with the U.S. Postal Service's plans to be fully automated by 1995, addressing guidelines (also known as "address standards") are complete and ready for mailers to implement. Below is an example of what address standardization does to an address:

Before:
Dave Manderfield
300 Second Street
Suite 100
New Brighton, Minn 55112

After:
DAVE MANDERFIELD
300 2ND ST NW STE 100
SAINT PAUL MN 55112

In simple terms, address standardization does three things:

* Inventories address elements and makes sure the address is complete
* Standardizes abbreviations of address elements
* Assembles mailing information in the proper order.

These guidelines can help you enhance your mailing efficiency and increase the deliverability of your mail, in addition to improving matching processes and the accuracy of barcoding.

Address standardization increases the deliverability of mail.

ATTENTION BUSINESS MAILERS!

Because of the number of elements in business addresses, business-to-business mailers face unique challenges during the merge/purge process. One business-to-business mailer recently asked CMS for help in overcoming two new challenges:

'Vary the number of books mailed by company size. This allows limits on the number of books mailed to an address according to the proportion of employees the mailer wants to target. The result: proportionate market penetration.

'Vary the number of books mailed by file type. This particular cataloger wanted to mail all unique *customer* names within a business while limiting the number of unique *rental* names within a business.

CMS custom-designed creative solutions to meet both these requests at no additional cost to the client—just another example of CMS's continuing commitment to innovation.

CMS welcomes challenge from business mailer.

IT'S NOT JUST INKJET ANYMORE...IT'S PERSONAL!

You already know that the proper use of catalog personalization can increase your response rates. Historically, the inkjetting process has not been sophisticated enough to personalize much beyond name, address and simple messaging. Additionally, most personalization has been limited to targeting *groups* within markets—not the *individual*.

Not anymore. You now have the ability to personalize to an individual level, enhancing your response rate even more. For instance, imagine having the ability to inkjet a picture of the last product your customer purchased as a reminder to re-order. With CMS's new custom inkjet graphic service, the limits of personalization stretch as far as the limits of your imagination. Other ways to personalize your catalogs include inkjetting:

* Maps directing recipients to retail stores
* Product cuts to promote special offers
* Graphic designs, including pictures and logos
* Custom fonts, such as handwritten fonts and signatures

CMS has developed formatting capabilities to support the Elmjet printer (SR50 inkjet device), allowing you to scan graphics, touch them up and convert them to an Elmjet-readable format for inkjet imaging.

Because inkjet imaging involves graphic design, CMS has also developed a proofing system for Elmjet formatting processes, to make sure your catalogs get the high-impact personalization you want. Call CMS today at (612) 636-6265 for a free test of customized inkjet formatting.

Looking for an attention-getter to increase response?

CMS Certifies With Publisher's Express

Because of the rapid increase in USPS rates, CMS recognizes the need to support mailers who want to use alternative delivery services. Publisher's Express is one such company, delivering magazines, catalogs and advertising mail to individual households at a cost less than USPS rates.

Like the USPS, Publisher's Express has its own mail preparation rules that mailers must follow to participate in the delivery program. CMS is now certified under these rules to prepare mailing lists for delivery by Publisher's Express.

Call CMS if you would like to explore the postal savings opportunities through Publisher's Express.

CMS supports alternate delivery.

It's 10:30 A.M...Do You Know Where Your Mail Tapes Are?

You're the circulation manager for a large cataloger, and you've just ordered your rental tapes from your broker. Your job is done, right?

Wrong. One of the many challenges catalogers face is tape management —making certain that all your rental files and house files get to your service bureau on time, properly labeled and with the correct quantities. CMS has a staff person dedicated to helping you manage this process.

CMS Tape Manager Kathy Bruzer's job is to keep you constantly aware of the disposition of your incoming and outgoing tapes. Kathy's team makes sure CMS has received what you've ordered, when you wanted it. For some clients, we act as the liaison between the circulation manager and the brokers for updates. CMS takes care of these critical details, so you can concentrate on the "bigger picture."

CMS provides database processing and maintenance services to large volume direct mailers nationwide... *When Performance Counts.*

♻ Printed on recycled paper

Figure 8-7. Your psychological weapon is to give your clients, customers, and prospects pertinent and useful information while reinforcing your company or organization.

Design Your Newsletter So It Attracts, Not Distracts the Reader

Callouts should be positioned so they stand out. Callouts in "The Listener" don't call attention to themselves. (In the original, they're printed in lavender.) For that matter they should be written with a single intent: pulling the reader into the article.

Take a look at the center callout on the back page: "Looking for an attention-getter to increase response?" This callout would attract the reader, but too few readers will see it at all. It's near-useless in small italicized type. All these callouts are designed the same way—too neat, too tiny, and floating aimlessly. The other two messages in the callout column of this page aren't even worth writing. Who cares if "CMS welcomes challenge from business mailer"? How would you have written this callout? If you were thinking in terms of a newsletter selling intangibles and building image, you probably would write: "Business mailer overcomes its greatest merge-purge problem."

Response Devices Can Help Guarantee Action

I don't have to tell you one key component missing from this newsletter: a response device. A call to action.

Of course, a call to action exists in almost every "news" item here. But because this newsletter only promotes the company, should they be so confident the reader is going to read their little company tidbits? For that matter, newsletters are skimmed for the interests pertinent to the reader of the publication. Not everyone will be interested in every article. So don't get overconfident and decide you don't have to print a call to action or use a response device, if you want the maximum number of people to respond.

The health care industry has to overcome numerous obstacles to get the attention of its target audience. No one likes to think of being hospitalized.

This newsletter is the perfect way of reinforcing the reliability and credibility of its doctors and hospital services.

At the end of each article (every one of which is informative and pertinent to the readers) is a call to action. Not only does each article include free information, but at the same time the totality adds credibility and stature to all the staff at this particular medical center.

The newsletter doesn't give any room to competitive pounding. Instead it reinforces a bond between the prospective patients or patients for a growing relationship even before someone might call for an appointment or information.

175

VOLUME

2

MARCH 1992

UCLA Medical Center

VitalSigns

A RESOURCE FOR YOUR HEALTH

Colon Cancer *is* Preventable

Michael Zinner, M.D., chairman of the Department of Surgery at UCLA, says that those who are most at risk for colon cancer have an inherited condition known as *familial polyposis* or have suffered for many years from *ulcerative colitis*. People with familial polyposis are twice as likely to develop colon cancer as those without.

"Most colon cancers evolve from 'polyps,' which are like warts in the colon," explains Dr. Zinner. "They are benign when they appear, and may take years to become malignant. Many polyps never do become malignant."

"Colon cancer is preventable," stresses Wilfred M. Weinstein, M.D., director of the Gastroenterology Proce-

dures Unit at UCLA. "Potentially cancerous polyps, known as 'adenomas,' can be identified *and removed* through a procedure known as 'colonoscopy.' If your parents or siblings have had polyps, then beginning at age 40 you should have a colonoscopy performed annually — it can be done on an outpatient basis. Even without a family history, if polyps are found and removed, you should be re-examined every three years."

Symptoms and Treatment

Colon cancer is the third leading cause of cancer death in the United States, after lung and prostate cancer in men, and lung and breast cancer in *Continued on page 5*

What You Should Know About Cancer Screenings

Inside:

There are several simple medical exams you can have, called "screenings," that help catch certain cancers at an early and more treatable stage. The earlier certain cancers are detected, the higher your chances of cure.

Robert Oye, M.D., medical director of UCLA's Internal Medicine Suite, explains that screening tests are methods of identifying disease in individuals before they develop symptoms.

Physician Relationship Vital

"Currently, younger, better educated adults are aware of health screenings more frequently than older people who

are more at risk for cancer," notes Dr. Oye. "Younger women are more likely to undergo mammography than older women, who are at higher risk for breast cancer."

This is why Dr. Oye recommends that health screenings be performed under the guidance of a personal physician. "A doctor should help prioritize which tests are important, taking your age, health, family history and other risk factors into consideration. Studies show that doctors are more apt to give advice on health screenings during regular check-ups. So, it's very important to *Continued on page 3*

Figure 8-8. This health care newsletter educates people about possible health problems and gives expert advice in preventing health problems. The entire newsletter is dedicated to this type of information. Notice the key words: expert advice.

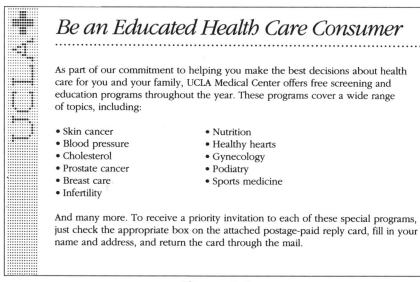

Figure 8-9

In the center of the newsletter is a bound-in response device. This way the center can track the response it gets from the newsletter. The response device helps the issuer keep score—what do prospects want to know about? This helps the medical center target readership more effectively.

Rule: Reader involvement is the natural parent of response.

Figure 8-10 shows a different approach for a health care newsletter which I think is very effective. This newsletter is squarely aimed at senior citizens in the community in which this hospital is located. The newsletter positions itself as an extra benefit for joining the hospital's senior citizen Golden Opportunity membership.

Because the newsletter is part of the membership package, its members are more likely to read it and view it as containing information and advice useful to them. The hospital takes full advantage of this opportunity by giving helpful and useful information in matters pertaining to these seniors, plus using this "in" they've created to get reader-members involved in hospital programs and to suggest that reader-members use their services.

At the end of each article is a call to action. Columns focus on upcoming events such as diabetes screening and exercise classes.

What does this do for the hospital? Obviously, it builds a lasting bond within the senior community and reinforces the credibility and reliability of the hospital. These seniors will grow to trust this hospital and its *proved* expert medical staff.

The main thrust this hospital uses is involvement in hospital activities; at the same time, they use the newsletter as a valuable and impressive

GOLDEN Opportunities™ NEWSLETTER

Good Health News for Seniors — Fall 1989

Everything you need to know about diabetes

More than 11 million people are afflicted with diabetes in the U.S. today.

- An estimated 5 million people have diabetes but do not know it.
- Diabetes-related complications claim 350,000 lives each year.

These statistics are not intended to alarm you, but to alert you to the potential severity of a disease known as diabetes.

Diabetes defined

In a healthy person, the body breaks down complex-carbohydrate foods, such as fruits, vegetables and whole grain products, into glucose. (Glucose,

> *Many diabetes-afflicted individuals can control their disease by maintaining healthy lifestyles.*

a simple form of sugar, is the body's primary source of energy.) As glucose travels through the blood stream, it fuels cells so that your body can perform routine activities. To use glucose as an energy source, the cells need insulin—a hormone normally produced by the pancreas.

Diabetes is a condition resulting from the body's inability to *produce* insulin or its inability to *use* the insulin it does produce. Without insulin, the bloodstream becomes overloaded with sugar, resulting in "high blood sugar."

Two types of diabetes

There are two types of diabetes: **Type I** (*juvenile-onset or insulin-dependent*) and **Type II** (*adult onset or non-insulin dependent*). **Type I** diabetics (about 10 percent of the diabetes-afflicted population) *do not* produce their own insulin, and therefore, must take regular insulin injections. **Type II** diabetics can produce varying amounts of insulin but can't use it effectively. Generally, Type II diabetics can control their illness by combining a healthy diet and exercise regimen with oral medications.

In either case, untreated diabetes prevents the absorption of blood sugar into the cells. High blood sugar can lead to kidney failure, vision problems, increased susceptibility to infection, circulatory problems, impotence, stroke and heart disease.

Treatments

Whether a diabetic falls into the insulin-dependent or non-insulin-dependent category, the afflicted individual must learn to monitor his or her lifestyle and "balance" blood sugar levels. Insulin, oral medication and exercise lower blood sugar; food, illness or stress elevate it.

Though insulin-dependent diabetes is not preventable, it is usually treatable. These individuals must adhere to daily insulin injections, strict diets and exercise regimens in order to maintain a balance in their blood sugar levels and health.

The good news about non-insulin-dependent diabetes is that the disease is usually both treatable *and* preventable. In most cases, Type II diabetes occurs in overweight people who have a family history of the disease. Excess weight is found to inhibit the cell's ability to utilize insulin.

A lifestyle change, however, may reverse or prevent a person from becoming a Type II diabetic. It is now commonly

Diabetes Screening at Lowell General Hospital

Lowell General Hospital will sponsor a Diabetes Screening on November 9, from 9 a.m. to 4 p.m., at *two* locations:

- **Clark Auditorium at Lowell General Hospital.** Call Maria Cameron at **937-6464** for more information.

- **Prime+Med Walk-In Center** on Rogers Street (Rt. 38) in Lowell. Call Mary Jane Caron at **937-9333** for more information.

The cost is **$2** for *Golden Opportunities* members and **$3** for the general public. **No appointment is necessary and no fasting is required.**

believed that weight loss makes the cells more responsive to insulin. Likewise, exercise not only helps in the weight-reduction process, it enhances the body's ability to use insulin more effectively and efficiently.

Take the time to learn

Many diabetes-afflicted individuals can control their disease by maintaining healthy lifestyles. This is why it's so important for diabetics, as well as family and friends of diabetics, to understand the disease. If you have any questions regarding diabetes, or would like to schedule a physical exam, contact the **LGH Physician Referral Service** at **937-6111**.

Lowell General Hospital **LGH**

GOLDEN Opportunities

Two important reasons why you should join Senior Stretch & Tone

Finally! An exercise class designed with *you* in mind. Senior Stretch & Tone is just one of the many benefits you can enjoy as a LGH *Golden Opportunities* member. We encourage you to take advantage of Senior Stretch & Tone so you can:

1. **stay physically fit.** Senior Stretch & Tone is a professionally orchestrated stretching and strengthening class designed to keep you feeling and looking great. Led by experienced and certified instructors, this hour-long class will teach you a variety of effective exercise techniques. Learn how you can stay in shape indoors this winter by using a chair for support! Regular attendance to Senior Stretch & Tone will help you:

- reduce your risk of heart disease;
- improve your respiration;
- attain or maintain your desired weight;
- improve your flexibility and coordination; and
- reduce anxiety and stress.

2. **meet fun and active people!** It's no secret that we have a fun group attending Senior Stretch & Tone. Bring a friend and enjoy the camaraderie of our exercise class. Both men and women are welcome.

Correction

An incorrect phone number appeared in the last issue of *Golden Opportunities* for the **Cancer Information Service (CIS) of Northern New England**. The correct number is **1-800-4-CANCER**. When you call, you'll be automatically connected to the CIS office in Boston at the Dana-Farber Cancer Institute. We apologize for any inconvenience this may have caused.

Senior Stretch & Tone is much more than a stretching and strengthening exercise class ... it's fun!

For more information ...

... call Maria Cameron, Health Education & Wellness Coordinator, at **937-6464**. Classes are held every Tuesday and Thursday, 9:30 a.m.- 10:30 a.m. in Clark Auditorium. The cost for *Golden Opportunity* members is $2.50 ($3 for nonmembers). We look forward to seeing you there!

Figure 8-10

medium to create the need for health care maintenance and to reinforce within the reader's mind the institution's ability to help the reader do just that.

A Case of Mistaken Identity?

Figure 8-11 shows us an obviously syndicated newsletter for insurance agencies. But take a look at the personalization. I'm confused. The newsletter states that it's from a financial services organization. I'd go to an insurance agent if I were thinking about retirement insurance, or long-term care insurance. (The person at whom they're aiming this newsletter is obviously retired.)

But the relationship between insurance and financial services isn't an obvious one. If, in fact, the local user of this syndicated newsletter *is* in the insurance business (and we have to assume he is, because the newsletter is issued by New York Life agents), to the unknowing recipient his company name is a misnomer.

The mismatch becomes even more confusing when, throughout the newsletter, text refers to a major insurance company. So what *is* the relationship with the guy whose name is on the newsletter?

Which is why I'll repeat an obvious point that isn't so obvious to every potential sponsor of a newsletter:

> If you're going to print a newsletter—especially a syndicated newsletter—don't waste your money by glorifying activities, services, and products in which you aren't involved but a semi-competitor might be.

Let's take a look at the contents of this newsletter's articles:

"Long-Term Care Insurance: What You Need To Know," contains valuable and specific information for retired people.

The next article, "Social Security and Medicare Changes in 1991," too contains a wealth of helpful and useful information for retirees.

The sidebar, "1990 Tax Changes Hit The Life Insurance Industry," tells clients and prospects why and how these tax changes affect them. It's a good article explaining why this particular national insurance agency wants its clients to know why they may have to endure an insurance rate hike. To the person who can't relate a "financial services" company to raw insurance, here's that confusion again, because the sidebar editorially mentions the major national insurance carrier who issues this newsletter.

The last page:

"Services To Help You"

What's wrong with this page?

Ostensibly, nothing much. It mentions beneficial services people can

David L. Levington, CLU, ChFC
Levington Financial Services
40 William Street, Suite 220
Wellesley Hills, MA 02181
(617) 237-2611 or (800) 427-2611

NUMBER 5   **with the company you keep**

Long-Term Care Insurance: What You Need to Know

BY DOUGLAS DAVIN

This year, over 2.3 million people will be living in a nursing home. Over the next 30 years, that figure is expected to double. Nursing home costs are also increasing at a dramatic rate. Currently, according to the Brookings Institution, a year in a nursing home costs $25,000 or more on average. By the year 2018 it will cost about $55,000. Who will pay the bill?

Such statistics go a long way to explaining the growing popularity of long-term care insurance. Since they were introduced on a widespread basis during the last decade, long-term care insurance policies have become among the most talked-about policies both within and outside the insurance industry. Designed to provide funds to cover nursing home costs, long-term care policies come in a variety of forms and are now available from over 118 companies. According to the Health Insurance Association of America (HIAA), over 1.5 million policies have been sold by these companies through 1989.

But as the number of policies sold increases so do consumers' questions. Among them:Who needs it? What does it cover? What is a good policy? And what are my rights as a consumer?

Who needs it?

To understand who may need long-term care coverage it is necessary to understand a few basic changes taking place in American society. First and foremost, according to the U.S. Census Bureau, America's Baby Boomers are aging. In 1990, there were 32 million people age 65 and older. By 2030, this figure will double to 64.6 million. Coupled with that is the fact that people are living longer today than ever before. Life expectancy is now pushing upward of 75; and by 2040 there may

Comparing Long-term Care Policies

Features	Recommended by Consumer Reports 5/88	New York Life Policy
Daily nursing home benefit	$80.00	$50-$200
Waiting period	20 days	20, 60, 90 days
Maximum benefit period for one stay	4 years	2, 5 years or unlimited
Maximum benefit period for all stays	unlimited	2, 5 years or unlimited
Does it pay full benefits in		
Skilled-nursing facility?	yes	yes
Intermediate facility?	yes	yes
Custodial facility?	yes	yes
If it has a prior-hospitalization rule does the coverage begin within 30 days after a hospital stay of at least 3 days?	yes	no stay required
Does it pay home-care benefits?	yes	yes (optional)
Does it pay these without requiring nursing home care, or a hospital stay?	yes	yes (if elected)
Does it have a waiver of premium?	yes	yes
Is it guaranteed renewable for life?	yes	yes
Is Alzheimer's disease covered by specific policy language?	yes	yes
Does the premium stay level?	yes	yes
What is Best's rating of the company?	A or A+	A+15

be more people over age 85 than there are over 65 today.

Not only are we getting older, but over the next 50 years working age population will increase by only two to 18 percent, while the elderly population is expected to increase anywhere from 139 to 165 percent. Traditionally, children were expected to care for their parents during old age. However, the increase in dual career families and family mobility have made finding alternate means of long-term care a necessity for many.

What does long-term care insurance cover?

Long-term care policies usually pay for skilled, intermediate or custodial care in a nursing home. They can also cover in-home care costs.

Generally, skilled care refers to round-the-clock treatment by a registered nurse under a doctor's supervision. Intermediate care refers to occasional nursing and rehabilitative care under the supervision of skilled medical personnel. Custodial care primarily meets personal

care needs in activities of daily living such as help in eating or bathing.

How LTC policies work

According to HIAA, almost all policies are indemnity policies meaning they pay a set amount, usually a fixed dollar amount per day. Others reimburse policyowners for expenses incurred. Few, if any, policies, however, provide full coverage for all expenses. Long-term care policy premiums range from $250 to $2,500, depending on age, elimination or deductible periods and the duration of benefits (e.g., a policy that pays $100 a day for five years will cost more than a policy that pays $50 a day for three years.)

How to pay for it

Who will support this population and help pay its inevitable medical bills? The writing is on the wall. "The aging of the Baby Boom generation combined with rapidly falling mortality rates for the aged inevitably will lead to sharply increased demand for long-term care that will require substantially greater

NEW YORK LIFE

Figure 8-11

public and private spending," write Alice M. Rivlin and Joshua M. Weiner in *Caring for the Disabled Elderly*, a new book published recently by the Brookings Institution.

But when it comes time to pay the bill, no federal programs—Social Security, Medicare, or Medicaid will be able to provide the funds necessary. Neither Medicare, nor private Medicare supplemental insurance will pay for most long-term care expenses.

Social Security is not the answer either. Social Security is not a savings account that builds up over time. It is a pay as you go system, paid for through payroll taxes on present employees to support former workers. Today, according to the Social Security Administration, each retired Social Security beneficiary is supported by the payroll taxes of 3.3 workers. By 2020 the ratio will have declined to 1:1.9. According to the Social Security system, payroll taxes would have to increase by almost 60 percent in order for the system to remain solvent and provide the same level of benefits.

Medicaid, on the other hand, is a major payor of nursing home care. Providing 42 percent of all payments

to those facilities, it is meant to help with expenses for the aged, blind and disabled poor. Many people who enter a nursing home and pay for it out of their own pocket then turn to Medicaid after their resources have been depleted.

Recent changes to Medicaid allow your spouse to keep only $786 a month and $12,000 (actual figures vary from state to state) in assets if you should become Medicaid-eligible for nursing home care. Long-term care insurance will help people avoid having to rely on Medicaid and spend down to poverty level.

Just what does a good policy include?

In May 1988, *Consumer Reports* published a study on long-term care policies. As the chart on page 1 indicates, *Consumer Reports* recommended policies that provided a minimum $80 daily benefit, a waiting period of only 20 days; paid full benefits for all levels of nursing home care facilities; was guaranteed renewable for life; specifically covered Alzheimer's disease. When it first appeared on the market, New York Life's policy was one of the first to meet all of *Consumers Reports'* requirements.

Consumers' rights

Recently the National Association of Insurance Commissioners (NAIC) has adopted a model act of consumers' rights which has been adopted in some form or another by approximately 40 states. A basic outline of the protections follows:

They prohibit: pre-existing condition exclusion periods of longer than six months; cancellation of a policy due to the age or diminishing health status of the insured; exclusion of the coverage for Alzheimer's disease; prior hospitalization requirements; and the practice of conditioning eligibility for nursing home benefits on receipt of a higher level of institutional care. The regulations also prescribe minimum standards for home health care benefits and inflation protection. A complete version of the model act and a buyer's guide can be ordered through the NAIC.

When considering long-term care, read the policies carefully and compare them. Ask for a disclosure form outlining the policy's features. Ask your agent if you have any questions.

Is long-term care right for you? Only you can decide, but with the help of an agent, you will be able to make an educated decision. ∎

1990 TAX CHANGES HIT THE LIFE INSURANCE INDUSTRY
BY GERALD KAPLAN

On November 5, 1990, President Bush signed the Omnibus Budget Reconciliation Act into law. This Act will reduce the federal government's budget deficit by almost $500 million over the next five years. One important provision in the Act will increase the life insurance industry's taxes by about $8 billion over the same period. This is an extraordinary 50% increase in the life insurance industry's taxes. This was by far the largest increase levied on any one industry in the Act, according to *The Wall Street Journal*.

The magnitude of this tax increase can be better understood in terms of effective tax rates. Under the new law, the life insurance industry's effective tax rate soars to almost 40 percent, significantly higher than the effective tax rates of competing financial businesses. Tax Analysts, an independent Washington-based publisher of tax materials and statistics, reported that under the previous law, the life insurance industry's effective tax rate was about 24 percent. This was about the same effective tax rate as applied to all corporations and was already higher than the effective tax rates of other financial corporations.

The new law increases taxes on life insurers by no longer permitting them to deduct their full costs in the year in which these costs occur. Under the new law, a portion of these expenses can be deducted only over 10 years. The law applies to all policies, new as well as existing. New York Life Insurance Company and its life insurance subsidiaries will pay about $480 million in additional income taxes under the Act during the five years following its effective date, September 30, 1990.

Although the Omnibus Budget Reconciliation Act substantially raises the taxes that life insurance companies will pay, Congress unfortunately did not make any offsetting changes in the amount of tax individuals pay on insurance products.

Because increases in our taxes of this magnitude are necessarily reflected in the pricing of our products, it is important to us to keep you informed. New York Life actively cooperates in industry efforts to protect your interests and to inform Congress about the importance of insurance and the need to maintain long-standing principles of insurance taxation.

Figure 8-11 (cont.)

Social Security and Medicare Changes in 1991

BY BRUCE SCHOBEL, FSA, CLU

The Social Security and Medicare programs change every year in certain ways. Some changes occur automatically, reflecting increases in the cost of living and in average wages. Other changes result from legislation, like the deficit-reduction law that was enacted in November 1990.

Because the programs affect 95 percent of American workers and their 40 million beneficiaries, we thought the following update of changes occuring in 1991 would be useful.

The best-known Social Security change is the annual cost-of-living adjustment, which technically was effective in December of last year, but first appeared in benefit checks received on January 3, 1991. This latest increase, 5.4 percent, is the largest since 1982. It is based on changes in the Consumer Price Index (CPI) from the third quarter of 1989 through the third quarter of 1990.

Because of the cost-of-living adjustment, a worker with maximum FICA-taxable earnings in every year who retired at age 65 at the beginning of 1990 saw his or her monthly benefit rise from $975 to $1,027. Workers who retired years ago or worked beyond age 65 can receive even larger amounts. The average monthly benefit for all retired workers is now $602.

While the FICA tax rate in 1991 remains at the 1990 rate of 7.65 percent, the amount of earnings subject to the tax increased for two reasons. First, the annual automatic adjustment raised the taxable earnings base from $51,300 in 1990 to $53,400 in 1991. This change is based on the increase in the national average wage from 1988 to 1989. Second, the deficit-reduction legislation enacted in November 1990 raised the amount subject to the 1.45 percent Medicare portion of the FICA tax to $125,000.

Thus, workers with high earnings this year will pay FICA taxes of 7.65 percent on the first $53,400 and 1.45 percent on the next $71,600, for a total of $5,123.30. These taxes are matched dollar-for-dollar by the employer. Self-employed people pay the combined employee-employer rate, but they can deduct half the tax as a business expense.

The amount that Social Security recipients can earn without losing benefits also rises automatically each year. Beneficiaries under age 65 in 1991 can earn $7,080 without any reduction; after that, they lose $1 in benefits for every $2 in earnings. Beneficiaries at ages 65–69 can earn $9,720, above which they lose $1 for every $3 in earnings. Beneficiaries at ages 70 and older are not subject to this retirement earnings test. Special rules apply for disabled people.

Medicare beneficiaries saw several important changes in 1991. First, the inpatient deductible that must be paid on first entering a hospital is now $628, up from $592 in 1990. After 60 days in the hospital, the patient must now pay $157 per day for the next 30 days. After 90 days, the patient can use up to 60 "lifetime reserve" days, paying $314 for each day used. The coinsurance for patients in skilled nursing facilities is now $78.50 per day, for the 21st through the 100th day.

No Medicare benefits are available after 150 days in a hospital or 100 days in a skilled nursing facility during a "benefit period." A new benefit period begins 60 days after discharge from a hospital or skilled nursing facility. A beneficiary who is readmitted to a hospital within 60 days after discharge from a hospital or skilled nursing facility does not pay a second inpatient deductible.

The monthly premium for Medicare Part B which helps to pay doctors' bills and other outpatient charges has been set by the new budget law for each year 1991–95. The premium for 1991 is $29.90 per month, up from $28.60 in 1990. The premium will rise to $46.10 per month in 1995. The Part B premium is ordinarily deducted from Social Security checks.

The annual deductible under Part B does not rise automatically, but it was increased by the new law from $75, the amount in effect since 1982, to $100 in 1991. No further increases are currently scheduled in the law.

The new law includes another change that is related to Social Security. The 1986 Tax Reform Act required taxpayers to show Social Security numbers on their tax returns for dependents age five or older. Legislation in 1988 lowered that age to two. The 1990 law lowers the age further, to one, effective with 1991 tax returns. To help taxpayers comply with the law, the Social Security Administration allows parents to apply for Social Security numbers for their newborn children at the same time they provide birth-certificate information at the hospital. The information is forwarded to SSA, which issues the Social Security numbers. No separate applications are needed. ■

Changes in Social Security and Medicare

Social Security

- Monthly Benefit: $975 / $1,027
- Earnings Base: $51,300 / $53,400
- Current Allowable Earnings: $7,080 (Under 65) / $9,720 (65–69)

1990 / 1991

Medicare

- Inpatient Deductible: $592 / $628
- Monthly Premium: $28.60 / $29.90
- Annual Deductible: $75 / $100

Figure 8-11 (cont.)

Figure 8-11 (cont.)

get directly from this major national life insurance company. It gives them the address of each service.

But wait! This newsletter supposedly is from someone in the retiree's own community. Are these references going to help this person who actually sent the newsletter?

Remember the triple-key to newsletter success?

> *1. Select topics of interest and value to your best reader-targets.*
> *2. Write with authority, knowledge, and clarity.*
> *3. Be sure you're the logical source of projected benefits.*

This one does quite well with the first two keys. But the supposed "issuer" is left out of the mix. We don't even have a letter or note from this person. (The newsletter is a self-mailer, with the return address of the major national insurance agency.)

Sorry mister, but you got gypped. Syndicated newsletters should be edited to benefit the actual sender. The response device should carry *your* name and address.

Member FDIC • Fall 1989

The SOVEREIGN Club

Introducing the Sovereign Club:
For those enjoying independent and active lifestyles

The Sovereign Club — the name conjures images of an exclusive organization. Its membership would, of course, hold a special rank, be of great size and seniority, and enjoy strong financial status. More important, the name implies a group of individuals leading healthy, independent lifestyles. That group is you.

The Sovereign Club should come as no surprise because it reflects a change in our former Retire-Amatic Checking Account. The central difference is a new name and several added benefits. We realize that you have been an important customer and believe you deserve greater recognition. After considering several ideas and giving much thought to the characteristics of your group, we chose *The Sovereign Club* — a club organized specifically for our **independent and active** customers who are 55 and better.

See Insert For Special CD Offer

You deserve the good life
As a former member of the Retire-Amatic Program, you enjoyed a special banking package. You'll be happy to know that with The Sovereign Club, you'll still enjoy the same package of free services and discounts — all designed to help you stretch your savings and income. As a member of The Sovereign Club, you'll still enjoy free checking with:

❑ no monthly service charge,
❑ no minimum balance,
❑ unlimited checkwriting privileges, and
❑ free checks.

In addition, you'll continue to enjoy:
❑ free Travelers' Checks,
❑ free Cashier's Checks,
❑ free Money Orders,
❑ free notary service,
❑ check-cashing privileges at over 150 First Security branches, and
❑ an identification card embossed with The Sovereign Club logo and your name — identifying you as a valuable customer of First Security.

In addition to the excellent value and convenience of The Sovereign Club, you'll also enjoy:

✔ **Direct Deposit/Automatic Savings Option:** You'll enjoy the option of having all your government or payroll checks conveniently and safely deposited directly into your checking account. This means no more waiting in lines to make deposits and, if you're on vacation, you'll know that your checks have been safely deposited into your account in your absence. Plus, with direct deposit, there's no need to worry about checks being lost or stolen. And, if you prefer to transfer funds from your checking to savings account, we can easily do so.

✔ **Financial newsletter:** You'll receive this informative newsletter, *The Sovereign Club*, quarterly with your checking account statement. Each issue will highlight money manage-

(Continued on page two)

First Security Bank

673 12394 45
James C. Morrison

As a member of Sovereign Club, you'll enjoy additional benefits such as this informative newsletter and periodic special offers. Present your Sovereign Club identification card at your local branch, and you'll be eligible for this quarter's special offer (see insert).

Figure 8-12

184

Secure your long-term goals with a CD investment

A CD investment allows you to earn high interest rates and retain yearly liquidity.

We live in a highly complex society. Everything talks to us today — from the cars we drive to the microwave ovens we use. Everything is computerized. Even the simple things in life, like saving for your later years, have become highly sophisticated.

There is one investment today that is still simple to use, yet provides the old-fashioned opportunity to earn secure, high yields — the Certificate of Deposit (CD). CDs are simple investments which allow you to invest your funds (from a minimum of $500 to a maximum of $100,000) in an interest-bearing account for a specified time period. This period may range from two months to five years. Upon maturity, you reap the competitive returns of your investment, which have accrued and compounded over the life of the CD.

CDs are flexible and convenient

With a CD, you are guaranteed a competitive rate of return for the term you choose. You also enjoy the security of knowing you'll have funds invested should an emergency arise, or should you need additional money to fund a specific goal or project.

For example, if one of your loved ones will be starting college within the next five years, you can invest funds in a 5-year CD which matures at the time of his or her high school graduation. Or, perhaps you and your spouse are planning to escape the cold for a vacation in Florida this winter. You can invest in a 3-month CD and collect your earnings prior to departure.

Regardless of your needs, you can match the maturity dates of your various CD deposits with those of your savings objectives.

Stagger your CD investments

One of the key ways to maximize CD investments is to develop a strategy allowing you to earn the high rates of long-term deposits while still enjoying the liquidity of short-term CDs. This is accomplished by "laddering" your CD investments.

For example, if you have $3,000, you can invest $1,000 in three separate accounts, a one-, a two- and a three-year CD. When the one-year CD matures, you reinvest the funds in a three-year CD. You continue this strategy with each CD. This allows you to earn high interest rates and still have funds available to withdraw every year without penalty.

Invest today

CDs are one of the safest, high-yield investments available. They can provide healthy earnings and financial security. For more information on how you can open a CD account, stop by or call your local First Security branch.

Sovereign Club ...
... from page one

ment tips, investment and tax information and estate planning news you can use.

The Sovereign Club also gives you an in-depth look at First Security's financial services — those we've offered for years and new services we're currently developing for *your* banking convenience.

✔ **Special Offers:** As an added bonus, we'll be offering you periodically, special investment opportunities, free gifts and other giveaways

— all because of your honored membership in The Sovereign Club. (See the insert for this quarter's special offer.)

Take advantage of your status

You've worked long and hard to establish your independent lifestyle — so take advantage of the special privileges that come with it. As a member of The Sovereign Club, you'll enjoy the benefits described and much more. For more information, stop by your First Security branch. And be sure to tell your friends and relatives about us.

Figure 8-12 (cont.)

Special CD offer with a one-time, no-penalty withdrawal

For a limited time only, First Security Bank is offering Sovereign Club members a special Certificate of Deposit (CD) — maturing anytime from two months to five years — with a one-time, no-penalty withdrawal.

The minimum deposit is $500. The maximum is $100,000. All we ask is that you leave your money deposited for at least seven days. On the eighth day or prior to maturity, if you wish to cancel your agreement or have a sudden financial need, we'll allow you a one-time, no-penalty withdrawal of any portion of your funds and any accrued interest — without penalty.

To take advantage of this special fixed-rate CD offer, present your Sovereign Club identification card to your local First Security banker. You'll automatically qualify. This offer is good through December 31, 1989. Sign up *now*.

Currently Giving 110%.
Member F.D.I.C.

Figure 8-12 (cont.)

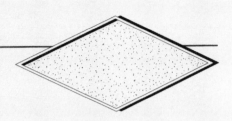

Annuities:

A tax-deferred supplement to your retirement savings

Planning for your future can be likened to a game of chess. The secret is knowing what's ahead and planning your strategy accordingly. Initially, your "game plan" should incorporate a savings strategy which maximizes your returns while minimizing the impact of taxes.

A tax-deferred investment can allow you to shelter your earnings until you begin receiving payments later. You'll benefit from delayed taxes while reaping the rewards of annual interest compounding on your principal.

Consider a **tax-deferred annuity** as a supplement to your other retirement savings. You'll not only provide for future income needs but also enjoy the tax benefits.

What is a tax-deferred annuity?

A tax-deferred annuity is an interest-earning account issued by an insurance company. (A tax-deferred annuity is available through First Security Bank.) You invest your funds in either a lump sum or installments. In turn, the insurance company invests your funds for growth, while they accumulate tax deferred. The minimum deposit required may be as low as $100. Unlike an IRA, which has a $2,000 contribution limit, you can invest as much or as little as you wish in an annuity.

An annuity lets *you* be in control. Upon your retirement or at a predetermined date that you establish, you begin receiving annuity distri-

butions through a variety of payout options. You can receive your distributions in either one lump sum or monthly, quarterly, semi-annual or annual income payments.

And, although an annuity is viewed as a long-term investment, you may withdraw up to 10% of your total account balance *once* each year without penalty.

Your "game plan" for the future should focus on having adequate savings in your later years. Consider a tax-deferred annuity as a supplement to your other investment savings.

A safe investment

The funds you invest in an annuity are safe both from an investment and legal perspective. As an investment, your funds accrue to their maximum potential and earn a competitive rate of return.

From the legal standpoint, your annuity investment is backed by the as-

sets of a major insurance company, which has received high performance ratings from A.M. Best, the foremost independent analyst of insurance companies. The insurance company must maintain adequate resources to guarantee the safety of your investment.

In addition, if after 10 days you are not satisfied with your overall annuity plan, you may withdraw from the plan and receive a full refund of your initial contribution.

Long-term tax benefits

With a tax-deferred annuity, your earnings are sheltered from all state and federal income taxes until you begin receiving payments. As a result, you benefit from the annual compounding of interest on your principal. Although you eventually pay taxes, you pay only on the portion of distributions coming from your accrued interest.

You deserve a secure retirement

You've worked hard your entire life to ensure a comfortable retirement. Make these years that much more secure by investing in a tax-deferred annuity. You'll not only reap the benefits of a secure investment, but you'll also enjoy substantial tax savings as well.

The advantages of tax deferral with an annuity investment are available to anyone up to age 85 with no charges or fees. For more information, call or visit your local First Security Branch. In Utah, call **1-800-548-7259**. In Idaho, call **1-800-433-8515**.

Figure 8-12 (cont.)

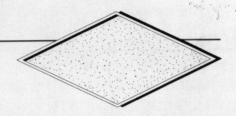

Don't let cold weather hamper your daily exercise and health habits

Winter. A relief from the broiling sun, it brings to mind peaceful snowfalls, festive holidays and family gatherings. The wintry season also brings those traditional holiday feasts — and excess calories — followed by a New Year's resolution to diet and exercise.

Too often, people use winter weather as an excuse to hibernate from daily exercise. Although chilling winds and banks of snow may hamper your usual morning walk, you can still maintain a daily workout even if you're indoors. The following home and outdoor exercise tips will help you maintain your health and spirits through the long cold winter.

Go for a brisk walk

Walking is a gentle sport that builds muscles and helps boost your cardiovascular rate, whether you decide to trek through the nearest mall or the snow in your neighborhood.

Although mall walking provides an escape from harsh weather, you may

Exercising indoors, on a stationary bicycle, is an ideal way to stay in shape during the long and cold winter season.

opt for a more tranquil jaunt through the snow. Before venturing outside, keep the following in mind:

● Avoid exposing your skin. Dress warmly to prevent frostbite and hypothermia (low body temperature). Individuals with diabetes and asthma should be extra careful in the cold because of related circulatory problems and pneumonia.

● If you tire when encountering strong winds, slow your pace. Be aware of wind chill factors and avoid venturing outdoors if the wind chill factor is 40 degrees or below.

● As you begin your walk, try to walk directly into the wind. Then, as you head home, you'll have the wind at your back.

● Beware of ice. Try to wear shoes with rubber ridges or those that attach metal cleats. If the ice is unavoidable, walk slowly with your knees slightly bent.

● Warm-up by stretching for five to 10 minutes or jogging in place before you venture outdoors.

Join a spa

Spas are not only great places to exercise, they are ideal for meeting people. Many of the larger spas provide a variety of exercise options, such as indoor swimming, Nautilus, stationary bicycling, free weights and aerobics classes.

Spas also provide trained fitness and nutritional specialists who will coordinate a proper exercise and diet program tailored to your health needs.

Turn your home into a private gym

By installing indoor exercise equipment, you can work out freely in the comfort and warmth of your own home. Some of the latest indoor equipment includes:

● rowing machines,
● stationary bicycles,
● treadmills (for indoor jogging),
● free weights,
● cross-country ski simulators, and
● aerobic videotapes.

For indoor exercise to be beneficial, it should:

● involve the large muscle groups,
● be performed three to four times a week at 20-35 minute intervals, and
● increase the heart rate from 60-75 percent of its maximum capacity.

A word of caution

All of these ideas are great ways to beat the cold and maintain your health. But with any exercise program, keep the following in mind:

● Start out moderately and slowly increase your pace.
● Try to exercise regularly.
● Do adequate warm-ups and stretching before any type of activity.
● If you are ill, take a break. Don't push yourself.
● And most importantly, consult your doctor before attempting any type of exercise program.

This winter don't let the cold weather force your daily exercise habits to fall to your "waist-side." Instead, maintain your already healthy lifestyle by exercising safely and regularly all year round — through rain, sleet and even snow.

Figure 8-12 (cont.)

When You Use Exclusivity As a Prime Motivator Sell Exclusivity

Take a look at this obvious introductory newsletter selling The Sovereign Club in figure 8-12. Although the first line of text says, "The Sovereign Club—the name conjures images of an exclusive organization," the headline is too all-encompassing to reinforce exclusivity. The second page and insert sheet sell CDs.

The last page—which might be a logical article in the pages of a health care newsletter—has nothing to do with the financial institution issuing the newsletter. Why include it? Because this newsletter is geared toward seniors, and seniors are the most health-conscious of all demographic groups, and obviously this bank wants to be "big brother."

The articles except for the back cover are hard, undisguised sales pitches. What's wrong with that? Contrary to what purists might think, only one thing. . .and it isn't the dynamics of the pitch.

Rather, it's overlooking the possibility to project *exclusivity*.

Exclusivity not only justifies membership in the "club"; it glorifies membership in the club.

Should we have criticized the bank for "pitching" the benefits of Sovereign Club membership? Only if we're one of the bank's competitors!

What to Remember When Selling Services and Products

1. You're selling your image.
2. You're selling promises.
3. You're making promises which come to life in your newsletter.
4. You're selling reliability.
5. You're selling expertise.

Give the reader something to believe. Follow-through in *credibility* and *benefit* within the pages of your newsletter is important whether you're selling tangibles or intangibles.

And you can't go wrong if you attach your editorial philosophy to the triple-key to newsletter success:

> *1. Select topics of interest and value to your best reader-targets.*
> *2. Write with authority, knowledge, and clarity.*
> *3. Be sure you're the logical source of projected benefits.*

CHAPTER 9

Achieving Maximum Results with Your Newsletter Program

Today we all have high expectations. We expect instant results, instant gratification...which mirrors our throw-away society.

But can we honestly expect to get high returns, achieve customer retention, and expect intramural and extramural loyalty on the basis of short-term goals?

In newsletter terms: Are your marketing efforts primarily focused on making a fast return, instead of aiming at long-term results?

If so, you're misinterpreting your newsletter program and literally selling it "short." You can't logically compare your newsletter with other advertising media.

Long-Term Viewpoint = Business Continuity Insurance

Your newsletter program is meant to build long-term results; it's your insurance against a future of lost attention—which means lost profits—down the road.

I certainly don't want to imply that even the first issue of your newsletter won't bring a response. But the longer your newsletter program is in effect, the more results you'll reap. Better than that: The longer your newsletter program is in effect, the more powerful each issue becomes in generating results.

What Time Period Should You Give Your Newsletter to Enable It to Take Hold?

The longer you invest in and take an ongoing serious interest in *any* relationship, whether personal or business, the more you cement that relationship. When you're beginning a newsletter program, how much time should you invest?

Blind opinion: I would give it two years. The more often you send the newsletter to your customers, donors, or prospects, the more you'll bond your relationship. (That's provided you and your customers, prospects and donors are reaping benefits from the relationship. And achieving this result is up to you.)

How Can You Tell If You're Making Progress?

As you're developing your relationships within your client base and initiating new relationships it helps to determine what serves or hinders your progress in this direction; what builds response, and with whom.

Before we cover ways and means to maximize response, let's take a look at how you can improve your distribution—which will also enhance response, if distribution is targeted.

Adding Mileage to Your Newsletter Distribution

Have you ever thought about the *variety* of ways you can use your newsletter to your benefit?

192

Of course, we have the standard method of distributing the newsletter, which is through direct mail. But other methods exist for distribution besides using it as a typical direct mail piece. Most of these methods can be used in tandem along with sending your newsletter by mail:

1. Distribute Your Newsletter Throughout Your Own Organization

Your marketing or fund-raising department had better not be encased in a glass bubble.

Before the newsletter gets shipped or circulated, the first step is to distribute it to key officials in your organization—sales people, customer service representatives, and on down the line.

Include a fact sheet for employees describing service and product offers in the newsletter. Let *everyone* know what offers have been included in the newsletter. This will help assure you won't lose sales because one of the key people doesn't know what's in the text. (Of course, it's up to all the key people to read it.)

Just imagine one of your customers or prospects placing a call to your customer service or a sales representative to ask about a specific offer stated in the newsletter. . . and your reps don't know about it! You can't allow even an iota of room for surprises and unprofessional reactions causing external guffaws.

2. The Newsletter as a Direct Mail Piece

Ordinarily all newsletters should be distributed by this method to your donors, prospects, and customers no matter what other methods you incorporate.

Why not try sending your newsletter to these targets: civic organizations, your directors, advisors, the chamber of commerce director, and other government bodies? You never know what piece of information they'll pick up and pass along to key individuals.

3. Display Your Newsletter

Be sure you have plenty of newsletters displayed in the lobby or reception room, for people to pick up and read.

4. Use Your Newsletter for Presentation Aids

Add newsletters to sales kits. Use them in your presentations or pass them out as part of your informational packet.

5. Newsletter Material for Follow-Ups to Inquiries

If someone calls to ask about a certain product, service, or activity send that person one of your newsletter issues which discusses that specific topic.

6. New Membership Packages

If your company or organization has a membership program, send the last few issues of your newsletter along with your ''welcome kit.''

7. Newsletters as Support Pieces

Hand out your newsletter to walk-ins and tours as background pieces.

8. Newsletters for Seminars

Use your newsletter as support pieces for seminars. They don't have to be *your* seminars. Maybe somebody else's seminar which pertains to your business is scheduled for areas in which you operate. Ask if they could use free support-pieces. This will benefit both you and the organization holding the seminars.

You or someone in your company may be a public speaker for certain conferences. Be sure to bring your newsletter for people to take away.

9. Newsletters for the Press

Send your newsletter to trade publications in your field, magazines which carry information for your target audience, and the business or city or feature editor of your newspaper. Include a note giving them permission to reprint the articles.

Turn on your imagination and think of different methods to use for peak performance through widest distribution. But before you can count your winnings, you have to have a means of measuring your results. Where are they coming from and why?

Let's take a look at response devices and how you can track them.

Boost Your Profitability: Identify Your Lead Sources and Test Your Response Devices

The newsletter medium is sometimes hard to track because many producers of sponsor-promoting newsletters may, as I've stated previously, forget why they're creating the newsletter in the first place.

Some may not include proper response devices or coding devices. Your response device isn't an afterthought. In fact, safety lies in thinking of your newsletter as the support piece for your offer as specified on the response device!

Each piece of the "newsletter package" should be coordinated to support the next piece. This means the envelope, response device, inserts, newsletter, and the appeals all support one another. They aren't separate mechanisms thrown together. They all are geared to getting a response.

A newsletter can be used as a one-step or two-step sales process. It's usually used as a two-step sales process. In other words you're more likely to be generating sales leads than trying to actually close a sale in a newsletter.

But this depends on what you're selling. If you're marketing a low ticket item under $30 within the newsletter, you can probably close the sale and ask for the order. Or if you're raising funds you can safely ask for the donation. (Obviously this depends on the amount of money you're asking for. If it's thousands of dollars you'll probably have to woo your targets beyond simply asking for a $5,000 donation in your newsletter's response device.)

Whether you're using a one or two-step process, your response devices need to be strong.

So let's take a quick overview about what to incorporate into the newsletter to boost your revenue and track results.

1. End Your Promotional Articles with a Call to Action

Use your article to entice the readers. Don't give them all the information they could ever ask for inside one article. You want them to ask for more.

At the end of an article ask the readers if they'd like more information about—whatever. Give them an exciting or provocative offer to find out more on the subject—something they may not have thought about before. Give them a phone number and the *specific* name of a real or fictional sales representative or customer service representative. But don't use this name anywhere else in your advertising mediums. This way you'll know where the response is coming from and which issue, so you can later tally the response

2. Include a Business Reply Card or Panel in Your Newsletter

Make that business reply card stand out. Make it reader-friendly. If you can, make it even easier for the reader to respond by including a postage-free business reply card. The only effort the reader has to take is "x" some boxes and drop the card in the mailbox.

Always code your business reply card. Here are a few ideas to use: Add the date of the issue on the outside return address or add a department number to the address.

But remember: If you code your different media advertising or news releases with the same number you won't know where the response came from.

Another tip to remember when you're using a business reply card: If it's not a fold-over don't ask for confidential information. As those who used to ask for credit card numbers on business reply cards learned to their chagrin, this damages response because the information is there for anyone to read. If you're going to ask for confidential information, use an enclosed response device or a fold-over business reply card.

3. If Cost Is a Factor, Use a Reply Flap

The reply flap is usually an extra flap of paper folded over so it won't take up editorial space. Readers can tear it out, fold it up, and mail it.

As effective as a bind-in card or coupon? In my opinion, no. All this effort can discourage readers from responding because they have a lot to do.

4. Consider Action-Coupons

The benefit of coupons is their instant recognizability. Every reader is used to coupons and regards them as non-threatening.

The bonus of coupons is that they're part of the editorial content: You cut down on production costs.

WARNING: The easier the means of response, the more *unqualified* leads you'll get. (*Conclusion*: You may want to test these different response devices to see which one works better. Use the same copy and art work on each so you get true test results.)

5. Use Reply Envelopes Where They Improve Response

Reply envelopes will obviously increase the cost of your mailing. But reply envelopes invariably get bigger response, possibly because the privacy of the reader is protected.

I suggest including a reply envelope for:

- readership surveys;
- closing an order;
- any donation;
- circumstances in which readers have to give confidential information;
- circumstances in which readers send checks, money orders or credit card numbers.

6. Include an Insert Where a Coupon Alone Won't Motivate

Include an insert with coupons for new products and services. The insert emphasizes the coupons as ordinary text never could.

7. Offer Free Subscriptions

Even though your newsletter is free, it has value. This suggests printing an issue price on the cover (apparent value!) and offering a no-cost subscription to your customer or prospect.

8. Use 800 or 900 Numbers for Interactive Communication

Interactive telephone numbers (800 or 900 numbers) can help make your newsletter program interactive. 800 numbers are great for response—they'll increase response by 300 to 500 percent.

The 900 number is just coming into prominence, after a shaky start and an image marred by high-profile sex lines. Now 900 numbers are ideal for two areas that complement newsletters:

First, for non-profits, a 900 number enables a participant to pledge money; unlike conventional pledges, which result in a 60 percent to 70 percent collection rate, a 900 pledge is almost universally good because the charge is against the donor's telephone bill.

Second, for information such as computer maintenance and technical help, a 900 number listed in the newsletter following an item describing a particular matter—can be a profit center as well as a subscriber service.

A Few Tricks to Include in Your Response Devices

1. Use an **URGENT** rubber stamp to provoke excitement.
2. Ask readers to recommend another person who could benefit from a free subscription.
3. Offer free material whenever possible.

How to Cut Your Response Time

Don't leave the readers with an open-ended response time. Doing this invites the reader to put the offer aside and forget about mailing or calling with a reply.

Rule #1: Give the reader a deadline or expiration date to respond.

Rule #2: Offer premiums, bonuses or free information if they respond before a certain date. Any response after that date doesn't qualify to receive the premium or free information offer.

How to Code Your Response Devices

If you only promoted one product or service and if you only promoted them in one medium to only one target, you wouldn't have to code your response devices. But that's not usually the case. Coding the response is the only true method of tracking response properly.

Different methods to code your response devices include:

1. Change the address for different offers. For instance if you have a post office box, change it to a suite number, or "Lock Box" number.

2. Add a department to your return address.

3. Add a name—John Brown, John Jones, Mary Jones.

4. Put a tiny code number in coupons and reply cards to tell you the medium, the issue, and the product. For example, 0101. The zero stands for newsletter, the 10 signifies the month of the offer, and the 1 signifies the product.

5. Telephone response: Give your readers an extension number to use. Or give them another name to ask for when they call.

Readership Surveys

A readership survey can serve as an important tool enabling you to really *listen* (in print, of course) to your customers and prospects.

Find out what your customers and prospects are looking for — in your editorial content, in a certain product, in the amount of information you transmit.

Communication doesn't exist if readers don't read. Ongoing surveys are ammunition for you, giving you direction for future issues.

Qualifying Your Leads

If your list is targeted you should get qualified leads, automatically. But for insurance, ask for specific background information in your response devices.

Qualifying questions include age range, lifestyle, number of employees, and business volume or income information.

WARNING! The more invasive the questions, the lower the response will be. A list of age ranges is less invasive than the question: ''Age?'' ''Household income range'' with multiple-choice entries is less invasive than ''Household income: $.''

Tracking Response

Compile a tracking form to track your codes by promotion code; the medium (phone, mail or walk-in); the advertising medium; the date of the response; and any specifics you want to have about *who* is responding.

Increasing the Lifetime Value of Your Existing Donors or Customers

The comparative expenditure of your marketing dollars-per-response or dollars-per-donor can *decrease* substantially if you cross-sell your products, services or fund-raising appeals, rather than spending your entire budget on cultivating new customers.

An absolute rule: Successfully cultivating long-term relationships increases profit-margins.

By measuring the results of your newsletter and other promotions you can determine the lifetime value of your customers and establish what you should focus on in upcoming issues. Think about this:

A single promotion in your newsletter may not appear to be very effective; but don't be hasty. The cumulative effect on customer retention and building a positive relationship and image within your client base might get you long-term results. Over a period of months or years one dollar might be worth five, ten, or twenty.

Measuring the lifetime value of a customer or donor can help assist you in evaluating and developing an effective more targeted newsletter and overall marketing plan.

How to Calculate Lifetime Value

In order to determine a customer's or donor's value you must first calculate your customer "loss rate" (losses of customers over a certain period of time). The loss rate gives you the "retention rate" (how many customers stay with you over the years).

So as a super-simplistic procedure, to determine your retention rate, just figure the loss rate of your customers and assume the balance. For example, if your loss rate is 25 percent for any given mailing program, your annual retention rate is 75 percent.

A variety of mailing campaigns can generate different retention rates. Usually, you'll notice the number of customers drops off most drastically the first year. If you already have a body of customers you can evaluate the drop off rate from previous mailings to learn your true retention rate, which is best calculated over a longer range than the first year.

The drop-off rate for products or services will be lower than the drop-off rate for one-shot or luxury items. For example, life and home insurance has about an 85 to 95 percent retention rate, consumer bank services 60 to 80 percent. For one-shots, the drop-off rate can be close to 100 percent unless you can keep up a flow of allied offers.

However, constant tracking of the results will tell you exactly how *your* customers perform, helping you cross-sell other services and retain your customers.

How to Expand on the Present Value of Your Customers

By estimating the present value of future profits from each of your customers you will be able to determine what they will be worth to you in the future.

Why is this valuable? Anyone who ever has sought investors can answer that one. Too, you can formulate a much sounder business plan and projection by being able to estimate with at least a moderate degree of confidence in your numbers.

Using Your Data Base

Once you've tracked response, estimated the lifetime value of your customers or donors, and discovered through readership surveys how to tailor your products and services more efficiently, what's left?

Data base—the darling (and often misused) buzzword of the 1990s.

Build your data base with this important information so you can segment and easily target your groups. You'll exchange guesswork for a more foolproof semi-scientific analysis.

What does your data base require? Input.

Your newsletter program will only be as good to you as the data, leads, donations, relationships you collect and act on. Efficient use of database means efficient editing and distribution of your newsletter.

A rule you certainly know already: Follow through on your collected information.

You can collect all the data and all the qualified leads. You can begin building strong relationships inside and outside your existing client base through your newsletter program and other advertising/promotional campaigns. But if there's no follow-through you're going to drown in your own efforts.

How much time should elapse before leads, especially qualified leads are followed up? Answer: No time. Follow them up immediately.

Ask any advertiser who uses "bingo cards" in trade magazines. Two to three months can elapse between the time the prospect circles a number, indicating "I'm mildly interested," and the time information actually arrives. By that time the prospect may have lost interest, bought something else, or forgotten that this is requested information.

You've spent a tremendous amount of time building better and stronger relationships with your existing customers and donors, plus the amount of time adding prospects to your list, increasing orders, and increasing donations; but all these efforts won't be worth a blue ribbon if you don't follow through.

The relationship building doesn't stop with the promotion; the most significant aspect is yet to come. So get your sales, customer service, and fulfillment processes in order.

Conclusion

The moment of truth is the moment of action. Are you helping or damaging the ease of response?

Don't let up. Don't separate response from editorial content, saying, "That isn't my job." If the newsletter is a flop because it doesn't generate response, the editor won't have *any* job.

CHAPTER *10*

What Does It Take to Get Into Print?

Getting into print in the mid-1990s is nowhere nearly as complicated as it was even a decade ago.

The difference, in two words: *desktop publishing*.

The first question to ask yourself is whether you're going to have your newsletter "camera-ready" by using a desktop publishing computer program or whether you're going to have it professionally typeset and laid out.

Which is it?

What happens after you write the text and make a rough copy of your newsletter layout? Do you tackle the desktop publisher, do you take it to an artist, do you let your office personnel handle it, or do you take it directly to the printer and let the printer figure it out?

If you do a little bit of all of the above you've probably figured out that if your newsletter is going to look professional you probably can't do it all by yourself.

Note that word "probably." In the desktop publishing ambience of today, more newsletters are desktop-prepared than not. And why not? Advanced word processing programs, graphics programs, a huge assortment of pre-kerned typefaces with limitless scalability, laser printers—these have made possible the preparation of a finished newsletter by a single individual.

Type doesn't fit? No problem: Instead of 11 point, try 10.4 point, an impossibility with conventional typesetting but a single keystroke with contemporary word processing software.

Need a banner or border or symbol? No problem: It's in one of the drawing or graphics programs.

Just one problem: You, or somebody, had better master those programs.

Want *total* professionalism? Then do what you can do well and entrust the rest to a professional. You'll pay more and get more.

When Should You Use Desktop Publishing?

Use a desktop publisher when you're comfortable with it. I wouldn't use a desktop publisher if it meant shifting a secretary or typist or anyone who's job it is to do something else in my company to do my typesetting or fit the copy or position my graphics on the newsletter. Since these people aren't trained in communication or design, they can give you a workmanlike but "flat" newsletter. They may know the basics of the technology . . . how to change typefaces and how to make columns . . . but do they know how to grab and hold attention through dynamic layout and typography?

Ask any "instant" printer how many half-baked newsletters come into his shop. He may fix up some, at a fee; others lurch through the printing process and spread an aura of semi-professionalism over the company's image when recipients get them.

So what would I do if I'm an average person with normal communications skills but no technical expertise . . . and I want my newsletter to look professional?

I would take it through the traditional stages of readying for the camera. I would *indicate* photographs and graphics and have them stripped in by the stripper at a printer or compositor; and I would have the printer make plates and then print the job.

I'll guarantee you that if you compromise quality, you'll compromise professionalism. And it could cost you more money, fiddling around in areas you're not comfortable handling, than it's ever worth.

How does the first-issue publisher nurse the initial issue through the traditional stages? My suggestions:

First of all, hire a freelance artist to position the elements and do a "type spec" (that is, specifying what size type each heading and text should have). Even if you have a desktop publishing rig, a professional will know how to use desktop publishing to its best—and best-looking—advantage.

(If you've hired a writer to edit your newsletter, usually he or she works side by side with artists and printers.)

Granted, *tons* of books exist on the art of desktop publishing. But these books are for professionals whose job it is to design and typeset. This is their chosen career path. It's not yours.

Do what you do best and hire others who can perform specialized jobs better than you can. You'll all make more money.

Before You Go to Print

Once your typesetting is done and the mechanical is ready, the next procedure is the "pre-press" phase. Most printers do pre-press as part of the service right on the premises, unless you go to a jiffy printer. In that case your mechanical would just be turned into a paper plate for fast printing.

But usually for a sponsor-promoting professional newsletter, you have to go through the pre-press phase.

What is pre-press?

Pre-press consists of a) camera (shooting the newsletter and developing the film negative), b) assembling the film (stripping), and c) the final phase, making the plate for printing.

Once the stripper has assembled the film, a "blueline" will be made.

Suggestion: Always ask to see the newsletter blueline. Avoiding this step can be woeful false economy. The blueline, all the elements in position on a sheet the color and texture of a blueprint, is your final look before the plates are made. If you catch a mistake *after* your piece has been printed, the printer has to go through the entire process again—and that will cost you money. (Worse: A reader probably saw the mistake before you did.)

Blueline checking can save you; but the most cost-effective way to catch an editorial mistake is to catch it before the job gets to the blueline stage. The advantage of blueline checking should be to catch a stripping or camera error.

Ten Potential Problems to Look for in Your Blueline

Usually the darker colors will be the darkest blue and your secondary color a lighter blue. Ordinarily the printer will vary shades to represent different colors and make note of them directly on the blueline.

1. Check to see if any copy is missing or placed wrong.
2. Check for breaks or spots in the type.
3. Are the type areas even?
4. Check for type, grammar, or content errors—again.
5. Check for misplaced photographs and graphics.
6. Are the photos stripped right side up?
7. Is everything facing in the proper direction?
8. Are screens proper and the proper color percentage?
9. Is the size correct?
10. Do the bleeds bleed?

(NOTE: Screen fineness depends on the type of paper. Newsprint holds 65-line to 85-line screens; supercalendared papers hold 133-line to 150-line screens; fine enameled papers can hold screens up to 200 lines. Never, *never* decide on screening before choosing the paper stock.)

Cutting Production Costs

It's not fun working on a meager budget but you can do it.

Before you begin your newsletter, the best advice I can give you is to ask for bids from a number of printers. Find out if these print shops do pre-press work too. If printers know you're getting bids from other printers you'll get the best price from them.

What information do you need to have before you ask for a bid from a printer? Here's a guide to follow.

1. Sizes of each component (Business reply card, newsletter, envelopes).
2. Quantity.
3. How many pages?
4. Is any folding required?
5. Does your piece require any binding?
6. When is your delivery date?
7. How many colors?
8. Any bleeds?
9. What type of photographs and graphics will you use?

All these items will affect the cost of producing your newsletter.

ABSOLUTELY: Get more than one printing estimate.

If bids are too high see what you can do about your paper stock. Consider one or two colors instead of full (four) color. Decrease the amount of your color work by using duotones and line art. (You can always do a lot with just one color, such as tints in different percents of the same color.)

It's your choice. You don't have to spend a tremendous amount of money to get your newsletter from the mechanical stage to the printed piece. So don't let your office assistant put it together. And don't let a printer push you around.

Just one determination should be in your mind from start to finish: Make it professional.

With that in mind, the only other component you need from me is the wish of...

Good luck!

INDEX